Paddling the Payette

A COMPLETE FLAT-WATER AND WHITEWATER GUIDE TO THE PAYETTE RIVER BASIN

BY STEPHEN STUEBNER

CREDITS

On the cover: Todd Walker rows a cataraft down Big Falls during his first descent in 1993. Photo by Mark Lisk. Steve and Alyson Townsley ferry a canoe across the Main Payette. Photo by Glenn Oakley. Cover design by Sally Stevens.

Photo on back cover: The author sports a big grin after a successful run of Little Falls, August 1987. Photo by Tom Shanahan.

Book design: Sally Stevens

Computer mapping: Rick Gerrard, Jan Sutter and Patrick Davis

Photos: All photos by the author unless otherwise indicated.

Copyright © 1995 by Stephen Stuebner and *Paddling the Payette* Productions. All rights reserved. No portion of this book may be reproduced without the written permission of the author.

ACKNOWLEDGEMENTS

The author was privileged to work with all kinds of great people to produce this landmark book on the Payette River. I interviewed dozens of boaters for the whitewater history chapter, including a number of folks who I had not met before, such as Mike Norell, Roger Hazelwood and Tullio Celano.

Everyone I interviewed for that chapter, without exception, was very helpful in piecing together the puzzle of who ran the river first, who named the rapids, etc. Remarkably, there was very little disagreement about those details. I've known Keith Taylor for several years from backcountry skiing, so it was fun to hang out on his dock at Payette Lake and listen to early Payette River stories.

Another pivotal source was long-time Payette River boater and conservationist Rob Lesser. Rob donated pictures for the book, took many hours of his time to show me around on the North Fork, and read over parts of the manuscript. I am grateful to Roger Rosentreter, Mike Ferguson and Mike Lyons for their personal anecdotes and views on Payette River history.

Steve Jones, co-owner of Cascade Recreation, has been helpful in many ways. Jonesy was the guy who suggested this book in the first place, and I thank him for that. Stan Kolby and Jo Cassin provided invaluable advice on what kinds of information paddlers want on the Payette River.

Several folks at the Idaho Historical Society were very helpful to me. I want to thank Judy Austin for her professional assistance in reviewing the chapter on Francois Payette. Diane Kromer was very helpful in assisting me with historical photographs. Boise State University history Professor Todd Shallat also provided his usual sage advice.

Finally, I was most fortunate to have a core group of smart, talented people to assist in producing the book. Rick Gerrard and Jan Sutter did a fine, meticulous job on the maps. Sally Stevens applied her artistic talents to the book's design and jammed late at night to help meet my deadline. And my wife, Amy Stahl, helped me in innumerable ways, as my fellow paddler and manuscript editor.

Thank you all.

TABLE OF CONTENTS

Meet Francois Payette..4
Early Indian occupation..13
Geology & mining...18
Log drives..21
Whitewater history...29
Whitewater safety..65
Main Payette
1. Banks-Beehive Bend...72
2. Beehive-Horseshoe Bend..84
3. Horseshoe Bend to Montour..88
4. Montour to Black Canyon..92
5. Black Canyon to Letha...96
6. Letha to Snake River..100
The South Fork
7. Upper Run, Bonneville Campground to Lowman....................106
8. The Canyon, Deadwood to Danskin......................................112
9. Swirly Canyon, Danskin to Alder Creek Bridge.....................122
10. Garden Valley, Alder Creek to Lower South Fork................128
11. Lower South Fork "Staircase"...132
12. Middle Fork Tie Creek...140
13. Deadwood Reservoir...142
14. Upper Deadwood — Class 5...146
15. Lower Deadwood — Class 4...150
The North Fork
16. Upper Payette Lake..160
17. North Fork Meanders..164
18. Payette Lake...168
19. Little Payette Lake...172
20. Sheep Bridge to Hartsell Bridge...174
21. Paddling Cascade Reservoir..178
22. Cascade to Cabarton Bridge..182
23. North Fork Cabarton Class 3...186
24. The North Fork, Class 5..194
River conservation...203
Flora & fauna...212
Key contacts: Outfitters, rentals, instruction, water flows.........213
Advertising gallery for boating businesses..............................215

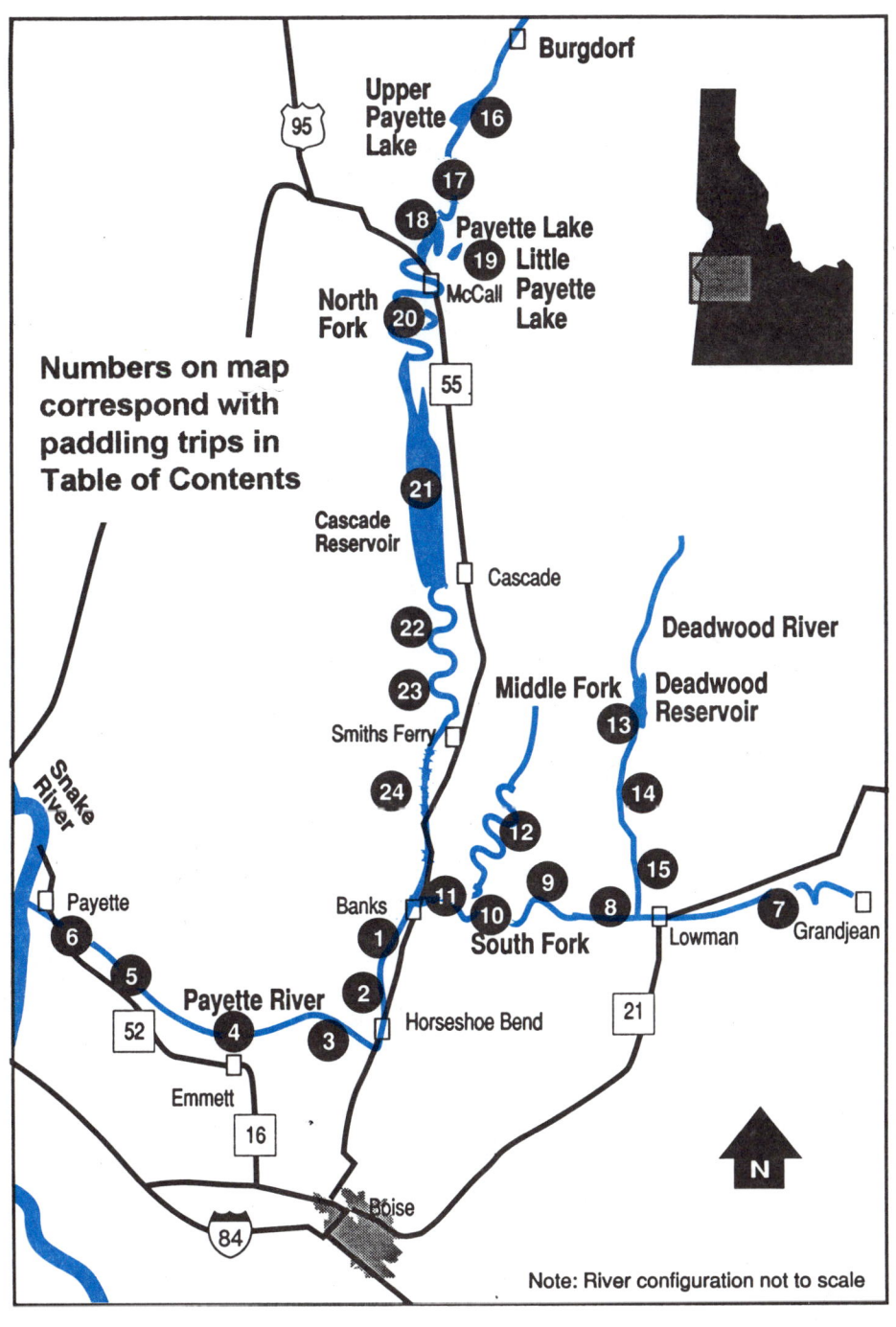

DISCLAIMER

WARNING: WHITEWATER BOATING AND PADDLING ON RIVERS AND LAKES INVOLVE A NUMBER OF AVOIDABLE AND UNAVOIDABLE RISKS THAT MAY CAUSE SERIOUS INJURY OR DEATH. THESE RISKS INCLUDE PINNING ON ROCKS AND LOGS, FLIPPING IN WICKED HYDRAULICS AND SWIMMING IN FRIGID SWIFT WATER. ANYONE WHO PURCHASES THIS BOOK ASSUMES ALL RISK AND RESPONSIBILITY FOR THEIR OWN SAFETY AND WELFARE.

The author has attempted to provide an accurate description of each paddling trip in this guidebook. However, a paddling trip listed in this book may or may not be safe for anyone to try at any given time. Paddling trips vary in difficulty, and boaters' abilities vary according to their experience, equipment and conditioning. River features change constantly as the river flow increases or subsides. River flows may change dramatically at anytime, depending on the outflow from upstream dams and reservoirs. Boaters should check on river flow before leaving on their paddling trip to ascertain river conditions. Boats also should be aware that river flows, river features and lake conditions may change at any time due to cataclysmic or climatic events.

Descriptions for paddling trips include information about the severity of rapids and the time required for each trip. Ultimately, boaters' decisions about whether to attempt a paddling trip on the Payette River are up to the individual as to whether they have the proper skill, knowledge and equipment to enjoy the river safely. The author attempted to provide ample warning about hazards associated with each trip, but boaters should be aware that they may incur additional hazards and be prepared to cope with them.

Please be honest with yourself and do not attempt paddling trips that are beyond your ability. Know your limitations and use common sense. It's far more honorable to walk around a rapid than to drown.

A rafting party takes the plunge in Staircase Rapids.

INTRODUCTION

It's a cold cloudy day in April. It looks as though it might rain, but hey, who cares? The Payette River is cranking down the mountains. The water is up, and it's time to seize the moment. The whitewater season has begun. Our paddle crew drives to Bonneville Hot Springs, 15 miles east of Lowman, to launch the raft for a fun-filled day of paddle rafting.

"Gawd, it's freezing out," one of the gals says as we climb out of the rig, and feel the cool drizzle on our faces looking into the gray sky. "OK, let's go hit the hot springs and tune up our muscles for the day."

We lie back and enjoy the 102-degree water. "Hit me," my buddy taunts the drizzle, emersing his body in the hot soothing water, leaving only his nose above the surface to breathe.

We finally climb out of the hot springs, blow up the boat, and begin a wild ride toward Lowman. We crash through Chapman Creek Rapids and Little Surprise, punching the hole nicely at the bottom. We salute our stylish runs by touching our paddles in the air and beaver-slapping them on the water. And then we settle in for a lovely glide through the upper canyon, surrounded by dense

1

forest, looking down into the clean, clear, emerald river, watching the trout dart around in the deep holes. We crash through some more rapids, Emma Creek, Pinball, Wangdoodle, Kirkham.

We're freezing from the chilly snowmelt water splashing our faces, but we're done. We leap into Kirkham Hot Springs and feel the sting of cold toes getting warm again. Even on a nasty spring day, the Payette River is just so much fun, so incredibly excellent.

No matter where you go, to spend a day on the Payette River can and should be a guaranteed good time. You just need to know where to go, how to get there, what to bring and you're home free — the river does the rest. The most important thing is to match your interests, equipment and skills with the immense variety of opportunities in the basin. For if you like to paddle canoes, touring kayaks, rafts, catarafts or whitewater kayaks, the Payette River Basin is waiting for you.

This book is the first-ever comprehensive guide to the entire sweep of the Payette River Basin. Several river guides have focused on the narrow kayaking aspects of the Payette's whitewater opportunities, but none have outlined what the whole basin has to offer for everyone. I have broken down the basin into 24 different paddling segments, including lakes, scenic canoe floats and all of the rollicking whitewater reaches of the Payette. And I have unearthed some little-known historical and cultural information about the Payette Basin so boaters can enjoy an interpretive journey as part of their float trips.

You'll meet Francois Payette, a fur-trapper extraordinaire. You'll learn about early Indian occupations, the geology of the basin, and fun facts about wildlife and the landscape. You can read about the early log drives down the Payette River, and the whitewater pioneers who struggled to tame the rapids. In short, I've tried to give boaters a greater understanding of what this wonderful mountain watershed is all about.

Many people associate the Payette River with world-class whitewater. Fifteen miles of continuous Class V rapids on the North Fork offer the ultimate paddling experience for the best experts in the world. For the masses, however, the Payette River offers something that many people don't know: it is the ultimate place to learn how to paddle, the consummate teaching river. It features many casual flat-water paddling areas for learning the basics, and then boaters can work their way up through Class II, Class III, Class IV and maybe even Class V rapids. Boaters can move up the scale as they see fit.

What most people don't know about the Payette Basin is that it features a number of gorgeous tranquil paddling areas, from the lovely lakes around McCall to winding meanders through mountain meadows and forests where bird and animal life abounds. These are the unsung parts of the Payette Basin. Here, boaters of all kinds will be thrilled to enjoy a relaxing non-threatening experience in beautiful settings. These kinds of float trips are tailor-made for families and kids.

Beyond all of that, there are a couple of other dimensions of the Payette River Basin that make it so unique and special. All of the 24 separate paddling adventures described in this book can be reached by road. No permits are required. There isn't another river basin in the world that's so accessible and so well-endowed with a diversity of paddling experiences.

Another key dimension is that the paddling season on the Payette never ends. Farmers and ranchers in the lower Payette River Basin teamed up with the U.S. Bureau of Reclamation to build a number of strategically placed water-storage projects that provide consistent summer-long flows on the North Fork, South Fork and Main Fork. There may be times when the lower North Fork is down after high water runoff in July, while farmers store water for later in the summer, but at the same time, the South Fork will have plenty of water. Then, when the South Fork's flow drops in late August or early September, the North Fork's level gets cranked up for late-season boating in warm water. All of the water has to funnel down the Main Payette to farms in the lower valley, so there's always flows in the main reach, even in October.

Finally, Idaho's consistently hot and sunny weather in the summer months — with temperatures in the 90s — provides an ideal climate for paddling the Payette. No matter how hot it gets, boaters can always count on the rivers and lakes to keep them cool.

I don't know how many times I've gotten up on a beautiful summer morning, packed up the boating gear, looked up at an immaculate blue sky, and whispered to myself, It's going to be an All-Idaho day on the Payette — guaranteed fun.

It's enough to make you smile.

FRANCOIS PAYETTE

MOUNTAIN MAN, TRAPPER, MASTER OF FORT BOISE

Mountain man by C.M. Russell,
courtesy Montana Historical Society

How appropriate that the Payette River was named by Francois Payette, a colorful French Canadian "free trapper" and mountain man.

For the man mirrors the river; and the river reflects the man.

Just as the Payette River carves a tempestuous course as it plunges down through the mountains, Francois Payette lived a dangerous and primitive life in unexplored, hostile territory. He survived bloody encounters with the Blackfeet. He thrived as a trapper, hunter and explorer, making a comfortable living off nature's bounty. Later in life, when Francois was a fat and sassy "elder" of sorts, the Hudson's Bay Co. made him master of Fort Boise, located at the mouth of the Boise River on the Snake. Here, Francois wined and dined Oregon Trail emigrants with dairy products from a milk cow kept at the fort, fresh salmon and sturgeon from the Snake, and other fineries.

Thus, just as the Payette River slows down and meanders at a pleasant pace through the Lower Valley in its final approach to the Snake, Francois Payette lived out his later years in relative luxury.

Payette was originally from Saint Roch de L'Assomption, a small town near Montreal. His birth date is not known. According to Francis Haines' article on Payette in *Idaho Yesterdays*, he was baptized on Sept. 27, 1793, the youngest of six children. His parents were Jean Baptiste Payette, a trapper, and Judieth Beaupied. Before he headed out West, Francois worked on Lake Ontario as a "canoeman" building log rafts and floating them 300 miles to Quebec.

In 1810, Payette went to work for John Jacob Astor, a German immigrant and early pioneer who organized the Pacific Fur Co. It's likely that Payette was a strong, energetic lad at this point who was uncommonly savvy about living off the land. He was about 18 years old.

Historical records indicate Payette came to the Pacific Northwest as part of Astor's small fur party, which sailed on "The Beaver" to the mouth of the Columbia River from New York. The journey took a year and a half. "The Beaver" arrived in the spring of 1812, only the second ship of whites to arrive on the Pacific Coast. The first task was to build Fort Astoria, a trading post. Initially, Payette was employed by the Pacific Fur Co. and collected furs in present-day Oregon, Washington and British Columbia. In 1814, he transferred to the Northwest Company when Astor sold his business to the Canadian firm.

The first Snake River expedition

Under the leadership of Donald McKenzie, Payette first set eyes on the Payette River Basin in 1818 on the first "Snake River expedition." He immediately bestowed his name upon the river, according to historical records. An 1821-vintage map of the Northwest, now stored in a British museum, shows that Payette's name stuck.

For the following four years in a row, McKenzie and his brigade worked the "Snake River Country," a vast area that stretched from the Grand Tetons on the east, the Great Salt Lake to the

5

south, the Cascades to the west, and the Salmon River canyon on the north. Two of McKenzie's trusted leaders on the expeditions were Francois Payette and Jack Weiser.

It was a wild and primeval time: Beaver pelts were abundant, white men were considered hostile intruders, and Indians tribes dominated the landscape. Most fur trappers did not stay long, if they were savvy enough to survive at all. Payette was apparently one of the best, a man who thrived and eeked out a living trapping and selling pelts at the same time that more well-known mountain men such as Peter Ogden, Jim Bridger, Jedediah Smith and Andrew Henry worked the region. During this era (1812-1830) — the heyday of fur-trapping in the Northwest — "beavers were as thick as fleas on a dog," wrote Carl Burger in the book *Beaver Skins and Mountain Men*. In the book *All Along the River* by Nellie Mills, she writes that McKenzie considered the Boise, Payette and Weiser rivers as "Idaho's best beaver streams."

" Beavers were as thick as fleas on a dog . . ."

If that's true, the Payette Basin must have provided quite the bounty of furs. For the McKenzie party's harvest of the Big Wood River in 1819 yielded 7,392 beaver in 13 months, according to Blaine County records. The author could not find any specific numbers on beaver harvest in the Payette Basin.

According to Burger, trappers were paid a salary of $200 to $400 a year, and then a commission on pelts. Manual laborers, by comparison, made about $1 day in that era. At the peak of the fur trade, pelts sold for $4 per pound or about $6 per beaver. Trappers called beaver pelts "plew," French for pelt. The furs were fashioned into felt stove-pipe hats and smart apparel for British and French aristocrats.

The trapping technique: "Drown 'em"

The typical method of trapping beaver worked as follows: They'd coat a large stick with castoreum, a heavily scented secretion from the glands in the groin of male and female beavers, and place it in the mud, over the top of a leg-hold trap, in the shallow end of a beaver pond. Once a beaver tried to yank away the stick with its teeth, it would get caught in the trap, whose anchor chain kept the beaver underwater and drowned it.

Trappers were inspired by their commissions to harvest as many "plews" as possible. But there was another factor at work: the British-Canadian fur companies were locked in a turf battle with American companies to claim the Northwest territories. The battle boiled down to a rampage on nature — each side rushed to trap-out the country first, and therefore, claim it as their own.

In the end, both sides succeeded in stripping most of the mountains streams of beaver by the early 1830s. The Hudson's Bay Co.'s annual harvest tumbled from 2,000 pelts in 1834 to 200 the following year. At the same time, Europeans started to make fancy hats out of silk.

The last rendezvous for mountain men was held in 1839 on the Green River. Of course, the Americans won the battle over the Northwest territories, which were purchased in 1846.

Idaho historian Merle Wells described Payette as the "most successful" French Canadian trapper, but surely, even if he was, his success has to be measured in more than just pelts. He was apparently very savvy about dealing with Indians — he had to be to survive.

A naked Payette flees the "Bloods"

According to Peter Ogden's journals, Payette led a party of 13 men into the Snake River country in southeast Idaho in early April 1825 to oppose an American trapping party working the same area. Several days after they arrived, Payette's party was ambushed by a group of Blackfeet, affectionately known as "Bloods," along the Raft River. Blackfeet Indians were notorious for being the most vicious tribe in the region. In short, they rarely took prisoners, only scalps.

Thus, Payette's party of trappers had to scramble for their lives. Five men were caught in the thick of the fight, including Payette, whose escape is best described by Ogden himself: "I sent out a party of 30 men, shortly after Payette ... arrived naked (in camp). He had a most narrow escape. He escaped in the bushes then left his horse & traps & swam across the river."

After Ogden's men returned, they reported that about 40 Bloods had attacked the trappers. Two men were missing. "Benoit and Gervais I fear are butchered," Ogden said.

As it turned out, they met up with Gervais a day later. But Benoit had, indeed, been killed by the Bloods. He had been "shot through the body and head as also three cuts with a knife in left side and his scalp taken off," wrote a man named Kittson, a member of Ogden's party.

Ogden's brigade retreated down the Bear River and made the British discovery of the Great Salt Lake that same year (1825).

In October 1826, Payette had another clash with a group of Indians, this time a small band of Shoshones. At this time, Payette was traveling with an Iroquois named Baptiste. The two were out tending their traps in central Oregon when they came across three "Snakes" who had seven extra horses in tow.

"Save yourself by flight. I am a dead man."

Immediately, they suspected the horses had been stolen from their camp and confronted the Indians. Ogden wrote the Indians did not put up any resistance and "delivered up the horses."

However, that didn't satisfy Baptiste and Payette. They demanded payment, and received some roots and arrows. Still, Baptiste was not satisfied. He "observed this is not the first time they have stolen horses from us and they never have been punished... let us beat and chastise them well but not kill ..." At this point, Baptiste "lost no time with his whip handle," Ogden wrote.

The Snakes put up with the abuse for a short time, but since they outnumbered the trappers three-to-two, they decided to fight and things got nasty. Two of them jumped Payette while the other tackled Baptiste. Payette killed one of the Snakes shortly after he was wounded and called out to Baptiste, "save yourself by flight. I am a dead man." Baptiste didn't get far — he received two arrows to the upper body and dropped to the ground. Payette took an arrow below his rib cage. "The two remaining Indians, finding they had gained so decided advantage began to fire their arms on the seven stolen horses and succeeded in killing four."

Upon seeing a white man approach on horseback, the Indians fled with three stolen horses and Baptiste's and Payette's guns and blankets, leaving them with nothing. "I have to remark we have sustained a most shameful defeat," Ogden said.

Payette recovered from the injuries. It's unclear what happened to Baptiste the Iroquois.

Payette the mighty hunter

Ogden's journals also reflect that Payette was one of his most trusted leaders, and that he had "great prowess as a hunter," writes Nellie Mills. "Frequently (Ogden) speaks of Payette bringing in game: two deer today, an antelope tomorrow, etc."

Several sources indicate Payette had a "spy glass," a tool he obviously used to watch for savages and search for game.

> Payette unsheathed his knife and glared at the Indian with daggers in his eyes.

In the late 1820s, Payette participated in the last three Snake River expeditions with leader Tom McKay. Mills points out that Payette's ability to endure the frontier life for so many years is hard to fully appreciate. "Back and forth across the burning sagebrush plains; down to the bitter alkali lakes of Nevada, up the deep canyons to the beaver lodges in the high mountain meadows; out again through the drifted snow, went the energetic Payette and his trappers. He must have known every Indian tribe and trail, every ford and boiling spring, almost every rock and tree in the Snake country," she wrote.

Yet, nothing ignited the fury of Payette more than an Indian horse thief. In September 1830, Payette was exploring in the lower reaches of his river when he came across a Shoshone camp and spied his old favorite saddle horse. In the presence of a "green" new commander, John Work, Payette walked directly into the Indian camp, snatched his horse and proceeded to lead it away. One of the Indians tried to stop him, arguing that they had traded for it, but Payette reportedly unsheathed his knife and glared at the Indian with daggers in his eyes. He was not challenged.

Although the beaver populations were getting trapped out by

the early 1830s, the turf battle for the Northwest continued. Reports that the American Fur Co. had built Fort Hall in eastern Idaho stirred the Hudson's Bay Co. to establish a fort on the west side of the Snake Plain. "Pay such prices for furs and furnish supplies at such rates as will make it impossible for (the American Fur Co.) to compete with us," McKay's orders read.

McKay took Payette with him to southwest Idaho and established Fort Boise at the mouth of the Boise River near the city of Parma and the Boise River Wildlife Area, on the east bank of the Snake. This occurred initially in 1834, and improvements were made afterward. Payette, who would have been in his mid-40s then, was named post master of the fort, at a salary of 75 lire per year.

Payette takes an Indian wife

Though reports are scanty, it appears that Payette got married in about 1830 to Nancy Portneuf, the half-blood daughter of French-Canadian trapper Joseph Portneuf, a good friend of Payette's. According to author Betty Penson-Ward, who briefly describes Payette's sexual escapades in her book *Idaho Women in History*, the man not only left his name on a city, county and river, he cast "his seed around a much wider area."

Kenneth L. Holmes, who writes about Payette in a 20-volume set titled *Mountain Men and Fur Trade of the Far West*, agrees with Penson-Ward. "This brings up the problem of Payette's marital affairs," Holmes writes. "He seems to have had several Indian wives at different times, possibly at the same time. The (latter) would not have been an impossible condition."

A member of the U.S. Navy, who visited the Northwest, reported that Payette had "a wife in every tribe," according to Holmes' account.

Before readers begrudge Payette as a philanderer, it should be noted that Indian women were routinely given to mountain men as a favor or a gift by tribal chiefs or elders. Sometimes it was for the night; other times the women became their wives. This was not an unusual circumstance. What would have been unusual is if Payette actually did have "a wife in every tribe."

In any event, there's human proof that Payette had at least two other wives than Nancy. Payette had a son named Baptiste with a Flathead Indian woman. Baptiste's journals show, he was sent to Cambridge, Mass., in 1833 to attend school. The boy was 13 at the time.

Payette also fathered a daughter, Marie Angelique Payette, with a Spokane woman. The girl was baptized in 1844. The girl did not live long. She apparently fell ill in her home in north Idaho and died in March 1847. Burial records list her as "une femme Pendoreil," Holmes reports.

Idaho State Historical Society
Fort Boise, on the banks of the Snake River, had adobe walls.

Missionaries, explorers and Oregon Trail emigrants wrote favorably of Payette's hospitality at Fort Boise. During Payette's first year at the fort, he traded with the famous missionaries, Marcus and Narcissa Whitman, to obtain a few dairy cows. Apparently the dairy cows were sore-footed from their long journey across the West, and Payette offered some of his beef cattle in trade at Fort Nez Perces in north Idaho, near the site of the Whitman's Mission. The dairy cows would provide milk and

Idaho State Historical Society
Interior view of Fort Boise

11

cheese for Fort Boise visitors, a rare treat indeed.

In the summer 1837, Nancy Payette fell terribly ill. Francois took her to Oregon's Willamette Valley where the Portneuf family resided at the time. Mills writes that Nancy Payette died "a beautiful death" and was baptized by a Methodist minister. It is not known what illness claimed her life.

Ever the adaptable survivor, Payette continued to preside over Fort Boise and regale visitors with fascinating stories. Thomas J. Farnham, who visited the fort in 1839, described Payette as a "merry, fat old gentleman of fifty."

Payette retires, returns to Montreal

After spending more than three decades in the Northwest, Payette retired from Hudson's Bay in 1843, and returned to his homeland, Montreal, in September 1844. Bank records show he withdrew 500 pounds from his Hudson's Bay Co. account, and made another withdrawal the following year. According to Haines in the *Northwest Quarterly*, for a man to retire on that sum of money in those days was very respectable.

No records confirm when Payette died or where he was buried. Haines suggests Payette remained in a French-Canadian village until his death. This seems to be the most likely scenario because it would have been a major ordeal for Payette to travel by wagon train back to southwest Idaho, and he would have known, having served many Oregon Trail emigrants, that the West would never be the same. He had his hefty retirement sum in Montreal, and all the luxuries of civilization. Thus, it's hard to foresee any reason why Payette would have made a cross-country journey back to the West as an old man.

Mills, on the other hand, reports that Payette's son-in-law, George Goodhart, told someone at the "Caldwell Old Fellows Home" that Payette died in the present-day town of Payette in 1854 or 1855 and was buried in the Washoe Bench overlooking the Snake River. Goodhart, who claimed to have assisted in the burial, offered to identify the grave, but unfortunately, that never occurred.

Without further proof, the truth about Payette's final resting place will never be known.

INDIAN OCCUPATION IN THE PAYETTE BASIN

The "Snake" Indians, or groups of the Shoshone, Bannock and Northern Paiute, lived off the rich bounty of fish and wildllife in the Payette River Basin for thousands of years.

The archaeological record shows that Indian occupations date back at least 5,000 years. Native peoples led a mostly peaceful existence. They gathered plants and roots for food, and they set up weirs to trap and catch chinook and sockeye salmon as the adult fish returned to home streams to spawn. A division of the Shoshone called the "Sheepeaters" or "Tukudeka" were very skilled big-game hunters; they harvested wild sheep with bows and arrows; and they were skilled at harvesting fur-bearing critters, using skins and fur for clothing.

From a geographic standpoint, archaeologists suspect that Mountain Shoshone established summer encampments at confluence locations in the Payette River drainage. These sites likely included the Payette Lake area, Banks, the Middle Fork confluence, Deadwood confluence, Horseshoe Bend, the Payette River confluence at the Snake, and points in between.

Mark Heath

Notched points found in the Payette River drainage.

Numerous hot springs in the Payette Basin also would have attracted Indian groups from time to time, archaeology officials say. A major obsidian excavation site, located on Timber Butte between Ola and Sweet, indicates that Indians roamed and worked the Squaw Creek country, too. Obsidian is a glass-like black rock that's used to make projectile points, knives, drills, scrapers and other tools.

Detailed information on early Indian occupation is limited to the results of several archaeological excavations in the Payette Basin, and the journals of early fur trappers. Explorers and fur trappers for Hudson's Bay Co., including Francois Payette (see Chapter 1) contain reports of Shoshone encampments along the Lower Payette River, and Sheepeater activity near Smith's Ferry, Cascade and Warm Lake. The site of Fort Boise, at the confluence of the Boise River and the Snake, was selected by Francois Payette and the Hudson's Bay Co., in part, because it was a well-known area where Shoshone, Bannock and Nez Perce Indians gathered to fish and trade skins, furs and other items.

The most recent excavation site in the Payette Basin occurred at Big Falls on the Payette's South Fork. This was a confirmed small Indian encampment, probably not occupied by more than three families at once, for catching chinook salmon and steelhead trout, according to archaeologists James Gallison and Kenneth Reid of Rain Shadow Research, Inc., in Pullman. Big Falls would have been a prime area for catching fish because the four-tiered 25-foot falls was too high for the fish to jump. As such, it was a natural fish trap of sorts.

In several small excavation plots on the south bank of Big Falls (near the portage trail), Gallison and Reid documented cultural deposits that date back about 2,000 years. "High densities of formed tools and obsidian debris occur in sandy sediments formerly armored by talus boulders but now exposed to heavy seasonal pedestrian traffic," the researchers wrote in their report. "Blood residue analysis on three projectile points resulted in a positive trout antiserum test on one specimen. This antiserum reacts with steelhead trout and chinook salmon."

More research may be conducted at that site in the future.

At Gallagher Flat on the South Fork, just downstream from the kayakers take-out below "Surprise" Rapids, evidence has been discovered from an Indian occupation about 1,000 years old. The camp was used by Shoshone, Northern Paiute and Nez Perce

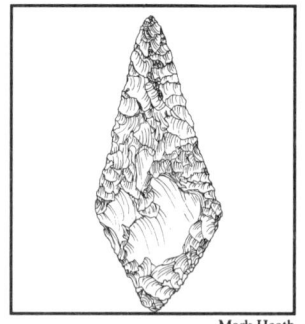

Mark Heath

Basalt shredder or scraping tool

14

people, Boise National Forest officials say. Many pieces of obsidian have been found at Gallagher, as well as some other artifacts.

Archaeologists and Passport In Time volunteers conducted excavations at the Deadwood River confluence area in 1992 and 1993. The main dig occurred immediately adjacent to the Deadwood Campground on the east side of the highway next to the Deadwood River. Radiocarbon dating shows the site was occupied fairly recently, between 500 A.D. and 1200 A.D.

Perhaps the most exciting find in that excavation were two well-preserved fire hearths, the first such discovery in the South Fork watershed, said Susie Osgood, Boise National Forest archaeologist.

"They were superimposed, one on top of the other," Osgood said.

In Reid and Gallison's summary report on the Deadwood excavation, they say the site was likely a warm-weather summer camp used for fishing and possibly fish-processing. It's possible that fish harvested at Big Falls may have been brought to the Deadwood camp for processing, given the relative close proximity, the authors said.

Beyond the fire hearths, excavators unearthed hundreds of flakes and lesser quantities of projectile points, points and tools. They also found pieces of charcoal, wood and ash by the fire hearths.

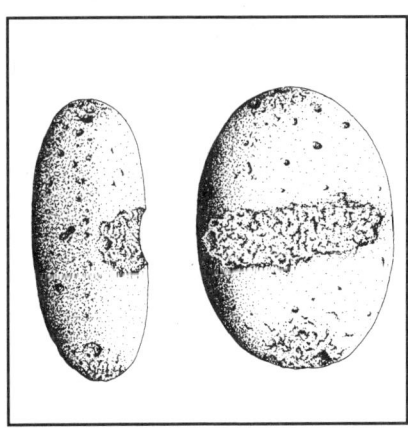

Mark Heath

Grooved maul

Some of the obsidian near these debris was blistered or floated from exposure to heat.

Excavators also found evidence that several different types of firearms had been discharged at the Deadwood site. They found a number of .22 bullet casings, .38 LONG cartridges, 7.65 cartridges from Luger automatic pistols, and 30.06 casings. All of the cartridges were probably discharged between the late 1880s and the early 1930s, Reid and Gallison's report said.

Ambush of four white pioneers near Cascade triggers war

Indian tribes in the Payette Basin led a relatively peaceful life until significant numbers of Anglos and Chinese moved into the Boise Basin and central Idaho in search of gold in the 1860s. As white man began to establish homes and settlements in the basin, the Sheepeaters generally gave them a wide berth and retreated into the backcountry. In the spring of 1878, a year after the Nez Perce War erupted up north, and the Bannock War broke out on the Snake Plain.

In August 1878, trouble erupted between the Sheepeaters and a handful of whites near Cascade. On the 17th of August, Indian Valley pioneer William Monday discovered that a pair of his mares had been stolen. "Indians! There was no doubt," wrote Nellie Mills in *All Along the River*. Monday saw moccasin tracks on the trail, and he was determined to get his team of horses back. Nearly everyone he knew, including his wife, strongly advised him to lump it. But he refused. Two days later, he gathered up three friends, Sylvester "three-fingered" Smith, Tom Healy and Jake Grosclose, and they lit out on the Packer John trail for Long Valley.

Mills wrote that the men, armed to the gills, crossed the Payette "above the falls" near present-day Smith's Ferry at about noon. They headed up a trail heading north. The Indians were hidden amongst large granite rocks, waiting for them with guns ready to fire.

Monday was in the lead. He took three bullets in the heart. He was dead. The others scurried for cover, but it was too late. Grosclose dropped in his tracks, killed instantly by gunfire. Healy tried to hide behind a rock, but he was quickly found and extinguished. Thirteen empty shells lay next to his body. Smith, the most savvy of them all, was shot through the hip and arm, but he quickly reversed directions on his mule and retreated. He apparently fell off the mule, tumbled down the mountain slope and hid inside a beaver lodge on the edge of the river. The Indians searched the area but the silent Smith was not detected. "Under cover of darkness, Smith swam to a little rosebud island ... and hid there for two days, exhausted and weak from loss of blood," Mills wrote.

On the third night, he hiked toward Payette Lake, 25 miles away, and intercepted the mail carrier. He was taken to New Meadows for treatment. A message was sent to Major Drum, who had a contingent of the U.S. Calvary camped near the headwaters of the Weiser River, just 13 miles from New Meadows. Meanwhile, a man named Edgar Smith made set a new record for traveling to Boise, the nearest location for professional medical help.

Major Drum immediately pursued the Sheepeaters, only to run across two more dead bodies about eight miles east of where the other three men were killed. After several days of pursuit, in which the calvary troop had only a few crackers apiece for food, they were forced to return for more supplies.

Combined with the murder of five Chinese miners on Loon Creek and an attack on Warren settlers that year, the death of the white settlers in Long Valley led to an all-out assault on the Sheepeaters in rugged Central Idaho, the Indians' home turf. Gen. Oliver O. Howard sent three troops of soldiers and Umatilla scouts to apprehend the Indians. It was nearly an impossible task. They had little success for months as the Sheepeaters started brush and forest fires to push the calvary back and they hid out in the gnarly canyons and mountain meadows they knew so well. By Oct. 1, 1879, one of the troops captured about 50 Sheepeaters, of which about 12 were warriors. The prisoners were taken to Fort Vancouver and delivered to Gen. Howard. The following year, they were moved to the Fort Hall Indian Reservation, north of Pocatello.

The end of the Sheepeater War capped the only major skirmish between Indians and whites in the Payette Basin. A peaceful sub-band of the Sheepeaters, which also has been identified as an off-shoot of the Lemhi Band, lived in the Dry Buck area above Banks and Squaw Creek Valley until the late 1800s, when they were relocated to reservations.

Author's note: *Archaeologists and the Boise National Forest remind the public that it is unlawful to excavate, remove, damage, alter or deface an archaeological resource, or attempt to do so, on public and Indian lands. If anyone has an interest in participating in the volunteer archaeological program in the Boise National Forest, please contact Susie Osgood or Will Reed, 364-4100.*

GEOLOGY & EARLY MINING IN THE PAYETTE BASIN

When you're boating on the Payette River, take a moment when you're on shore to pick up a rock. Pick up a few on the shore, next to the river, or from the river bed or lake, and take a close look at the rock.

Most likely, you'll be holding a chunk of granite. That's because most of the Payette River Basin cuts through a large homogenous granitic rock formation known as the Idaho Batholith. Including all of its parts, the formation extends from Boise in a northeasterly direction to the Idaho-Montana border, south of Missoula. The southern portion of the batholith, the part dominating most of the Payette Basin, is called the Atlanta Lobe.

In general terms, the granitic formation thrust upward 50 million to 75 million years ago. Rounded granite rock outcroppings, such as those lovely columns, spires and fins commonly seen in the South Fork Payette River "canyon" section, typify the landscape shaped by the Idaho Batholith. The granites "consist essentially of feldspar crystals intergrown with much smaller numbers of quartz grains," according to *Roadside Geology of Idaho*, by David Alt and Donald Hyndman. Shiny rock flakes known as mica also are embedded in pieces of granite.

Take a look at the crystals in the rock. In general, the crystals indicate how quickly the rock melted during its formation inside the earth's core. Large crystals indicate slow, cool or wet melts, and small crystals indicate a quick melt. "If you can see crystals with the naked eye, it was a subsurface melt," says Doug Lawrence, a Boise earth-science teacher and long-time Payette River kayaker and guide. During wet melts, large seams of crystals formed bands of quartz or gold.

The South Fork tracks along a number of fault lines in the batholith. Faults create conduits for water to flow into the earth's core, and in some cases, water to flow toward the surface. This, in very rudimentary terms, is how hot water rises to the surface from the earth's core and forms hot springs, Lawrence says. Cool water trickles into fault lines, and since it is more dense than hot water, the cool water pushes hot water to the surface as it sinks, he says.

Long Valley, the broad swath of land extending from McCall

to Cascade, is a classic glacial-formed valley from glaciers in the present-day Payette Lake area. Less than 15,000 years ago, a 900-foot-thick glacier covered the present-day location of Upper Payette Lake. Over time, several small valley glaciers formed. As the cold period continued, the glaciers grew and moved in a downward direction toward McCall. When temperatures grew warmer, the glaciers retreated and melted, leaving mounds of sediment, rock and debris in their wake. Payette Lake, Upper Payette Lake and Little Payette Lake all served as catch-basins for glacial melt. The city of McCall lies on top of the southern terminus of the glacier. Large boulders scattered around town were deposited by the ice flows.

The Grandjean area, near the headwaters of the South Fork, also was glaciated, following the rise of the Sawtooth Batholith, a later intrusion about 50 million years ago.

The Lower Payette River Valley is the only branch of the Payette Basin that does not lie inside the zone of the Idaho Batholith. But there's an interesting transition from the batholith to a geologic zone formed by many basalt lava flows some 15 million years ago. Since the batholith formation came first, there are sites, such as at Black Canyon Dam, where the batholith and lava flows intermingle.

Gold discovered in Boise Basin

Gold strikes in the Grimes Creek area of the Boise Basin in 1862 brought hundreds of white miners to southwest Idaho. Although the big strikes were over the hill, in the Grimes Creek and Idaho City areas, miners had to travel through the Payette River country to get there. The typical route from the West was the Brownlee Trail, which intersected the Main Payette River near Gardena. Miners with gold fever had to cross the Payette River just upstream of Frenchman's Island by ferry or other means, and then they headed into the Boise Basin via the Harris Creek toll road. Miners coming from the north climbed into the basin via Alder Creek and Grimes Pass.

And so, the Payette River did not play a major role in the gold rush, except in the Deadwood area. In late 1864, after the area had been placered for about a year, miners made 50 cents to

$1 per pan, said Merle Wells, author of *Gold Camps and Silver Cities*. When word leaked out, miners from the Boise Basin flocked to the area. One company reportedly made $600 in one day. Mining activity continued at a consistent pace through the 1860s, justifying a post office and a town, Deadwood City. It's likely the area was named for all of the standing dead wood and a river full of dead snags (as it still is today). But in *Idaho Place Names*, Lalia Boone writes that the town and river may have been named after "Deadwood Jim" a miner.

Wells reports that miners left Deadwood City for other promising areas, notably Loon Creek, in 1869. Deadwood City had become a ghost town by 1876.

On the South Fork of the Payette, limited placer-mining development occurred. An operation at the present-day site of Oxbow Rapids, in the canyon reach, was launched at the turn of the century. It never produced much (see Canyon narrative).

Paddlers will notice the tell-tale signs of placer mining — neatly stacked piles of river cobble — a few miles below the old Grimes Pass Dam site on the South Fork, on river-right. It is possible that these placers were worked by Chinese miners, who moved into the area after completing the Central Pacific Railroad in 1869.

Signs of erosion; look into the river bed

A natural consequence of the Idaho Batholith geologic formation is highly erosive soil. Snowmelt, rainfall, wind and other natural forces cause large amounts of silt and sediment from the steep mountain landscape to drain into the Payette River. Logging, skidding and road construction, as well as mining and recreation activity all have accelerated the erosion. During high runoff, much of this sediment is picked up by the river and deposited on the shore, in the form of beaches.

As granite rock breaks down from erosive forces, mica and feldspar break apart first, while the quartz — one of the hardest minerals on earth — is the last to go, Lawrence says. Sand particles from quartz form the beaches, he says, while mica and feldspar particles can be seen on the river bottom.

"RIVER HOGS"
PAYETTE RIVER LOG DRIVES

Idaho State Historical Society
Loggers gather scattered logs in the Payette near Emmett, circa 1906.

Long before roads or rails provided a transportation route up the North or South Fork of the Payette River, logging pioneers tried to turn the gnarliest sections of the Payette into a log highway. These wild and wooly dudes — the first white boaters to challenge the Payette's rapids — were known as "river hogs."

Log drives on the Payette were an immensely daring and dangerous undertaking, for the loggers not only floated logs and railroad ties downriver, but they also followed them in narrow deep-hulled wooden boats called "Wanigans." The boats, which were designed for use on the much flatter Minnesota and Michigan Rivers, swamped and flipped frequently. Loggers, who of course had no life jackets or wet suits, drowned nearly every year that log drives occurred. The deaths helped inspire sawmill owners to push a railroad up the North Fork and put a stop to the river carnage. Log drives occurred sporadically on the Payette from the

1880s to 1916.
A shortage of railroad ties for the Oregon Short Line's new line across southern Idaho created the need for the first Payette River log drive in 1883. The logging contractor, Coe & Carter, of Omaha, Neb., collected woodsmen from Maine and the Midwest

Idaho State Historical Society

"River hogs" try to negotiate the Payette in a wooden boat with a pole.

to cut 300,000 ties out of trees in the North Fork drainage. "Lumber was sawed by hand from the native timber. Rivermen drove the ties down the river, and boats were built to follow the drive down the canyon and carry the men from shore to shore," wrote Elizabeth Smith, in her *History of the Boise National Forest.* "Long, strong cables were used to line the boats down the rapids," she wrote.

It is unclear from Smith's report how far the men floated the ties down the North Fork. She mentions a packer delivering the ties to Payette by overland route.

No deaths were reported during that early drive of ties. The entire quota was delivered in the city of Payette (called "Boomerang" at the time), near the river's mouth.

In 1890, attempts to float wood and men down the upper South Fork claimed seven men at Big Falls, Smith reports. Trees harvested in MacDonald Creek, some 12 miles upriver from Lowman, were driven to the river bank with oxen, stacked on the bank, and then released the following spring in high water. The logs were destined for the Horseshoe Bend sawmill. During this drive, the seven men drowned at Big Falls, either by failing to pull their boats out before the falls or during a hazardous lining operation around the falls.

Logging pioneers rode logs in rapids for sport.   Idaho State Historical Society

Log drives on the South Fork continued through the 1890s, sending timber from the Garden Valley area to sawmills in Emmett and Payette. Nellie Mills, in *All Along the River,* provides an apt description of these logging pioneers. "The old-time logger and river-driver was a big-hearted daring character whose utter abandon and fearlessness have seldom been equalled," Mills wrote. "Every year, the roaring Payette, in a terrible mood, claimed one or more victims, but always there was another ready to shoot the foaming rapids in a skiff or ride a whirling log, balancing with his peavey and singing as he went."

Early sawmill owners Jim Wardwell and Joe Reed of Emmett used oxen teams to haul logging equipment and river boats over the Boise Basin trail to South Fork logging sites in the fall, and then their crew felled trees and set up log decks on the river all winter long. Loggers were apparently "easy to come by," Mills writes, since ranch and farm hands were idled during the winter. In the spring, they'd release the log decks and follow the logs downriver in their wooden boats. Historical photos show the Wanagans carried about six to eight men — two in the bow and stern who used poles to steer, and several men in the middle, seated, pulling on oars.

Even though drownings were frequent, it wasn't uncommon for people to drown on log drives or for any other reason in the pioneer days. In the spring of 1904, the Payette River Basin was heavy with deep snowpack. Newspaper reports predicted big floods. A May 25 Idaho Statesman dispatch, dateline Emmett, read as follows, "As a result of the late warm weather, the usually placid stream, the Payette, has swollen into a turbulent river and extremely dangerous river. The river is bank full and the complete

Idaho State Historical Society

Early log-drive boat carries loggers down the South Fork.

inundation of many of the prosperous farms in the lowlands is threatened.... The lumbermen from the hills tell of the enormous quantities of snow and say a prolongued duration of hot weather will result in a flood which will surpass any of the high water marks reached in this valley."

A day later, the lead story in the Statesman's "News from Idaho Towns" cries out: "FOUR MEN LOST IN RIVER — Payette claims a quarter of victims."

"Four men were drowned in the rapids of the Payette River this morning between the point where the South and Middle forks of the stream join and where the united streams flow into the North Fork. The remains have not been recovered.

The four men were part of the crew that was bringing down the big log drive for Prestel's sawmill at this place (Payette, Idaho). They were attempting to come down the rapids in a boat, when in some manner it became overturned and all four occupants of the boat were drowned."

There was no follow-up story the next day. It was just part of life in those days. Events like that drowning — most likely in present-day Staircase Rapids — led loggers to call that cataract "Hells Half-Acre," according to local legend. As whitewater boaters approach Staircase now, in modern times, and feel their gut churn at the possibility of flipping or swimming, think how terrified logging pioneers must have been of the entire Lower South Fork. It had to a be a roll of the dice every time they went through.

Pioneers were a little too bold for their own good at times. They lacked good river sense, and given the poor equipment used to navigate the stream, catastrophes were common. In May 1906, for example, a 50-year-old man and a 15-year-old boy drowned in high water when the man, Joseph Lang, tried to row a small boat across the backwaters of Grimes Dam to fetch a letter on the other side. "They made the attempt to cross, though the river was running swiftly, making it desperately dangerous to undertake such a crossing," a Statesman report said. "Caught in the swirling current (this is in Swirly Canyon), the boat soon swamped and both its occupants were carried to their death without hope of being saved. They disappeared in the boiling waters and nothing more was seen of them excepting that the body of Lang was seen as it went over the dam .... A message from Centerville last evening

Idaho State Historical Society
Logs released off log decks began the "drives" to sawmills downstream.

stated 40 men were working on the river in an effort to find the bodies ... The river is very high. It has swift current for a long distance, and unless the bodies lodge, they may be carried many miles."

In 1902, the Payette Lumber and Manufacturing Co. made a move to move logs down the gnarliest reach of all, the lower 17 miles of the North Fork. Payette Lumber created a subsidiary, the Payette Improvement and Boom Co., to "beat the rapids into submission," writes Jim Witherell in *Log Trains of Southern Idaho*. The Boom Co. "lavished $100,000 on flumes and dynamiting channels in the Payette." In addition, the Boom Co. built a river-wide splash dam at the present-day site of Big Eddy Campground on the North Fork.

Smith reports that a man named "Roaring Jack" Bell — named so because his booming voice could be heard over the river's rapids — supervised the splash dam construction project.

The first log drive on the North Fork resulted in chaos — only half the logs made it to the Emmett mill and four men reportedly drowned. It's unclear whether any of the men tried to boat the North Fork in Wanagans or whether they died trying to unlock log jams in the middle of frothing rapids. Smith reports in her account that the men followed the logs downriver on a pack trail on the west side of the river canyon — the first route to be established in that area. As for the dynamiting, she writes, "tons of powder were used; and for several years the stream flowed through the canyon with more freedom and smoothness than at any time in its existence. But winter avalanches and spring freshets brought huge trees and stones to dam the channel, and 15 years later, it was difficult to find a trace of the great labor performed in that summer of 1903."

As crazy as either scenario sounds on the North Fork, it wasn't uncommon for these "River Hogs" to jump into the river to deal with log jams with their feet or ride logs downriver (see photo). Another spring-time drowning reported in the Statesman in 1905 involved a River Hog who fell through a log jam on Grimes Creek. Log drives on that stream occurred at the same time of the Payette River drives, but the logs from Grimes Creek were floated to the Barber Mill, near the present-day Barber Park in east Boise. The report said, in part:

"A small jam had been broken about four miles above the mouth of the creek and (Nels) Bradley started to cross the creek on the moving logs. In jumping from one to another he struck a small log which rolled with him. He lost his balance and fell into the stream. The logs floated over the place where he went down and he did not come to the surface. Eighty men in the employ of Barber Company spent all of Friday afternoon and all day yesterday searching for the body without success.... Cutler Lewis, logging boss for the drive ... stated that the water was not over three feet deep where Bradley was drowned but very swift. The search will be resumed today."

Obviously, if men died attempting such antics on Grimes Creek, a comparatively tiny stream, there must have been many who reached the same fate on the powerful Payette River.

Several railroad outfits competed for rights to build the rail line to Cabarton and Cascade. Finally, the Idaho Northern Railroad finished the rail line up the North Fork in 1915, the same route that exists today. As construction proceeded upriver from Horseshoe Bend, a separate crew cut trees in Long Valley and fashioned ties by hand. Then they apparently floated the ties downriver and collected them at strategic points for building the track. The new railroad eliminated the need for log drives on the North Fork. The South Fork drives apparently petered out soon afterward, as there is no mention of them after 1917 in the literature.

Thus, a colorful chapter closed in the pioneer days of log drives on the Payette River. What the loggers learned about the Payette is a lesson that all boaters learn and relearn on a constant basis — that is, the Payette's South and North Forks pack a powerful punch and demand the utmost respect. Anyone who fails to heed that advice ultimately suffers the cruel wrath of the river.

Idaho State Historical Society

The Payette Lumber Co. built a splash dam three miles below Smith's Ferry at the Big Eddy wayside for the first North Fork log drive in 1904.

28

PAYETTE RIVER
WHITEWATER PIONEERS

Rrrrrrrrrrrrrring. Rrrrrrrrrrrrrring. Rrrrrrrrrrrrrring.
"Hello?"
"Hi Tullio, it's Walt Blackadar. I've been thinking about running the North Fork of the Payette. Wanna go?"
"Hmmmm. That sounds interesting. When do you want to run it?"
"Next weekend. Next Saturday. I'll be coming over with Al Beam. Wanna go?"
"Ah ... yeah, sure Walt. I'll give it a try. I'll go up there before you come and take a look at the rapids."

Tullio Celano, a 27-year-old medical officer at Mountain Home Air Force Base, was excited. Here he had met this country doctor and kayaking pioneer from Salmon, Idaho, a week ago, and he had a chance to become a regular paddling partner. But Celano didn't know diddly about paddling whitewater, much less the ferocious North Fork and its Class V rapids.

"I guess he assumed that to paddle," Celano says.

"I guess he assumed that since I could roll, I knew how to paddle."

— the peak of the psychedelic era, the rock generation and the Vietnam War. It was a crazy time. Many people did foolish and outrageous things. Few compared to what Celano did next, however, sans drugs. After scouting the lower five miles of the North Fork, he decided to pre-run it before **Walt Blackadar** showed up.

"I put in just below Hound's Tooth, made it a couple hundred yards, and then I flipped over and swam. I lost my paddle and my boat and got out on the left side of the river," he says.

The wrong side. He had to get across the river to the highway. So he jumped back in and swam across. Somehow, he made it. "That was pretty stupid, huh?" he says now.

Celano found his Urban-Penall fiberglass boat broken in half just above "Crunch" Rapids, the last big drop on the North Fork above Banks. He called Blackadar and says sheepishly, "Gee, Walt. The water was pretty fast. I lost my boat."

Blackadar didn't skip a beat. "Don't worry. I'll bring you another one next week."

Blackadar and Ketchum boater **Al Beam** showed up a week later, and they scouted the lower North Fork. "Al Beam was white as a ghost and I was just totally ignorant," Celano says. "Walt said he felt like he had to get in there, and Beam said he'd drive. At the last minute he got in with us."

Keith Taylor
Tullio Celano on the South Fork, early 1970s

Blackadar assured the rookie paddlers that he'd watch out for them in the raging mish-mash of swift water, curling waves and big stopper holes. To be on the safe side, Celano wore a full wet suit and two life jackets. They pushed off just below Hound's Tooth Rapids, and within seconds, Blackadar got washed into a hole and swam. The next thing Celano sees is his mentor madly swimming for shore. Then Celano got sucked into a hole and swam, but this time, the river wasn't so forgiving. "I remember my whole life passing by me," Celano says. "I was losing it; I was getting tunnel-vision and everything," Celano recalls. "The hole finally spit me out sideways just by the grace of God."

Mike Ferguson
Walt Blackadar heads into Crunch Rapids, circa 1975

He swam like hell for the shore and pulled himself out. In the Blackadar biography, "Never Turn Back" author Ron Watters writes that Blackadar, his legs bruised and bleeding, and Beam found Celano collapsed on the rocky bank, his lungs heaving. "Come on!" Blackadar yelled. They had to retrieve the boats.

"I was pretty intimidated after that," Celano says. "Every time I got in my kayak again, my legs started shaking."

Nevertheless, Celano had been the first-known kayaker to try running the North Fork, and Blackadar and Beam were the second and third. Of course, none of them had done it with style, and they hadn't run the South Fork or Main Payette to become acquainted with the river and build their skills. They just blindly leaped into the boiling caldron of the North Fork, which was widely considered to be unrunnable, a death trap.

Much like the early loggers who challenged the Payette's gnarliest rapids at the turn of the century, the first whitewater boaters on the Payette didn't have any teachers or role models to show how it's done. Being totally ignorant, they had leaped into the worst of the whitewater fury and nearly drowned. The most experienced boater in the state, Walt Blackadar, had led the way. Blackadar already had had several close-calls on the Salmon River, including a nasty swim through Dagger Falls. But "fear" wasn't part of his vocabulary. The brash and gutsy Blackadar, who had more than 15 years of whitewater boating experience in rafts and sweep boats, didn't think of breaking in green kayakers with a step-by-step progression that's used today. These early Payette whitewater pioneers simply had to learn by the seat of their swim trunks, in the cockpit of a hard-to-maneuver fiberglass boat.

Keith Taylor, an athletic Boise orthopedist, got ideas about kayaking as early as 1966. He remembers reading an article in "Popular Mechanics" about building a kayak with plywood and door hinges. "It was like nothing you could imagine," Taylor says. He built a couple of them, but if you tipped over, you sank to the bottom of the river.

Taylor found a real kayak in the summer of 1969 while on vacation in western Washington. He spied a bunch of kayakers paddling on the Wenatchee River near Leavenworth, Wash. Turns out it was the National Kayaking Championships. Ever the gregarious guy, Taylor asked the coach of the U.S. kayaking team where he could buy a kayak, and the guy said, "Here's one." Taylor bought a nice fiberglass kayak and a paddle for $125. He stopped at a whitewater shop in Seattle to buy a second kayak for his wife, Dawn.

Keith and **Dawn Taylor** practiced kayak rolls in Payette Lake, and then they tried to paddle the "easy" Boise River, from Barber Park to Boise. The last big diversion drop on the river, across from the old Gate City Steel building, had a row of wooden posts sticking up several feet. There was enough room between the posts for a kayak to slip through going straight ahead. Keith made it through, but Dawn floated up to it sideways and pinned upstream. The force of rushing water pushed her head below the water and flattened the fiberglass kayak against her legs.

Rob Lesser

Dawn, right, and daughter Kari Taylor get ready to run the Payette with Keith.

Keith quickly got out of his kayak, and waded out into the river to save his wife.

With water up to his thighs, Keith held Dawn's head above the water so she could breathe, but every time he tried to pull her out of the boat she screamed "Stop! You're breaking my legs!" She was trapped.

Then some guy driving by on Warm Springs Avenue saw them in trouble and asked, "Do you need any help?" Keith Taylor asked him if he had any tin snips. The guy was from out of town and had borrowed his brother's car. Sure enough, he had some snips. Dressed in a suit coat and tie, the guy waded out in the river and gave the snips to Keith, who proceeded to cut the kayak in half and freed Dawn. "If that guy hadn't stopped, I don't know what we would've done," Taylor says.

"Stop! You're breaking my legs!"

Now that his wife was spooked, Taylor needed a paddling partner. He called Blackadar in Salmon, who told him that two boaters lived nearby in Mountain Home, Celano and fellow airman **Roger Hazelwood**. The trio got together and paddled the Main Payette many times in that summer of 1970.

Hazelwood benefitted from Celano's hairy experiences on the North Fork in terms of preparation. He and Celano practiced rolls in C.J. Strike Reservoir; they trained in the air base pool and practiced holding their breath underwater; and they practiced paddling on the South Fork Boise. "We were into survival tactics," Hazelwood recalls.

Keith Taylor still has his fiberglass kayak.

Midway through the summer, Keith Taylor showed his kayak to Boise school teacher **Mike Norell** at Payette Lake. Taylor and Norell knew each other from the Boise Symphony: Keith played the oboe and Mike played the French Horn. Taylor taught Norell how to roll at the lake, and then in a pool session.

Aside from what little paddling technique they had gleaned from Blackadar, the quartet of Payette pioneers engaged in true survival paddling. "Our philosophy was to paddle as hard and fast as you could," Taylor says. "We had no concept of eddying out and working down the river. It was just point it downriver and paddle like hell."

"Everything in those days was having a good roll," Celano adds.

Together, the four of them named the biggest rapids on the main that season — "Mike's Hole," "Mixmaster" and "AMF." (See Main Payette description for details).

All of them looked pretty funny in those big, puffy Mae West orange life vests, long and bulky fiberglass boats, beige nose plugs and the huge Illiad paddles. But it didn't matter. They had the river to themselves, and they were having a good time.

"In those days, there were only five or six people boating on the whole river," Norell recalls. "Today, there's five or six people on every wave."

33

Taming of the South Fork

Blackadar had arranged for a large plane to fly about 25 kayakers into the Middle Fork of the Flathead River over the July 4th holiday in 1971. A number of eastern boaters, including **Barbara Wright** and **Mary Nutt**, the eldest of the Nutt paddling clan from Pennsylvania, were part of the crew. After the Flathead, part of the group moved on to tackle the Selway, and run the first descent of several upper sections of the South Fork of the Salmon. Nutt remembers rounding out the trip with a stop on the South Fork of the Payette River, mostly likely the Lower South Fork. Blackadar was with her, along with her 18-year-old brother, Billy. "It was fun but it wasn't terribly challenging," she says.

Mike Ferguson skirts the whale rock in Staircase Rapids in the mid-1970s.

Nutt didn't run the North Fork, but she remembers driving along it, and Blackadar saying, "I can run that." Actually, he hadn't paddled it yet, and he had bigger plans that summer: A solo descent down Turnback Canyon on the Alsek River in British Columbia.

By virtue of her short trip on the Payette, Nutt was probably the first woman to paddle the South Fork "Staircase" run. "This was back in the days when girls weren't paddling rivers," she says.

By this time, the original gang of four had graduated to boating on the South Fork of the Payette. Celano showed them the way, when he ran and then named Staircase (while a friend drove along the highway to watch) in August 1970. "I had to go to the bathroom three times before I did it, but I did it," Celano says.

Early in the spring of 1971, Blackadar paddled Staircase in high water. "I remember standing in front of Staircase thinking it could be done, but it'd be the maximum thing that someone could do in a kayak," Hazelwood says. "We called Walt and said, "You've got to come look at this rapid." "

He did. It was pouring rain in May, and all the rocks were covered in Staircase. That means the river must have been running about 10,000 cfs or more. Blackadar said in his usual brash way, "I can run this thing." He carried his kayak 100 yards above the rapids and launched. He crashed through the big curling waves without a problem.

"The following week, we went out and ran it ourselves," Hazelwood says. Taylor, Celano and Norell were with him. "It was so phenomenal compared to the Main," Norell says. "Once we graduated to the South Fork, we never went back."

Early loggers who shepherded logs down the North and South Forks of the Payette referred to the entire reach of the North Fork as the "Stairs." They called Staircase "Hell's Half-Acre" due to loggers drowning in the rapids. But given the stairstep-nature of Staircase Rapids, Celano's name seemed to fit the cataract, and the name stuck.

The original kayaking group had developed big-water skills by now to the point where they could have lots of fun on the south fork. They ran many other rivers, too, such as the South Fork of the Salmon, a Class IV-V stream, depending on flow, the East Fork of the South Fork Salmon, another gnarly run, and the middle section of the Owyhee, a solid Class IV section with a Class V-plus rapids commonly known as "Widowmaker."

In August 1972, Hazelwood one-upped them all by joining Blackadar and paddler **Kay Swanson** of Montana on the first descent of "Devils Canyon" on the Susitna River in Alaska. "It was a trip of a lifetime, Hazelwood says.

By the spring of 1973, several new paddlers had emerged on the Payette River scene, including **Ron Frye**, a Pennsylvania school

Rob Lesser
Ron Frye surfs the South Fork play wave in his C-1 boat.

35

teacher and experienced C-1 paddler who moved to New Meadows, Boise State University student **Mike Ferguson**, and Payette auto mechanic **Tom Murphy**. Frye remembers that he met the Boise-based kayaking gang when he spotted a vehicle parked in front of McU Sports with a kayak on top. It was Hazelwood's rig, and he was instantly plugged into the group. **Rick Mellen** would join the group in a few months. He found Ferguson through a bartender at the Trolley House restaurant.

Being an experienced Class IV boater, Frye says his first day on the Payette was on the Lower South Fork. "I came from the Youghegheny River in Pennsylvania, which was mobbed with kayakers and rafters all summer long," he says. "To see some-

Mike Ferguson
Tom Murphy and others frequently boated the Payette in the winter in the early 1970s.

thing like the South Fork of the Payette with no one on it at all was truly amazing. We had the whole river to ourselves."

Murphy, who came to Idaho from Ohio, also met Hazelwood at McU's. Hazelwood sent him to Salmon to buy a fiberglass kayak from Blackadar. That fall and winter, Hazelwood and Murphy paddled on the Payette in the snow and ice. "It was all I could think about," Hazelwood says.

They were obsessed. Ferguson taught himself to roll in Lucky Peak with the aid of a book on whitewater kayaking. He started paddling with Taylor, Celano, Frye, Murphy and Hazelwood on the Main Payette and then the South Fork. "I remember the tension and the butterflies would build up all week long, and then you'd get in the river and you'd be totally focused, and then afterwards, you'd get this incredibly huge adrenaline rush."

The thrill of running and surviving whitewater had seized them to the core. "It was some kind of bizarre lure to fulfill some kind of primal need," says Ferguson, now the state's chief economist.

It should be noted that by this time, Taylor's wife, Dawn, Hazelwood's wife, Betsy, Celano's wife, Marilyn, and Murphy's wife, Irene, were paddling the Main Payette and parts of the South Fork with their husbands. Taylor also taught his daughter, Kari, how to paddle at age 15 and later, his son, Steve, would learn to be an expert boater.

Taming the North Fork's "Lower Five"

Come spring of 1974, the Boise big-water paddling gang still had several challenges on the horizon. No one had ran the South Fork "Canyon" as yet, and no one had successfully run the North Fork. They still were no rafts to be seen. Turns out, they tackled both runs that year. They ran the canyon without incident at medium flows, and in the fall when nothing else was going on, they went for the North Fork "Lower Five" section.

Hazelwood remembers the water was low everywhere on the Payette in August 1974 except on the North Fork. It was a typical August flow, about 1,500 cfs. "We kept looking at it, and looking at it, and wondered if it could be done," he says.

"We kept looking at it and wondered if it could be done."

There was another element that added weight to the gravity of the situation. **Julie Wilson** had died on the Bruneau's West Fork, upsetting all of the party members, including trip leader Blackadar. They realized that there were limits to running Class V whitewater, and that witnessing a drowning was a real bummer.

Even so, Hazelwood says, "I figured I had a good roll and I could hold my breath forever. I said to Murf, "Let's go up after work and run this thing and get it done." "

Taylor joined them for that first descent of the lower North Fork. They put in below Otter's Run and paddled through the two Class V drops above Banks, "Juicer" and "Crunch." All three of them made it without swimming.

The barrier had been broken. The paradigm that the North Fork couldn't be run safely was shattered. Blackadar showed up several days later and the local boaters, including Frye and Norell, ran from Hound's Tooth on down, conquering what is known today as "the Lower Five," the beginning of the North Fork progression.

Norell remembers the thrill to this day. "Boy, when you pull into Banks after making that run, it's a real mind-blower," he says. "But I decided after that, that I'd had enough. Those guys (Taylor, Hazelwood, Blackadar et al.) just kept pushing the limit, doing bigger water and tougher rapids, I didn't feel I needed to push the envelope any farther."

Not everyone had smooth runs on the North Fork that fall. Norell remembers a guy named **Steve Jolly** got window-shaded in a hole in Juicer and swam. His bright orange kayak remained lodged in the rapid for three weeks, a bright beacon warning others of what could happen to them.

Just how high is high water?

The following spring, the Boise gang was still testing the limits of high water. It had been one hell of a winter, and the mountain snowpack was deep. Spring runoff was enormous. Blackadar called Taylor and said, "I'm coming over this weekend to run the canyon." The South Fork was beyond bank-full — it lapped at the edge of the Banks-Lowman highway by Bronco Billy Rapids.

Glenn Oakley
Rob Lesser in Jacob's Ladder, North Fork.

Not to be outdone by Blackadar, Taylor, Murphy, Hazelwood and Norell went up to run the canyon the day before Walt was due to arrive. Taylor borrowed a boat for "some rookie boater" named **Rob Lesser** who came along for the ride. What a ride it must have been.

The river was so high it was flying through the notch at Big Falls, the notch between the bank and the peninsula point below the falls. The river level would have been about 6,000 cubic feet per second. It was an insane level to be in the canyon. "We didn't know any better," Taylor recalls.

"We'd been running high water all spring," Norell adds. "We figured that was what kayaking was all about. Running big water."

Lesser, who had grown up in Boise but hadn't paddled the Payette yet, recalls, "I was thinking, man, this is a pretty radical thing. The water is cooking pretty high. It was like, oh boy, here were go."

John Wasson

Big Falls at 6,000+ cfs in 1982 — a similar flow to the 1975 high-water trip.

They put in at the Deadwood confluence on a hot sunny day. No one remembers much about the trip until they arrived at Big Falls. As they squirreled into micro eddies or grabbed bushes to get out above the falls, Norell lost his paddle next to the rocky shore. The paddle ran down the falls and swirled around in an eddy on river-right below the falls.

At this flow, the eddy below Big Falls turns into a giant whirlpool. "It was a really violent, recirculating eddy moving up and down 3-4 feet," Norell recalls. "And there were logs flying around in the eddy. It looked really dangerous."

"I'm not going to make it, Mike, kick like hell!"

Somehow, they had to retrieve Norell's paddle. Hazelwood

and Murphy lined up on shore with the nose of their kayaks facing the current. Norell was poised to leap onto the back of their boats for a quick tow across the river. They had to make it before Blackadar Rapids, just 200 yards below.

They went for it. Norell made the leap and grabbed the boats. Lesser remembers Murphy saying, "I'm not going to make it, Mike, kick like hell!" Norell kicked and kicked. His legs cramped up in the freezing water. But they made it to the right side after the first wave flush below the falls.

Taylor and Lesser waited for a while, and then headed downriver. Lesser got hammered in Blackadar Rapids. "There were huge eight to 10 feet waves leading into it," he says. "I got dumped and didn't make my roll. I swam and lost the boat."

He swam around the corner through Blackadar II and managed to get out on river-right. He ran up to the dirt road above and flagged a car down to look for the borrowed kayak downstream.

> "I grabbed the cliff and climbed up the wall, hauling my boat with me."

Meanwhile, Taylor was chasing it down the river. He'd chase the boat, get close to grabbing it, and then he'd get trashed in the rapids. When Taylor ran through "Trash Can," where the river piles into a cliff wall on river-left, he got flipped over, missed his roll and swam, holding onto his paddle and boat. He reached an eddy on the left bank. "I grabbed the cliff and climbed up the wall, hauling my boat with me," Taylor says.

Once on top, he spied a cable spanning the river nearby. He decided to climb across it hand over hand. "It was a little spooky," Taylor says.

Three days later, Lesser paddled the length of the Payette River, searching for the lost boat, with Norell. They paddled from Deer Creek to Black Canyon Reservoir. Nothing. Then they put in above Little Falls and found the boat just upstream of the Deer Creek Bridge, about 40 miles downriver from where he lost it. It was damaged to the point where he had to buy the loaner a new one. Hazelwood, Norell and Murphy had decided to bag the trip below Big Falls and climbed out.

Keith Taylor

Roger Hazelwood on the South Fork, circa 1972.

"It was such a stupid incident," Lesser says. "It was reflective of the times. We didn't even think about bringing break-down paddles. We didn't think about throw ropes. It was just a guy thing — we were testing our mettle. We were there to match ourselves with the high water and try to survive."

Even though Lesser had grown up in Boise, he had left Idaho in 1963 to attend Whitman College in eastern Washington and then graduate school at the University of Montana in Missoula. He jumped in a kayak for the first time on the Blackfoot River near Missoula in the spring of 1969. He paddled for 2.5 miles and eventually he swam. He loved it. "I was absolutely hooked," he says.

Although he was a new face to Taylor, Lesser says he was not a rookie boater in the mid-1970s. "I had been doing a lot of boating, it was just in Montana, Alaska or other places."

Always in search of wild adventure, Murphy went back to the canyon a few days later with Ferguson, Mellen and Frye. The river was still booming. As the group approached the Big Falls portage area, things went awry, again. Murphy got flipped over as he tried to get out of his boat and he had to swim. His kayak went flying over the falls. Frye, with a single paddle and his C-1 boat, successfully ferried Murphy across the river below the falls. It must have been close.

Mellen, meanwhile, got stuck in a small, explosive eddy against the right cliff in Blackadar Rapids. "Occasionally, we saw the tip of his paddle or the tip of his boat from above, but we couldn't see Rick," Ferguson says.

Mike Ferguson

Tom Murphy in Juicer, which is also known as Murphy's Maelstrom.

Somehow, Mellen clung to the cliff with a fingertip-hold and began to climb up the wall. Frye had a rope in his boat, and was in a position to scale the rocky slope and lower a rope to Mellen. Ferguson chased Mellen's boat. "We were stupid to be there, we knew that," he says. "But we didn't know any better."

A fresh face on the scene

In the spring of 1975, Ferguson befriended **Mike Lyons** at BSU. Lyons was particularly memorable because of how he learned to kayak — the swimming way — and what he achieved later. Ferguson and Lyons both enjoyed the outdoors a great deal — still do. They went backpacking together and climbed Mt. Borah. Ferguson talked about boating on the Payette and Lyons wanted to give it a go. But he didn't want to spend any time learning how to roll when all of his friends were out running rivers. "The trips kept coming up, and it was either stay home and learn how to roll, or just go swimming all the time when I got knocked over," Lyons says. "It didn't bother me to swim. I had been around water all of my life. I had no fear of the water."

"I swam almost all the way to Banks."

He ran Hells Canyon at 55,000 cfs that spring with Ferguson and some friends, and he had several hellacious swims. After that, he ran the Owyhee and the South Fork of the Payette. Indeed, he had no fear of water, and he had no trouble swimming to shore. But his fellow paddlers were tired of chasing his gear. "After a while, I remember Keith Taylor telling me, "OK, Mike, you're not going on another trip until you learn to roll." "

So he went to Lucky Peak and learned to roll with his dad. He went back to the Payette and boated a ton. By the end of the summer, the Bureau of Reclamation turned off the Deadwood River, and the South Fork was done for the season. Lyons decided to try a lower piece of the North Fork. He and John Hall, a C-1 boater, put in below Juicer, about 2.5 miles above Banks. When he entered Crunch, he got flipped. "I swam almost all the way to Banks," he remembers. "I got kind of bruised and battered in there. The rocks are so sharp in the North Fork, it kinds of beats you up."

Rob Lesser

Mike Lyons in Crunch at 5,000 cfs, early 1980s

Lyon's first fiberglass kayak, a Lettman Mark I, was destroyed by the North Fork. It wrapped on a rock and busted into pieces.

The following season in 1976, Hazelwood purchased 12 Hollowform plastic boats for McU Sports, the first plastic boats available on the market. Lyons pounced on one of them. During that season, Lyons began running the North Fork all the time, often in a quarter-inch- thick wet suit with no life jacket. Even though there were other guys who ran the North Fork occasionally, Lyons just loved the thrill of running the Lower Five. Often, he was forced to paddle it by himself for lack of a willing partner.

"I loved how the North Fork tests your reflexes and your skills," Lyons says. "It's scary to be upside down in there. At 1,500 to 2,000 cfs, it's Russian Roulette. So paddling the North Fork is just like survival. You've got be totally focused on the river."

That season, Lyons named the three main rapids in the Lower Five: Otter's Run, Juicer and Crunch. (See the narrative for the North Fork Class V section for details. He also ran pieces of the upper North Fork, and named "Steepness," the first major drop below Smith's Ferry.

Lesser was back in Idaho that spring and summer from Alaska. He recalls paddling the North Fork a few times with Lyons that year. He also ran the Middle Fork of the Salmon River with the "Crunch Bunch," a wild group of Kentucky Class V boaters.

Idaho's reputation as a whitewater paradise was beginning to ripple across the country among the tight kayaking network. Small groups of paddlers showed up from New York, New Jersey, California, Illinois and Wisconsin. The Midwest group came from "The Hoofers" an outdoor club from the University of Wisconsin-Madison.

"Fearless Freddy" Young, the leader of the Hoofers who ran 25-30 foot waterfalls in a C-1 boat along the north coast of Lake Superior, says they discovered Idaho by running the Middle Fork of the Salmon in 1971. They came out every year, and paddled more and more of what Idaho had to offer, including the Payette River. They ran the Upper South Fork, the South Fork Canyon, the Staircase run, and later, the North Fork, possibly as early as 1975.

"I remember going right over the pinnacle of Hound's Tooth, even though I knew I was supposed to go to the right or left of it," Young said. "I had been on stuff that was much steeper than that, but it was still a scary moment."

One other significant event occurred toward the end of the 1976 paddling season. Hazelwood, Frye and Murphy ran the first descent of the Class V Deadwood River, a 15-mile roadless canyon from below Deadwood Dam to the end of the Julie Creek Road. "We had talked

Linda Olson on the Salmon River in the mid-1970s in her K2 sunglasses and water-skiing vest.

about doing it a lot but no one had run it," Hazelwood says. "One guy told us there was a 25-foot falls in there. We told our wives it might take us two days to get through. Heck, it turned out we ran it in three hours."

For Hazelwood, running the Deadwood was a thrill. "That was, in my mind, the most enjoyable run we'd done on the Payette. No one had been down it, so we didn't know what to expect. There was a lot of dead wood, and one drop so choked with logs we had to portage it. But you could run everything else. It was great Class V stuff."

By this time, another rare female boater, **Linda Olson** of Boise, began boating the Payette with her ex-husband, **Ron Butler,** Lyons, Taylor, **Dick Knapp**, and others. A solid skier and natural athlete, Olson enjoyed running rivers. But she remembers there were very few women around. "It was pretty much a guy thing, but I thought it looked like fun," she says. "I might not have gotten into it if my husband didn't kayak."

It was 1977, a watershed year for the North Fork. The final big nemesis that remained was the steepest, middle section, later named "Jacob's Ladder." Here, the river drops 240 feet per mile — twice the average drop of 120 feet per mile on the North Fork. The "Crunch Bunch," **Bob Walker, Dennis Whitehouse, Bob Latter**, and **Craig Perdue**, was in town from Kentucky for two weeks of solid paddling in Idaho.

Rob Lesser
Dennis Whitehouse swam Jacob's Ladder during the first descent in 1977.

They hooked up with Lesser for the first descent of Golden Canyon on the South Fork of the Clearwater, and then the returned to paddle the whole North Fork.

Chuck Horrell, one of the Kentucky boaters, kept a journal, titled "Idaho 77." "This has got to be one of the most challenging runs in the country," he wrote. The 18 miles between Smith's Ferry and Banks "are absolutely continuous Class 4/5 water with at least one 6. On the enter run there are only three short pools."

They ran through Steepness, Nutcracker, Disneyland, S-Turn and the entire top section of the North Fork, pulling out before Jacob's Ladder. They named one section of the river "Golf Course," because it had eight consecutive "stopper" holes over a length of 50-75 yards. Golf Course was later applied to a section of the North Fork below Jacob's Ladder. After that day, Lesser had to return to Boise for nose surgery, scheduled months earlier.

"I felt cheated by the timing," Lesser says. "They're a really fun group of guys to hang out with — just a bunch of crazies."

On Day 12, the Crunch Bunch — named so because they lead with their nose — tackled the Jacob's Ladder section. "After an almost total sleepless night, Bob, Bob and Dennis started the last four miles," Horrell wrote. "After 30 minutes of paddling and three hours of scouting they pulled into an eddy near milepost 86 to look at the most God awful rapid I've ever seen.... After two hours of scouting and discussions, Bob W. in his usual conservative manner, said "There's no way." He promptly jumped in his boat and started the run. Forty-five seconds and four rolls later, he was sitting in an eddy below the fourth drop still saying, "There's no way." Dennis came next and once again exhibited the Crunch Bunch way. He flipped in the first drop, ran the second drop backwards, ran the third drop upside down and swam the fourth. Luckily, he flushed into an eddy below the last drop and got out with just a few bruises."

> Forty-five seconds and four rolls later, he was sitting in an eddy below the fourth drop still saying, "There's no way."

Walker, who had named Hound's Tooth Rapids the year before, says he was impressed with the continuous nature of the North Fork. "We'd run other stuff that was steeper, but the North Fork has the most continuous Class V water I've ever seen. It's obvious that if you go swimming, you're going to swim a long ways."

The water is powerful, too, Walker says. "I remember flipping in that thing and almost getting ripped out of the boat."

Even though the Crunch Bunch thought Jacob's Ladder was unrunnable, at least Bob Walker and Bob Latter showed it could be run with guerrilla whitewater skills. "It was definitely the highlight of my paddling career," Walker says today.

A week after the Crunch Bunch left Idaho, Lesser and fellow paddler Al Lowande had to run Jacob's Ladder, too. "We figured, By God, if we couldn't do Jacob's Ladder and everything else, we weren't ready for the Susitna," Lesser says. They survived Jacob's without any serious problems.

Lesser joined Blackadar on the Susitna that year with Frye and Lowande. All Payette River boaters, and now, all world-class boaters. See Watters' account of Devils Canyon thrashing Blackadar and Lowande, both of whom barely survived awful swims. Lesser was the only one who made it through intact.

But still, no one had run the North Fork top to bottom in one day....

Modern-day rafters discover the Payette

Not a single kayaker remembers seeing any rafts on the Payette River in the 1960s or much of the 1970s. Surely there were a few isolated rafters here and there who ran the Main Payette or parts of the South Fork. But surprisingly, the people who were rafting a lot in Idaho at that time — guides on the Middle Fork, Main Salmon and Hells Canyon — didn't spend any time warming up or pleasure-boating on the Payette, as some guides do today. Access to the Middle Fork is blocked by snow until late May or early June, when the water is honking. Access to the Payette, of course, is year-round.

"We were all based out of Salmon," says **Charlie Thompson**, who has run hundreds of trips down the Middle Fork and Main Salmon rivers, since 1966. "We just didn't think about coming over the hill and running the Payette."

It's possible that the first raft trips on the Payette River were done by Idaho Fish and Game officers on fishing patrol. **Martel Morache**, a long-time F&G biologist and enforcement officer, started running the Cabarton reach of the North Fork in the early 1960s. He used a Udisco rubber raft with a make-shift wooden frame and an oar set-up.

Morache checked anglers on the way down the river for work. On his own time, he also ran the river to catch a hefty rainbow or two. Starting in the late 1950s, Morache began to explore many of the Payette's flat-water runs. He paddled from McCall to Hartsell Bridge, the Deadwood River, above the reservoir, Cascade to Cabarton, and the Lower Payette River for duck and pheasant hunting. He did all of these things years before hardly anyone else thought of it.

Brock Loveland, a veteran Payette River rafter and catarafter, started doing private trips on the Main Payette in 1974. He recalls paddle rafting the Grand Jean section of the South Fork and paddle-rafting Swirly Canyon as a fishing trip. "It was a virgin water feeling," Loveland says. "Floating rivers at that time was how you really got away from people."

Blackadar dies in South Fork Canyon

Mother's Day weekend 1978. Blackadar invited a bunch of Sun Valley boaters to accompany him on a tune-up trip down the South Fork Canyon. He also invited Keith Taylor and Tullio Celano, who were busy. Taylor warned Blackadar on the phone about a big log spanning across two-thirds of what would become Blackadar Rapids. Lesser has photographs of the mucho ugly "sweeper" sticking upstream, but when Blackadar scouted the drop from the highway some 250 feet above, it was hard to see anything. The water had come up a bit, covering much of the sweeper with white foam.

As the group portaged Big Falls, Blackadar told the Sun Valley boaters, "It's paddleable," Watters wrote. Typical Blackadar bravado. He didn't try it that day, and it'd be 13 years before someone tried it — on purpose.

Below Big Falls, the South Fork zooms toward Blackadar Rapids in less than a minute. There were eight boaters in the party: Blackadar ran third behind **John Petit** and **Jeff Bevan**. As they approached the Class IV drop, Petit and Bevan pulled off in small eddies in the enclosed granite canyon. Bevan saw the outline of the log, Watters wrote, and then saw Blackadar drift by. "He smiled at me," Bevan told Watters, "and floated by as nonchalant as hell."

As Blackadar entered the drop, he didn't line up for a hard

ferry to the right or paddle to the right to miss the sweeper log, as Taylor had warned him to do. He rammed into it dead-on. "He hit the log hard with his bow, jarring him badly," Bevan told Watters. "The bow slipped all the way under, so the log ended up resting on his lap and against his large life jacket, which stopped him from going further. He was trapped."

The mighty Blackadar, the godfather of kayaking in Idaho, was pinned in a brutal position. He grabbed for a high brace, pulling down on his Illiad paddle to keep his head above water, but the force of the current sucked the boat into the log, and his Lettman Mark IV fiberglass kayak stood up on end. Petit and Bevan ran around the obstacle and eddied out on river-right, completely powerless to do anything. They saw Blackadar's life jacket float free, but his body wasn't with it. The seemingly invincible Blackadar was dead.

Celano and his friend **Del Stubblefield** came up the next day to search the river for the body. They found it on the right bank about 15 miles below the rapids, which instantly bore his name. "His boat was still trapped on the log Sunday morning," Hazelwood recalls. "It was pretty eerie."

For Blackadar to drown in a whitewater river almost seemed appropriate, because he had predicted it himself. "Walt talked a lot about living," Hazelwood says. "He always said, You'll bury me next to a rapid."

As it turned out, the family could have buried Blackadar next to the rapids but the Blackadars were worried the burial site might be drowned by a proposed high dam for the South Fork. So they got special permission to bury his body in the Pioneer Cemetery in Garden Valley. The plot sits on a hill with a gorgeous view of the valley, through which the river cuts a meandering course. "We had a fitting burial," Hazelwood says. "We made a circle, held hands and told Walt stories."

The moment still lingers in Hazelwood's mind. About 20 of

Blackadar's closest friends and family members attended.

In a way, Blackadar's death signalled the end of an era — and the gutsy, brutish, almost reckless kind of paddling style he represented. Younger kayakers, such as Lesser and many others, brought more finesse, caution and safety skills to the sport. Still, armed with greater ability and better equipment, they would push the envelope beyond what even Blackadar thought was possible.

A month later, in June 1978, expert Colorado boater **John Wasson** met Lesser that year while filming an ABC-TV "American Sportsman" segment on running the Yampa's Cross-Mountain gorge at flood stage. It was huge water, and the two excelled and bonded on the trip.

Later that month, a number of hot kayakers converged in Idaho. "It was a kayaking rendezvous in a true sense," Wasson says. "It was this great congregation of old cars and pickups and kayaks." Fred Young and the Hoofers were there, as was Al Lowande. They paddled the upper South Fork Payette, the canyon and parts of the North Fork, as well as many other Idaho rivers. "I realized this was a great place to be, hanging out running rivers," Wasson says.

Leonard, Guinn launch raft companies

Stanley boater **Joe Leonard** set up the first kayaking school in Idaho, possibly in the West, while he worked at the Robinson Bar Ranch in 1979. He held the first whitewater rodeos on the upper Salmon in the mid-1970s. He was a man of ideas. So Leonard decided to start the first raft-guiding service on the Payette that year. He ran trips in the upper South Fork, the Grand Jean section, and **Mary Naylor** ran trips on the Main Payette.

"I felt like kind of a hooker, going around to the hotels looking for clients," Naylor says, laughing at the thought.

They booked trips with out-of-staters in Boise for business

for $40 a head. "We'd pick up the customers at the hotel, drive them to Banks and float the Main," she says. "If we had enough customers for two raft-loads, I'd guide the second raft and hitchhike to run the shuttle at the end of the trip. If there was only one raftload of folks, I'd run the shuttle, park the van, and then ride my bicycle back to Boise."

The Lower South Fork of the Payette was considered "treacherous" in those days

Brock Loveland rows a boat filled with guests through Staircase in the early 1980s.

for rafting, Naylor says. "I still remember two people getting into innertubes above Staircase and drowning," she says. "It was just deadly."

Leonard, meanwhile, was entranced with the upper South Fork. Early in the season, they'd go downriver in kayaks, armed with saws. They'd float downriver and saw out logjams.

Leonard, who now lives in Tucson, Ariz., didn't make a big bundle from the outfitting business, but he adored the Payette River. "Boy, I miss that river," he says. "It has the best water in the world. Nothing I've been on gives you the versatility that the Payette has."

Long-time Idaho rafter **Steve Guinn** started renting rafts in the spring of 1979 when he opened a whitewater shop in Boise. At that time, Guinn ran the Barber Park rental business for Boise River floaters and most of the people renting went out to run the Boise. A few wanted to run the Payette, though. Guinn would fill out the forms for folks, outfit them with a raft and life jackets, and then he'd ask, "Have you been up on the Payette before? What part are you going to do?"

As an experienced rafter, he knew people could get into trouble in a hurry if they didn't have a clue. He worried about renting equipment to people who weren't experienced. "There wasn't anybody out there to get people into the sport safely," Guinn said. So he tried to start a training school on the main Payette, until he got a call from the Idaho Outfitters and Guides Licensing Board. They told him he couldn't run a training school without an outfitting license. So he obtained the second outfitters license on the Payette, and started running trips mostly on the main Payette.

Guinn remembers an early training trip on the Lower South Fork, in which he rowed a 16-foot raft down the left side of Staircase Rapids and got hammered. "We knew we wanted to be on the right side of the whale rock, but we got pushed left before we knew what was going on," he says. "We had quite a wild ride down that left side."

Once in Banks, they got out and took the boat back up the road for a second run. This time, though, Guinn nailed a T-shirt to a power pole next to Staircase. He'd be ready the next time.

First top-to-bottom big-water run on North Fork

That October of 1979, Lesser, Wasson and a group of expert kayakers who had been teaching at the Sundance Kayak School in Oregon stopped in Banks on their way to West Virginia. Late fall releases for irrigators had pumped the North Fork to 2,250 cfs. The group had four days to kill, so they began to tackle the North Fork piece-by-piece, much like the Kentucky group had done two years before. After three days of paddling, they got ready to leave, but a few of them thought about paddling the North Fork one more time. Rick Fernald shocked everyone when he said, "If I ever go back up there, it'll be to run the whole thing, top to bottom, in one day."

To Lesser's knowledge, no one had done to that, at least not at 2,250 cfs, a much more difficult flow than 1,200 cfs.

And so, on their fourth and final day on this Payette trip, the group paddled the whole North Fork top to bottom. Lesser skipped out on that run to take historical photographs for *Outside* and *Canoe* magazines. Wasson, **Don Banducci, Paul Hoobyar** and Fernald made the run. Oregon expert kayaker **Kathy Blau** ran the Lower Five with them. In doing so, she was the first woman to run the Lower Five, and she did it with total style.

Lesser says the top-to-bottom run scared the bejesus out of all of them. Banducci even wrote a will and penned a last-wishes letter to his girlfriend. "It was a primordal experience for Banducci," Lesser says. "It was his vision quest. It took him to the core."

He probably wasn't alone.

Jacob's Ladder, the steepest drop on the North Fork, was uppermost on their minds, of course. Banducci, Fernald and Hoobyar made it through without getting creamed in any number of horrifying holes. Wasson missed a critical move, though, and was forced to swim along the right shore. Miraculously, he got tossed out of the torrent by a wave and knocked onto the sharp rocks on shore. He was happy to be alive.

For a moment, Fernald had trouble, too. The front of his kayak slammed and pinned on a rock on the right shore. He was stuck. Lesser, who was watching on shore, took 3-4 minutes to wrestle his boat free. "He was cool as a cucumber and waited for me to unhook him," Lesser says.

The rest of the group was tempted to can it right there. Wasson urged them on, telling them the worst was behind them. Now they just had hundreds of holes, Golf Course, Screaming Left, Jaws, and the Lower Five to run through before Banks. It was daunting, but "John's brief show of faith turned that day around," Banducci wrote.

The trio paddled to the finish line, the confluence at Banks, and celebrated. The entire North Fork had been tamed. Soon, the word was out. Banducci's article in *Canoe* magazine and Lesser's photographs in *Outside* brought national attention to the feat. The idea of paddling the toughest continuous Class V river in North America would entice world-class boaters to the Payette for many years to come.

It also was a crowning event that convinced Wasson to buy property on the South Fork next to the old Grimes Pass Dam. He bought 12 acres initially, and later purchased the whole site of the historic Grimes Pass community, a beautiful river-bank flat of 140 acres. "The Forest Service and the river are our only neighbors," he says.

For several years, Blau and Wasson lived in the house together. Blau, now married to Oregon expert boater **Bo Shelby**, remembers it being a blissful time. "Oh gosh, it was great," she says. "The South Fork had clear water and hot springs, and lots of diversity. There's just nothing else like it."

To live above great Class IV river and have a play wave in your front yard was tough to beat, too. "Our friends would drive up and beep their horn from the other side of the river, and John and I would run down to the river with our boats, paddle across and go up and paddle the canyon back to our house."

Rob Lesser

They also ran the North Fork together. Blau ran the Lower Five at 5,000 cfs once, and did fine. "I've definitely never been as strong or on top of things as I was then," she says.

Kathy Blau glides through Hound's Tooth Rapids at high water.

Payette gets "busy" in early '80s

In the early 1980s, boating began to boom in a modest sense on the Payette. Guinn's outfitting business, Whitewater Shop River Tours, was beginning to boom. Several new lines of rafts enticed private boaters to leap into the whitewater world. A young new generation of kayakers entered the scene from Ketchum and Boise. Advanced equipment, instruction and the added experience of veteran boaters created a more inviting environment for adventurous folks to join in on the fun.

Loveland recalls how the scene changed. "It was as if someone had flipped a switch. All of a sudden you had private boaters (rafters) on the river, and the outfitting business was really starting to take off."

Guinn hung whitewater posters at Barber Park and selected

hotels, enticing folks to give the Payette a whirl. They ran oar boats down the Lower South Fork and paddle rafts on the Main Payette. Leonard's skeleton crew also ran Main Payette trips, with people like **Jo Cassin**, co-owner of Idaho River Sports, and **Bob Henry**, a veteran Middle Fork boater, as guides.

They only ran high-water trips in May and June and bagged the season in July. Loveland remembers taking two customers down the Lower South Fork when the water lapped against the oil on the Banks-Lowman highway. They got stuck in an eddy on river right and whirled around three times before Loveland could power the raft through the eddy fence. "They asked if it was going to get any worse than that, and I said, "We haven't even started." Then they gave each other that 'we are deadmen' look."

They made it down OK. But Loveland, an expert catarafter and safety instructor today, says "we were really hanging out in the wind" in those days. "We didn't have flip lines; we didn't have throw ropes, and often times, the guests weren't dressed in proper cold-water gear. I can not believe we got away with what we did."

Guides feared a flip more than anything else in those days, Loveland says. "To guides in those days, the lowest of the low was flipping. If you flipped, it was like tattooing a scarlet F on your forehead, and you'd get hammered for the rest of your career."

And so, we have to tell a Brock Loveland flip story. In the early '80s, he was taking Barbara Mandrell's country western band down the river. They decided to take them on the Main Payette to be on the safe side. After all, Guinn recalls Loveland saying, "What can happen on the Main?"

Well, Loveland had five band members in his raft, and they were having a good 'ol time on the main. Somehow, he came into Mixmaster's powerful left-lateral wave sideways, and boom, they flipped and everyone was pitched into the drink. Everyone was laughing in the boat behind them, and then they realized, Oh no, we're next!

Loveland remembers the ego-blow was uppermost in his mind when he surfaced. "All I could think of, was, Oh, my god, I flipped. I flipped. I didn't get on the raft and start pulling customers out of the water. I was in shock. That was a total wake-up call for me."

That night, Loveland went to the Snake River Stampede and got a royal ribbing in front of thousands of fans. "They put the spotlight on me and the announcer said, "Don't go boating with that guy, he'll kill ya." I've never lived that one down."

Wildman "Banana Boy" Mark Fraas

Mark Fraas, a late '70s and early '80s-vintage North Fork kayaker, may have a trend-setter without even knowing it. Fraas was one of those immensely athletic guys who picked up new sports quickly. **Roger Rosentreter**, who came onto the Payette scene in the late 1970s, helped teach Fraas how to kayak. They became quick buddies and once Fraas got the hang of things, they started boating together frequently.

Rob Lesser
Mark Fraas pops an ender at the Payette Whitewater Rodeo.

Before he got into kayaking, Fraas was a motocross champion and he set the speed record at Jackson Hole ski resort on telemark skis. To excell in motocross or set the speed record on "pins," you've got to be just a little bit nuts. Obviously, Fraas would enjoy kayaking.

Rosentreter remembers a downriver race in Salmon in 1980, featuring some of the nation's top boaters, who were paddling specialized racing boats. "Fraas beat them all in his Dancer," Rosentreter says, referring to the Perception plastic whitewater boat. "He was so phenomenal."

Much like Lyons, Fraas didn't know any fear. He loved to play in holes and get "elevator" rides in the surging reversals. He frequently boated the North Fork solo, sometimes without a life jacket. He was that comfortable in the big water and that crazy. "Fraas used to drop into holes just to feel what it was like in there," Rosentreter says, smiling. "One year, he ran the North Fork 40 times," Rosentreter says.

The guy was prone to playful antics, too. In one of the early whitewater rodeos, Fraas was doing endos on a play wave and got flipped. When he rolled up, he had a giant fish in his mouth. He also had a nail atop his kayak helmet, and he drilled a hole through the middle of his paddle handle so he could insert the paddle atop his helmet and twirl it while he rode a wave.

Eventually, Fraas left Boise and went to Hood River, where he runs a store called "Air Time." He apparently is one of the best board-sailors in the gorge, which doesn't surprise anyone who saw Fraas paddle the North Fork.

First North Fork raft descent of Lower Three

Sometime in the spring runoff of 1981, maybe 1982, a big burly rafter from California made the first raft descent of the lower three miles of the North Fork. Boise boater **Sandra Gebhards** was on a Selway trip with **Peter Ryan**, a professional guide who ran trips on the Tuolomme River in Calif., in mid-May. The Selway was booming at seven feet on the gauge. "We ran it in a day and a half," she said. "There were 10-15 foot waves in some of the rapids. It was like nothing I've ever seen in my life."

Ryan handled the big water in an Avon raft with strong skills, Gebhards says. "He was this big Viking type of guy. He was 6-5, and super strong and really good on the oars."

On their way home, they drove by the North Fork and Ryan announced that he was going to run it. Gebhards said, "Oh no, you can't do that, you'll die in there."

Ryan asked her to go along, and Gebhards had to decline. Her father, Stacy, was an experienced kayaker and rafter. He was very safety conscious, and she knew "if I didn't die on the river, my dad would have killed me afterwards."

Rob Lesser

Roger Rosentreter hams it up on the South Fork.

Ryan needed someone to ride with him to bail the boat. Legend had it that since no one would ride with Ryan, he picked up a hitchhiker on the way to the put-in and put him in the front of the boat. It was a great tale because the hitchhiker obviously wouldn't know any better. But the true story is a kayaker drove up as Ryan was getting ready to launch and volunteered to go along.

Ryan filled several dry bags with rocks to weigh down the front end of the raft, and the two shoved off. They made it through Juicer and Crunch without flipping, and landed safely in Banks. Yet another paradigm on the Payette had been pierced — a raft had survived the lower North Fork. Suddenly the kayakers didn't have exclusive title to the North Fork — a "lowly" rafter had conquered a piece of their river. It would be years, however, before a bunch of wild guys ushered a new kind of craft down the whole thing.

Equipment innovations raise outfitting to new level

Through the 1980s, new equipment created new horizons for the daring and adventuresome. The advent of self-bailing rafts, catarafts (double-pontoon rafts) and solo canoes all added new dimensions to whitewater boating. The hot new rafts, which eliminated the need to bail water out of a boat, drew hundreds, if not thousands of new people to the sport.

These boats made running Class IV and V rapids easier than in the old "bucket" boats because the old crafts filled up with water, became heavy and unmaneuverable, and the boaters soon got into trouble, being subject to the river's whims.

Steve Jones
All of Cascade Raft Co.'s gear fit on one trailer in 1985.

Steve Jones and **Cully Erdman** took advantage of the new self-bailing raft technology to introduce commercial paddle-rafting to the South Fork Canyon. They formed Cascade Raft Co. in

1985, and pushed the outfitting business to a new level on the Payette River. Jonesy, as he's commonly known, had been paddle-rafting on the Lochsa and rowing dories for Grand Canyon Dories. Erdman was a world-class Class V kayaker who owned Slick Rock Expeditions, a river outfitting business based in Moab and Mexico. "I remember those early trips on the Payette as being pretty exciting," recalls **Mary Williams**, one of the original guides. "Nobody had the canyon wired like they do now."

Idaho Whitewater Unlimited, owned by **Dave and Shelly Fisher** of Meridian, followed Cascade's lead with paddle-boat trips in self-bailing rafts in the summer of 1987. "We got into whitewater rafting privately for recreation about 15 years ago when we were first married," Fisher says. "We floated all kinds of rivers just for fun. Then we decided, why not turn our hobby into a business, and so that's what we did." IWU also ran trips in the canyon and elsewhere on the Payette on a routine basis.

By 1989, outfitting was really started to hop on the Payette. Some of their customers decided to buy their own equipment and get into rafting, with the Payette being so close to Boise. In 1989 Bear Valley outfitters went into business under different ownership than today. It has passed hands twice until Liz and Steve Boren, sister and brother, bought the business in 1995. They also boated on a private basis until they started their own company.

Conrad Fourney, an expert Class V kayaker from back east, launched his business in September 1992.

The Aire boys reach for the sky

"Cats," as they're commonly referred to today, took an even bigger technological leap by eliminating the floor of a raft altogether. The twin pontoons slice through rapids and holes with ease, and they can take rocks up the center, a deadly problem for regular rafts.

Nolan Whitesell, an Atlanta, Ga., based boater, designed a low-volume solo canoe with a high bow and stern that was built especially with running Class V whitewater in mind. Whitesell's boat started a whole new trend. Local boaters such as **Phil Lansing, Stan Kolby, Rick Katucki, Amy Haak**, and **Denny Mooney**, among others, made solo canoes a permanent fixture on the

Payette. Whitesell traveled to Banks, Idaho, in August 1987, to see if he could run the entire length of the North Fork. "Anywhere you go, advanced boaters know about the North Fork of the Payette," he said at the time. "Very advanced expert boaters view it as being the ultimate."

With safety kayakers around him, Whitesell conquered all of the different sections of the North Fork during a week-long stay in Idaho. He helped bring attention to the river, too, at a time when whitewater boaters and environmentalists were working hard to protect the North Fork from being dammed and diverted into a tube (See River Conservation chapter).

Glenn Oakley
Nolan Whitesell makes first solo canoe descent of North Fork, circa 1987.

Just days after Whitesell's first solo canoe descent of the North Fork, **Kris Walker, Ned Cox, Alan Hamilton** and **Mark Dunn** attempted the first top-to-bottom run of the North Fork in catarafts. Video camera crews were on hand to document the run.

Hamilton had run the Lower Five in 1986 in a Northwest River Supplies Argonaut, and he'd been looking at the rest of the North Fork for a long time, wondering if it could be done. At the time, Hamilton worked for Northwest River Supplies, and he had a ton of whitewater experience. Walker ran a mountaineering equipment-design business in Colorado, and he, too, had lots of whitewater experience. He ran part of the North Fork in 1986, including the horrific-looking "Screaming Left" drop. Naturally, these two wildmen had a hankering to do the whole North Fork, the grandaddy of all Class V rivers.

It was a sunny, hot day, perfect conditions for the top-to-bottom run. The North Fork was pumping at 1,800 cfs, a good flow that would provide some cushion on sharp rocks, but the holes would be huge and powerful.

To prepare, the crew had scouted the whole river. Walker, who would run the lead boat, wrote out an elaborate cheat sheet and duct taped it to his left tube. The sheet contained notes and little drawings. "I'd put a Big X mark and Do Not Enter in places where I didn't want to go," he says.

They ran the upper section without incident, knifing through holes and waves and getting tossed about on their cats. They got a breather in Big Eddy, and then headed down toward the big daddy-o, Jacob's Ladder. Walker punched the hole below the steepest part of Jacob's and emerged in one piece. Whew! Cox wasn't so lucky. The huge stopper hole lurched the raft sideways and he got tossed into what kayakers call the "taffy puller," a powerful hydraulic with revolving whip-action. He got egg-beatered and then swam to his boat and got back in.

"He's the only guy I've ever seen act like a flying fish," Hamilton says.

Then Dunn got surfed in the "ocean wave," a giant wave at the bottom of Jacob's, for about five minutes, giving the camera crew time to run downriver, get set up, and film him hanging 10 in the wave. Ever the jokester, Hamilton yelled at him, "Hey, you're hogging video time."

After running through a set of nasty holes and rocks known as the Golf Course, the group settled in for a thrilling ride to Banks. They knew they had gotten through the worst of it, their skills were sharp, and they started to have heaps of fun. "After you've run the top-half, you're trying to hit the biggest stuff you can find," he says. "It's one rapid at a time; one peg at a time."

In Banks, it was time to clink beer cans.

"We felt we were on top of the world," Cox says.

"It's the ultimate adrenaline rush," Hamilton says. "You run the whole North Fork like that in one day, and you feel like you're invincible."

Walker puts it this way. "You feel like you've cheated death."

Mark Lisk

Alan Hamilton of Aire cruises down the North Fork in a cataraft.

In April 1989, Walker and Hamilton formed a cataraft- and raft-manufacturing corportation called Aire, short for Argonaut Inflatable Research & Engineering Co. They specialized in cats.

First descent of Big Falls

After the North Fork had been conquered, there was really only one major deal left: No one had run Big Falls in a kayak or a raft ... on purpose.

In 1989, **Grant Amaral**, an expert Class V kayaker, first-descent creek boater and author of an Idaho boating guide, decided he was going to give Big Falls a try at low water (300 cfs). After his successful first descent that year, other Class V kayakers started to join Amaral for late-season runs down Big Falls. Boise kayaker **Tim Shanahan** has organized the event in the last four years, calling it the **Larry Dunn** Swimvitational, after a boater who accidentally swam Big Falls in the 1980s.

> "It must have been 12 hours before I came to the surface."

Not to be outdone, the Aire boys decided to give Big Falls a whirl in 1993. **Todd Walker** ran the first boat down in a 12-foot cat, and Hamilton followed in a 15-foot boat. Walker made it in one piece, although he got stuck several times on the way down. Hamilton had a smoother ride at first, but he flipped at the bottom of the falls.

"It's the longest I've been under water," Hamilton says. "Everyone talks about time-expansion, and it must have been 12 hours before I came to the surface. I went down about 20 feet, and I remember looking up toward the surface, thinking, anytime I break the surface would be cool."

He finally emerged above water and got a big breath. Next time Hamilton runs Big Falls he says he plans to do it in a shorter boat.

What's next?

Who knows what's next on the horizon for new challenges, new feats on the Payette River. Since Fraas's era on the river, top-

Rob Lesser

Jim Grossman as a teen-ager on the Ultimate play wave.

to-bottom runs on the Payette were pushed to multiple runs in one day. Expert kayaker **Bob McDougall** was the first boater to complete three top-to-bottom runs in a day to clock a vertical mile. Missoula Class V paddler **Doug Ammons**, who started boating the North Fork in the mid-'80s, has run the North Fork five times in day — whew! that's 75 miles of hair-ball water in a single day.

Others, such as Boise boater **Jim Grossman** and Salt Lake boater **Mark White** have hand-paddled various sections of the North Fork, and then Ammons did the full 15-mile run with hand paddles. He's since done multiple complete runs with hand paddles.

Grossman learned to kayak as a young teen-ager, an increasing trend on the Payette. Boise teen boaters like **Adam Shandro** and numerous others have cut their teeth on the Payette, and the North Fork in particular, vaulting them to new heights. Cascade Recreation lured California expert kayaker and instructor Tom Long to the Payette in 1993, and more and more kids are being seen on the river all the time. The kids include Long's three teen-age sons, all of whom paddle the North Fork.

Ammons, meanwhile, is constantly challenging himself, trying to learn new things from the river. It's not a "showboating" kind of thing to paddle the North Fork with hand-paddles, Ammons says, it's skill-enhancing experience to become one with the river. "I learned as much as I did that day as I had the previous three years," he says.

Ammons also ran the North Fork at 6,100 cfs in 1993, a super-high level that provided a new challenge for him, a challenge that brought everything together he'd learned in kayaking over a decade in one day. A classic guitarist, he likens it to playing a complex musical score without making a single mistake, just turning his mind and body over to the river and letting everything flow.

"I could close my eyes and feel the whole river at once," he says. "I could feel all of these nuances of the current, all of the patterns, all of the lines.... To me, water and music are flowing emotions; one is not like the other, they are the same."

Still, even when one becomes that comfortable in the middle of so many complex forces, Ammons says the river is still ever-powerful to him, always the master. "All you can do is keep asking questions, and the river will give you an answer," he says.

Payette Visions
Safety kayakers help rescue swimmers after a flip.

WHITEWATER SAFETY

World-class rivers such as the Payette demand the utmost respect from boaters of all kinds. The Payette is a big, powerful river with chaotic hydraulics, strong eddy lines and cold water. Unfortunately, some beginning boaters are too ignorant or head-strong to grasp the danger — much like a few incidents involving Payette River pioneers. Let me share an anecdote to illustrate the point.

Early Payette River outfitter Steve Guinn ran across two couples near Staircase Rapids on the South Fork on a spring day in the early 1980s. The river was honking high, and the water temperature couldn't have been over 40 degrees F.

Payette Visions
Paddlers should get out of cold water quickly.

65

Guinn spied the young couples and noticed that only the women had life jackets. The men thought they were too manly to need life jackets, and Guinn's couldn't talk them out of running the South Fork.

The ignorant idiots launched, flipped and drowned, and the wives survived.

The moral of this story: It's not macho to run whitewater without a life jacket, it's stupid.

It's not macho to run whitewater without life jackets, it's stupid.

To ensure an enjoyable experience on the Payette River, the author recommends that boaters learn the basics about whitewater safety. In general, that means being prepared for the worst, carrying key safety gear for coping with rescues and knowing how to respond to emergencies.

Safety experts recommend the following equipment for a whitewater trip on the Payette River:

■ Cold-water garments: Layering is best, much like for active winter activities. Start with a bathing suit on the bottom, and then add layers of polypropelene or capaline underwear for cold water and cold weather. Then top it off with a wet suit, dry suit and/or paddle jacket, and wet suit booties.

■ U.S. Coast Guard-approached lifejacket.

■ Solid hard-plastic helmets with foam-padding. Helmets are required for kayakers and solo-canoeists for obvious reasons. Rafters attempting Class IV and V water should wear them, too.

■ Throw ropes. Rafters should have at least one throw rope within easy reach of paddlers in the bow or the paddle captain in the stern or both. It's a good idea for kayakers to carry a throw rope inside their boat. Make sure you know how to use a throw rope; it's a good idea to practice.

■ Flip lines for rafts and catarafts. Another option for self-bailing paddle rafts is to run a strap or rope across the bottom of the boat and tie it off to each side of the self-bailing floor.

■ Tow lines for kayaks. You can set up a line with a caribiner on one end and a jam cleat on the other. That way a kayaker can clip the biner on the loose boat and tow it to a landing, instead of trying to "herd" it with the nose of the kayak. The jam cleat allows the towing kayaker to quickly release the other boat, if necessary.

■ Extra oar/extra paddle. Rafters should count on losing a paddle to a swimmer or losing an oar to a rock. Be sure to tie safety lines from your oars to the frame in the event that the oar gets popped out and falls into the river.

■ Whistle. It's hard, if not impossible to hear people screaming something at you in the middle of a rapid. A whistle will get their attention, and agreed-upon hand signals will help communicate what to do next.

■ Carabiners. Pop a few 'biners on your life jacket and have some spares in the boat. Biners are great for attaching gear to the boat for quick access and release. They're also great for using as a pulley in the event of a pinned boat.

■ River knife. Several manufacturers make excellent quick-release river knives for emergency situations or spreading a sandwich. Knives can help boaters get untangled from loose ropes during a flip, and they serve many other purposes when lines get tangled or caught at inopportune moments.

■ Portage line. For the South Fork Canyon, boaters will need about 100 feet of line to portage rafts around Big Falls. Several throw ropes clipped together with a 'biner will do the trick, too.

■ Sun screen, lip balm and hand lotion.

■ First-Aid Kit. At minimum, a kit should include band-aids, adhesive tape, butterfly pads, gauze pads, pain-killers or aspirin, fold-up saw, lighter, Swiss Army knife.

■ Duct tape. You've heard of it, no doubt, the river runner's "everything" tool.

■ Z-drag kit for raft or canoe pins. See the book "River Rescue" by Les Bechdel and Slim Ray for details on how to set up a z-drag with slings, caribiners, prusiks and rope.

River safety courses

Boaters who live in southwest Idaho have a variety of whitewater safety and rescue courses to choose from every year. At this time there are three options:

■ International river rescue expert Les Bechdel offers several river-rescue courses on the Payette River every spring. For more information, call 208-634-4303.

■ Boise State University's Outdoor Adventure Program offers river rescue and safety courses, taught by veteran Class V boater Brock Loveland. For more information, call 385-1374.

■ Cascade Recreation offers river-rescue courses taught by Tom Long, Steve Jones or Denny Mooney. For more information, call 1-800-292-RAFT.

Safety talks

Before any whitewater river trip, someone in your party — presumably your leader — should give everyone a safety talk. Novice boaters should request a safety talk if their leader doesn't offer one voluntarily. The talk should cover:

■ Lifejackets. Everyone must have a life jacket. Be sure to adjust the jackets to fit snugly. That way, the jacket won't smother your head during a swim and people will be able to yank you into the boat by hauling on your tight-fitting life jacket.

■ Swimming ability.

■ The potential dangers faced that day — high-water or low-water hazards.

■ High-siding when the boat flips to one side or during pins.

■ What to do in the event of a swim: Hold onto your paddle, get your feet downstream, stay with the boat or get to shore, whichever looks best, etc. etc. Don't panic.

■ What to do in the event of a flip.

■ How to use a throw rope.

■ Water fight technique.

Drownings

There have been seven drownings in the Payette River Basin since 1975, according to the Idaho Parks & Recreation Department statistics, compiled from sheriff's reports. The list is not complete, to the author's knowledge, but it provides a glimpse of how boaters have gotten into trouble on the river and on Payette Lake.

1. Walt Blackadar's kayak pinned on a log in the South Fork Canyon below Big Falls in May 1978. Blackadar, 55, had been

warned about the log, but he failed to avoid it. See page xx for details.

2. A 17-year-old boy was struck by an outboard motor propeller after falling overboard. He drowned in 1988. Victim was reportedly doing circles around a canoe while seated on back of driver's chair. Boat was at full throttle. Victim and second person were thrown overboard when they hit their wake. The boat circled and struck the victim in the head and arm. Life-jackets were on board but not used.

3. Tim Houlihan drowned in 1988 after getting ejected from his 14-foot self-bailing raft and swam an ugly hole, the "Taffy Puller," in Jacob's Ladder Rapids on the North Fork, near Swinging Bridge Campground. Houlihan, 40, was launched out of the raft when he hit the stopper hole below the rock drop in Jacob's. He was wearing a life-jacket and helmet. The moral of this story: Swimming the North Fork can be a roll of the dice.

4. Mark Schirmer, 32, Boise, drowned on the South Fork after his raft flipped in Little Falls in the spring of 1989. Schirmer and two others were thrown into the river. They stayed with the raft and floated downriver. Schirmer already had had a tracheotomy and knew if he got thrown into the river that he'd have trouble surviving.

5. A 28-year-old male kayaker, Jim Yetter, drowned after his kayak slammed into a log on the North Fork, and pinned. It took four hours to extricate the body. Accident occurred in the summer of 1992.

6. Anna Korstad, an 18-year-old Boise woman, drowned in 1994 after the raft she was riding in got wrapped on a large boulder in Dog Leg Rapids on the lower South Fork. The raft was overloaded with 15 people. After the raft wrapped and passengers got thrown into the river, the victim became entangled in loose ropes, was trapped under water and drowned.

7. A 39-year-old Boise man, Les Benson, drowned in the South Fork Canyon in the spring of 1995 after a raft flipped in the Lone Pine section. Victim swam with the boat for 15 minutes in cold water, but did not get on top of the raft. Passengers swam to shore. Victim got separated from the raft and drowned. The moral: After a raft flip, be sure to get on top of the raft or swim to shore. Freezing-cold water saps a person's energy quickly.

Map Legend

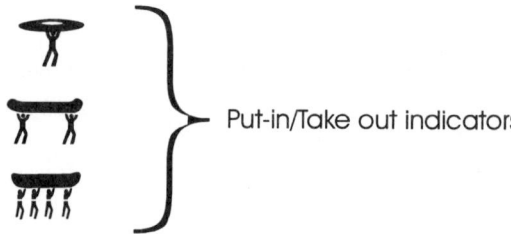 Put-in/Take out indicators

 Direction of Travel
✹ Scout

∼ Class I Rapid
≈ Class II Rapid
≋ Class III Rapid
≋ Class IV Rapid
≋ Class V Rapid
≋ Class VI Rapid

🚶‍♂️ Trail
[555] Forest Service road
(72) State Highway
(30) U. S. Highway
(84) Freeway

[3,780'] Elevation
△ Mountain
◆ Historical Site
⌒ Spring

🍴 Restaurant/Food
🚻 Rest Area
P Parking
▲ Campground with services
▲ Primitive camping area (no services)

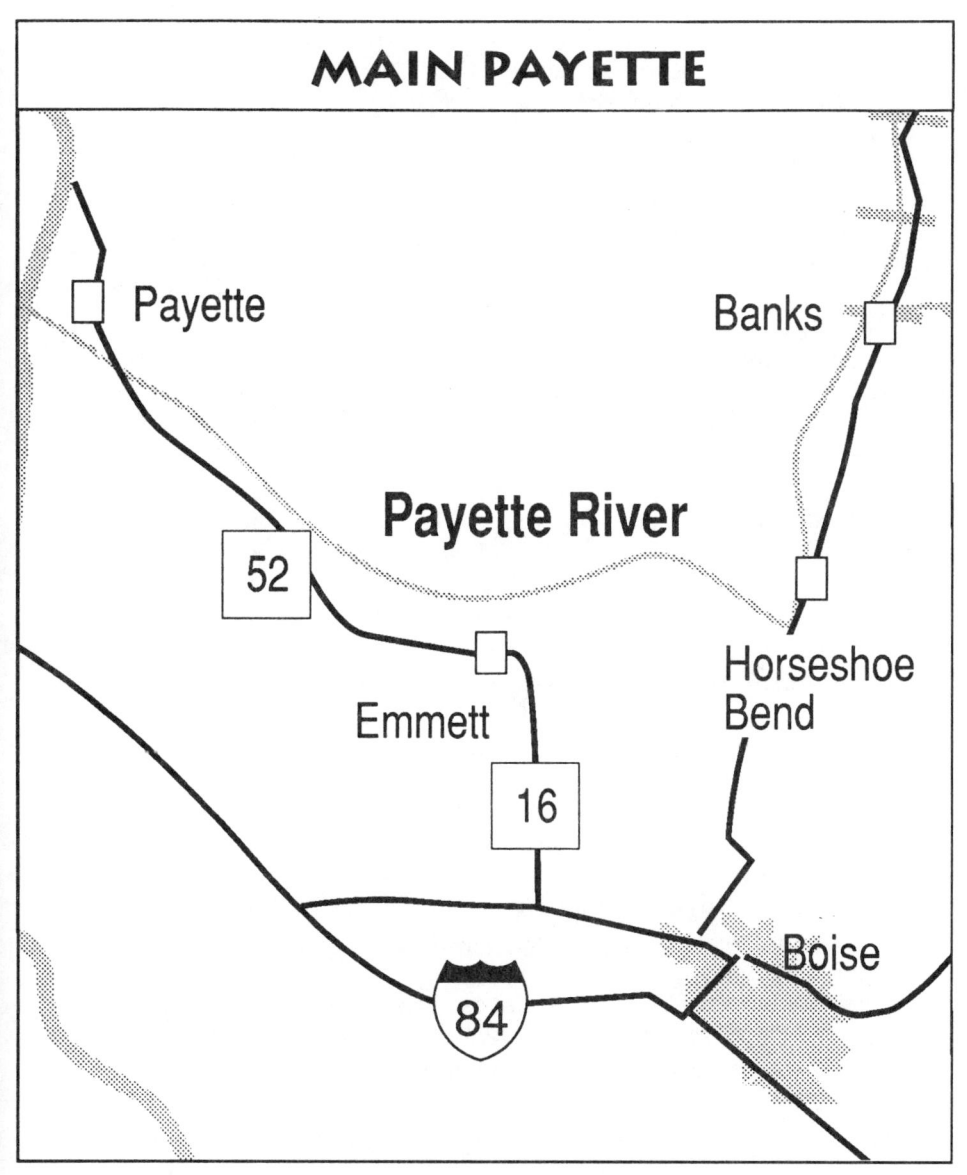

BANKS TO BEEHIVE BEND

Difficulty: Intermediate & up (Class III)
Put-Ins: Banks; Sandy Beach; Surf City; Chief Parrish.
Types of craft: Kayaks, rafts, canoes, duckies
Distance: 7 miles
Float time: 1-4 hours
Take-out: Beehive Bend; Gardena; Gravel ramp; Horseshoe Bend.
Steepness: 26 feet per mile
Season: March-October

Getting there: Drive to Banks, Idaho, on Idaho 55. It is 35 miles to Banks from Boise, and 70 miles to Banks from McCall. Banks lies at the junction of the south and north forks of the Payette, and therefore, is a key put-in/take-out point for floaters who are ending their trip or just beginning it. Just past the Banks store, watch for a left-hand turn across the North Fork to the Main Payette launch site. Alternative put-ins include: the Sandy Beach, about 1.5 miles below Banks; Surf City, about 2 miles below Banks); and Chief Parrish, about 4 miles below Banks. (see map)

Shuttle: Drop a vehicle at your preferred take-out: Beehive Bend on the main Payette (five miles north of Horseshoe Bend); Chief Parrish (eight miles north of Horseshoe Bend), or at points downriver toward Horseshoe Bend.

The Float: The Main Payette is the consummate Class III whitewater playground for boaters of nearly all abilities. It's a kick just to be in Banks, Idaho, "River Central," the epicenter of whitewater madness. At the Banks launch, one can feel the electricity just by hanging out, listening to boaters rave about their runs upstream, or about the excitement of what lies ahead. Every possible brand of boater and craft can be found here at the Banks put-in. The Class III-level of "The Main" — as locals know it — makes this a perfect run for families and novices. Big features, waves and holes, offer up some hoots for kayakers in search of play spots. Hopefully raw beginners, especially kayakers and canoeists, will have the sense to run the lower main or the Middle Fork Tie Creek reach as a "warm up" to the Main Payette. For

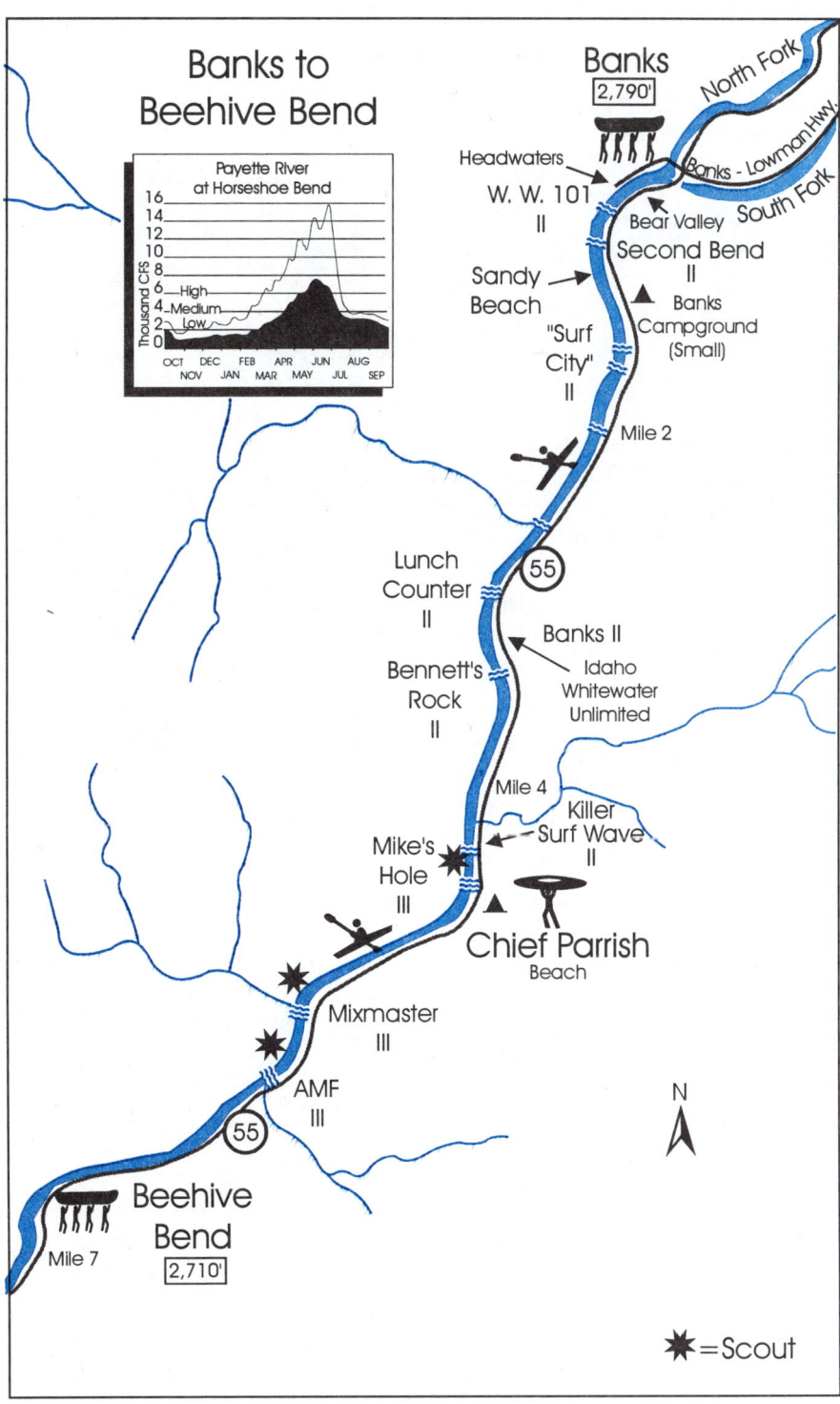

Top: The Banks boat ramp on a typical summer weekend. Right: Banks, Idaho, hub of Payette River whitewater madness.

this is the real McCoy. The Main Payette features a number of Class II drops with tall waves, three named Class III rapids, and powerful river dynamics. In high water, novice kayakers should expect to get knocked over in powerful eddy lines, and novice rafters often get whirled around in holes, flipped in rapids or wrapped on rocks. But once you've acquired the skills to enjoy Class III water, the Main provides for a fun-filled experience. It's also a beautiful place to spend the day. Numerous sandy beaches provide nice stopping points for lunch or just hanging out and relaxing. Advanced kayakers revel in the main's plentiful play spots, including the main play wave at "Surf City." Fishing for rainbow trout can be decent on this reach, too. All in all, floating the main is a guaranteed good time.

To begin, head out of the Banks put-in and shoot into the current. Kayakers can use a spacious eddy at the put-in for practicing rolls or they can warm up playing in small holes and rollers in the adjacent rapids. Once you head downriver, it's less than a

Sandy beaches are abundant on the Main.

half mile to the first Class II drop, which Cascade Raft Co. calls **Whitewater 101** for lack of any other name.

A gradual left-hand bend and the roar of whitewater signal the rapids is coming up. The run here is typically in the left-center portion of the river, at most river flows. Canoes may want to sneak the main wave train to avoid getting swamped in three-foot waves. After the first drop, there is a short break before a second Class II rapids comes up, again after a gradual left-hand bend. The run here is normally about the same course as the first drop, left-center. Kayakers should watch for numerous playing opportunities in both drops. At certain flows, a nice endo hole is located at the tail-out of the second rapids on the left side of the river.

Floaters will drift into the **Big Sandy Beach** after Second-Bend Rapids. If boaters encounter serious trouble in the first two drops, they should pull out of the river here. The rapids will get bigger and more challenging downstream. The beach area is a nice place to rest, practice kayak rolls or play volleyball (if you get a court set up before the masses fill in the beach). But since the beach is a major hangout for road-weary travelers and tourists, floaters should consider looking for their own private lunch beach farther downriver.

Anything goes on the Main Payette.

Around the bend from the beach, a small rapids provides some mini-play waves for kayakers. Look ahead after that, and kayakers will see a nice river-wide curling wave in the next drop. You guessed it, this is **"Surf City,"** the most popular play wave on the Payette.

This wave changes dramatically at different flow levels, as do many play spots on the Main. It's a good idea for kayakers to line up backwards and try to catch the wave as they drop into Surf City, or if you miss it and get blown off, paddle for the river-left eddy and try again. It's possible to park above the wave in a road-side pullout if kayakers or solo canoeists want to focus their river trip on the Play Wave.

Proceeding on, the river flows through some Class II drops and then smoothes out for a piece next to some nice beaches as the Payette winds toward what a few people call **"Lunch-Counter Rapids."** This is a straight-away Class II drop down the center of the river, with a big churning hole near the top of the drop on river-right. It's not real obvious from above, but kayakers who want to give the hole a go should pull into the right-side eddy next to the rapids and take a look. Roger Rosentreter says some of his kayaking buddies call this drop "Lunch-Counter" because it's fun to pull over and eat lunch on the right bank and watch 'yakers get launched out of the hole or get trashed.

Since this rapid doesn't seem to have a commonly used name, we'll use Roger's to see if it sticks. Below here, the river bends to the left and spreads out in a wide spot in the channel. At low water, the river splits around a low gravel bar and then narrows up

The Main Payette play wave, a.k.a. Surf City, at 3,000 cfs.

before the next rapid at Banks II.

The rapid, caused by a large boulder in the center of the river, is known as **Bennett's Rock** or **Bennett's Hole**, after the last name of a man who used to run a restaurant in Banks II. At high water, the river washes out the hole that forms behind Bennett's rock at low flow, and forms a set of huge ocean-like waves behind it. Rafts can run center at this level. At medium- to low-flows, the rock emerges out of the river and forms a mammoth hole behind it. At these flows, the raft run is on the right. At high water, the giant waves at Bennett's form one of best surf spots in the Payette drainage. Kayaks can catch the first glassy wave in the series, or eddy out on river-left and rudder into one of the steep stacks of your choice. I recall surfing one of those hugies in the spring of '95 and feeling as if I was inside a giant room-full of water. Catch one of those puppies and it'll put a big grin on your face.

Once boaters pass by Banks II, they enter the second half of the Main Payette whitewater reach. **Mike's Hole** is coming up in about a mile — at the end of the long straight-away. In the meantime, floaters can look forward to a nice set of deep roller-coaster waves in a Class II rapid immediately upstream of Mike's. The smooth entrance wave in this drop is another gorgeous place to surf. After that drop, it's time to psych-up for Mike's Hole.

Keith Taylor
Mike Norell, of Mike's Hole, circa 1972

The scout is on river-right, if you want to pull out and take a look. It's also possible to eddy scout on the right bank.

At medium flows (3,500 cfs), **Mike's Hole Rapids** has several notable features — a rock shelf on the left, which pushes the current to the right, and a large rock on the right, which pushes the current back toward the center. So the run at this flow involves lining up on the right, following the current toward the rock, and then paddling toward river-center to avoid getting washed over the rock into the hole. In essence, it's a classic little S-turn run around the rock and hole. Long-time Boise kayaker **Mike Norell**, who paddled with a handful of kayaking pioneers on the Main Payette, got washed into the hole the first two times he ran the rapids in the fall of 1970. As a result, fellow boaters Keith Taylor, Roger Hazelwood and Tullio Cellano christened the rapids after Mike

A typical scenario for beginning kayakers: Flip trying to miss Mike's Hole.

"I was at the tail of the pack, thinking about how much fun we were having and looking at the scenery, and suddenly I'm floating sideways into this big hole," Norell recalls. "I remember I dropped right on top of someone else who was already in there, and knocked them out.... I bailed out and went straight to the bottom of the river, and I was stuck underneath there bouncing around for 15 seconds, and finally I came out."

After that kind of experience, you'd think Norell would remember the hole and stay the hell away from it. But noooooooo. He did it again. On his second trip down the Main, Norell recalls he was having another great day. He remembers that from Banks on down, he had gotten knocked over three times and rolled up twice. Then Mike's Hole comes up, "and I forgot about it. I was sideways and too far to the right, and I dropped into the hole sideways again," he says, laughing at himself. "I bailed out and swam and came right out that time." He was happy about that. His second swim dropped his rolling percentage to 50 percent for that trip, but he didn't forget about the hole again. I kayaked the Main with Norell in the summer of 1995, and I asked him if he wouldn't mind dropping into his own personal hole for a photograph? He politely declined, shaking his head adamantly, "No way I'm going in there. Do you want to drop in the hole? I'll be glad to take your picture." I politely declined. Norell, 58, stopped boating in 1975 for almost 20 years and then started again in 1994 to join his teenage son on the river. "I was really surprised to learn that 20 years later, there was a place on the river called "Mike's Hole," he says. "I didn't know it had stuck. But I'm honored nevertheless to have a rapids named after me. I'm sure there's lots of kayakers who've gotten washed into that hole."

Proceeding on downriver, boaters will float through a small wave flush with a large rock and hole on the right, and then run a nice roller-coaster rapid around a right-hand corner. Below this drop, a large eddy and small beach on the left signal the take-out for the **Chief Parrish** BLM site. A toilet, parking lot, picnic area and small orchard are located on a nice flat above the river. A well-constructed trail provides easy access to the flat. Chief Parrish was named for a half-blood Indian who used to live at this site before the BLM purchased the land and turned it into a river access point. Below Chief Parrish are several surfing possibilities, particularly about 200 yards downriver next to a rock wall. Here, a river-wide glassy wave forms at flows below 5,000 cfs. Early boaters used to call this drop **Ouzel Wave** for a pair of water ouzels that nested in the rocks nearby. Below Ouzel, the river flattens out for a half mile or so.

A large left-hand bend and a brushy draw on the right signal that **"Mixmaster Rapids"** is coming up. A big pool forms above the rapid at the corner, providing easy access to a scouting position on the right bank. A Class III drop, Mixmaster grows bigger and more ferocious with flow. At levels above 5,000

Mixmaster has a strong left lateral wave that'll flip rafts at higher water. Payette Visions

cfs, a vicious left-lateral wave can flip rafts if they don't make an effort to stay off the left bank in the main drop. At flows of 3,000 cfs and less, it's usually safe to just blow through the middle of the main drop. Canoes frequently sneak Mixmaster on a diagonal run toward river right to avoid the biggest waves. Keith Taylor, Tullio Cellano and Mike Norell named Mixmaster after the first couple times they ran the Main in 1970. "We just thought, Boy, that thing hits you from all directions — it's like a mixmaster," Norell recalls.

A large runout and pool follows Mixmaster for a half mile before the river begins to bend toward the right for the final big drop on the Main, **AMF Rapids.** A cool little beach on river-right provides for a nice stopping point just above AMF. The run here is typically in the center to right-center side of the main drop. A large hole on the left pushes the main current toward river-center. It's usually possible to sneak this drop on river-right. Taylor, Tullio, Norell and Roger Hazelwood settled on the name for AMF in 1970. The acronym stands for Adios Mother F——r. I had always thought the acronym was reversible, and if boaters have a good day on the river, they can look back at AMF and whisper, Adios My Friend. But those early guys say they never looked at AMF in those days with any reverence at all.

Payette Visions
Boaters can count on AMF for a good splash.

"There was a hole in there that just beat the shit out of you," Tullio recalls.

"We used to think the Main was pretty big-time stuff," Taylor says. "We'd just be damn happy that we'd survived the run."

The runout of AMF provides some big playful waves and a enjoyable ending to a beautiful day (let's hope). It's about a mile to the take-out a **Beehive Bend**. It's possible to pull-out in an eddy below AMF and climb up to the dirt pull-out above if you want to end your trip here. Other floaters can relax and enjoy the scenery as you drift toward the take-out. Beehive Bend is located on river-left just before the river bends to the left. If you're so inclined, boaters can continue downriver to other take-out points mentioned in the next section. It's about five miles of mostly flatwater from Beehive to Horseshoe Bend. Beehive Bend, by the way, was named for a bunch of beehives — the kind in the white boxes — that a rancher used to keep at that corner before the BLM and Idaho Parks & Recreation Department purchased the site and developed the take-out. A toilet, large parking area and dirt ramp are available here. The agencies and volunteers plan to build an access trail for disabled folks at this site in 1996.

MOTOR HOME MAYHEM
Tourists set Payette Canyon ablaze

Fred and Jeanne Howard, a retired Pennsylvania couple, cruised along on Idaho 55 on a hot sunny day in July 1992 in their luxury 32-foot motor home, towing a 1982 Honda Civic wagon. The Howards, aged 67 and 70, were enjoying fetching views of the Payette River Canyon as they drove north past the little town of Gardena.

Little did they know that they were about to begin "THE VACATION FROM HELL." The right-rear tire of the Howards' old Honda wagon blew out as they rounded the bend past Gardena.

Idaho Department of Lands
Half-melted rim of the Howards' station wagon.

As the Howards drove by Cascade Recreation Co.'s office, shuttle driver Ken Conroy was standing by the highway. He noticed that the Honda was swaying back and forth behind the motor home. He heard a "thump, thump" noise

81

from the flat tire, and he noticed the blown tire was throwing off sparks.

The Howards didn't notice. "We were watching the river because it was such a lovely river and we were just enjoying the scenery," Jeanne Howard told a reporter for NBC-TV's "Dateline."

By the time the Howards drove past Beehive Bend, sparks flying off the blazing-hot tire ignited the brush on the east side of the road. Due to tinder-dry drought conditions, the sparks turned to flames in milliseconds. A fire raced up Cottonwood Gulch, and the spark-throwing tire ignited dozens of other fires along Idaho 55 as the Howards cruised toward Banks.

Idaho Department of Lands

The Cottonwood Creek Fire charred 6,268 acres and cost $1 million to put out.

Ed Fear was driving a diesel tanker combination rig behind the Howards that day. He saw "little balls of fire" bouncing down the highway from pieces of rubber that flew off the flat tire. Fear started to blow his horn. He flashed his headlights and a gazillion other truck lights at the Howards. He even pulled into the left lane and flashed the motor home.

Fred Howard apparently couldn't see the sparks or flames, and he didn't pull over.

"He just acted like he was ignoring everybody," Fear told KTVB-TV news. "I don't know how or why they couldn't see the flames. I did everything I could to get him to pull over except to run him off the road."

Howard told "Dateline," I saw him flashing his red lights but I've driven my motor home for 20,000 miles. I would say I'm a little hardened to people blinking their lights and stuff. I go, The heck with you, you know?"

By this time, the Howards had driven almost to Banks, setting the entire canyon ablaze. Finally, at the road-side pullout next to Banks Campground, the oblivious tourist pulled over. HE

WENT EIGHT MILES! He saw the Honda's rear-end smoking and quickly unhitched the vehicle from the motor home. The car caught fire and burned by the road.

Meanwhile, alert citizens between Cascade's office and Banks had seen the flames and called 911. Firefighters were immediately dispatched to the scene. The highway was shut down and remained so for the weekend, cutting off the main artery for Payette River floaters and Idaho 55 travelers.

The wildfire, which raced up the grassy pine-dotted mountainside on the 90-degree day, took three days to suppress. More than 1,000 firefighters were called to the scene, in addition to 32 fire engines, five bulldozers, and several fire-retardent tanker airplanes and helicopters hauling water-buckets. Most fortunately, private homes and businesses in Banks II were saved.

The fire burned 6,268 acres and cost $1 million to suppress. Most of the charred land was state property.

By state law, if a private party is found to be negligent in starting a wildfire, the party is charged for full fire-suppression costs. Attorneys for the state of Idaho reviewed the case, talked to witnesses such as Mr. Fear, and sent the Howards a bill for $1 million.

The Howards were aghast.

"I hope the people of Idaho don't think I'm stupid enough to drive a motorhome and pull a fire bomb for that length of time and know it," Fred Howard told KTVB news. "If I knew it, I definitely would have stopped many miles before it happened."

The state of Idaho ultimately settled with the Howards' insurance companies for $300,000.

It's a story to think about when you float down the Main Payette, and see the dead trees and bulldozer cuts high on the mountain slopes. Forest fires frequently occur in these parts when dry lightning strikes or stupid campers forget to suppress campfires.

BEEHIVE BEND — HORSESHOE BEND

Difficulty: Novice-Intermediate (One Class III rapid).
Put-In: Beehive Bend.
Types of craft: Kayaks, rafts, canoes, duckies
Distance: 5 miles
Float time: 1-3 hours
Take-out: Horseshoe Bend Bridge; Gardena; Gravel Boat ramp, Cascade Recreation Co.
Steepness: 5 feet per mile
Season: March-October

Getting there: Drive to Horseshoe Bend on Idaho 55. It is 20 miles to Horseshoe Bend from Boise, and 90 miles from McCall. Proceed about five miles, past the wood-carving shop, to a left-hand turn marked by a Sportsmen's Access sign. This is the turnoff for the Beehive Bend launch site.

Shuttle: Drop a vehicle at the Horseshoe Bend Bridge, on the north side of town, at Gardena (three miles north of Horseshoe Bend), Cascade Recreation or the jet boat ramp (two miles north of Horseshoe Bend).

The Float: The lower main Payette, below Beehive Bend, is a perfect "warm up" section for novice whitewater boaters, especially kayakers and canoeists. It features mostly flat water, with strong eddies in high water (perfect for learning eddy turns in a kayak and canoe ... get ready to swim!), one Class 3 rapid called "Climax" and a scenic tour of the lower Payette gorge. Some folks who float the main Payette from Banks on down like to continue drifting through this section on hot summer days.

Historical Notes: This river reach is loaded with history. The first ferry established on the Payette was located on the upstream end of Frenchman's Island, a large cottonwood-forested island above Gardena.

Frenchman's Island is named so because two French trappers built a cabin on the island and lived there for a number of years after the 1830s. A man named Phillip Remmil obtained a license

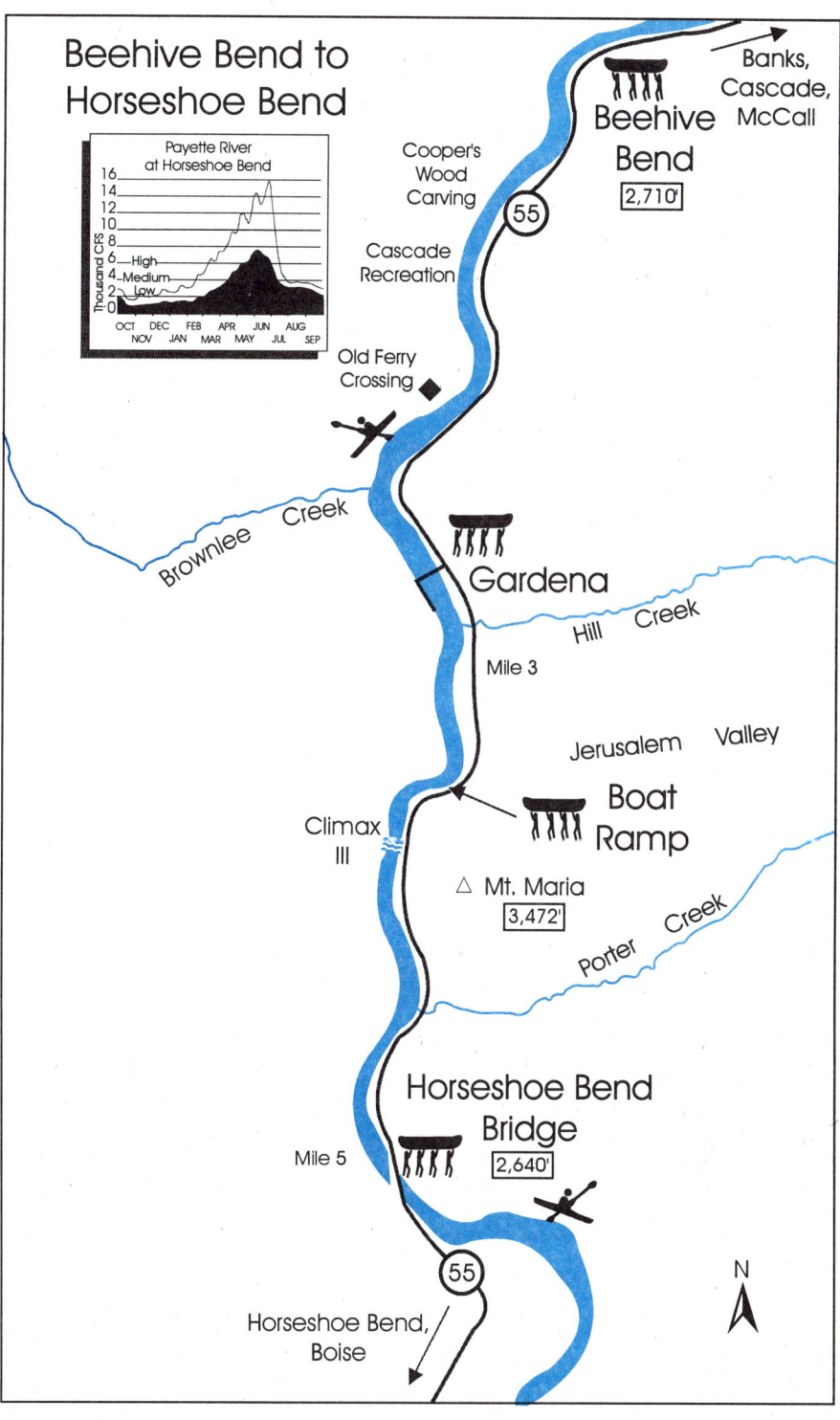

to operate the Payette ferry on June 2, 1863, at the beginning of the gold rush in Boise Basin. The ferry served hundreds of gold miners who came to the Payette country via the Brownlee Trail from Oregon and California as it was the first ferry for miles. Miners crossed the Payette at Frenchman's Island and then continued downriver to the Boise Basin via the Harris Creek Toll Road, operated by a fella named Felix Harris. He was a wealthy guy, who made a fortune in the California gold rush and he held several gold claims in Centerville and Placerville, reported Nellie Mills in *All Along the River*.

When you float by the mouth of Harris Creek, a few miles upstream of Horseshoe Bend, think of Felix and his wife, Anna, homesteading eight miles up the creek in a beautiful nook next to the golden hills. They built a $100,000 road to their home, and built a gate across the road. Knowing miners were packing tidy sums of gold, Harris was known to charge as much as $1,000 to swing the gate, Mills wrote. Several years later, Harris was riding the 12 miles from Placerville to his home at night, and some thieves beat him up and stole his gold cache. He died a year later; he apparently never fully recovered from the attack. Harris' widow, Anna, ended up marrying the man who handled the dead man's estate, and raised three sons and a daughter at the Harris Creek ranch. The Harris Creek Toll Road still leads to Placerville and the Boise Basin, but of course, there's no charge today.

Below Gardena, a rural valley unfolds above the river to the left. This was known as the settlement of Jerusalem in the 1860s. Several families homesteaded here and established the first orchard in the Payette drainage.

As boaters drift by Jerusalem, the river bends 90 degrees to the right, and flows by a large gravel bar on river-left. This is a gravel ramp area that can be used as a take-out for drift boats and dories. Jet boats have been known to launch here, too. The large gravel area is usually frequented by families picnicking on the beach, anglers and swimmers. If boaters want to bypass Climax Rapids, they should take-out here.

Around the next bend, boaters get a small break before Climax Rapids comes up, the only Class III drop — and the only rapids of any consequence — in the "warm up" run. The river course swirls from right to left at the entrance of Climax, and a set of waves form on the left side. The initial impact in this rapids can cause a jolt, typically flipping first-time kayakers. A large pool forms below the rapids for recovering swimmers.

It's a gentle coast toward Horseshoe Bend from here. Not too far below Climax, a cool jump-off rock comes up on the left in about a half-mile. This nose-shaped rock provides some good structure for fishing, but if boaters care to pull off here, it's a fun place to leap into the Payette's refreshing water on a sweltering summer day. The current moves slowly past the rock here, making it easy for swimmers to return to the rock face, climb up through the nooks and crannies, and leap off again. Watch out for poison ivy growing in the cracks of the rock.

It's about a half mile to the road-side take-out on river left before the first concrete bridge on the north end of Horseshoe Bend. This is the final take-out for the Main Payette. The Horseshoe Bend-Montour canoe float begins at this same point.

HORSESHOE BEND TO MONTOUR

Difficulty: Class I-Class II-plus (Diversion Drop)
Suitable crafts: Canoe, kayak, solo boats, rafts, dories
Put-In: Horseshoe Bend upper bridge
Distance: 13 miles
Float time: 2-5 hours
Take-outs: Montour Bridge, earlier road-side sites
Steepness: Less than 5 feet per mile

Getting there: Drive on Idaho 55 to Horseshoe Bend (20 miles north of Boise), and look for a large concrete bridge that spans the Payette River on the upstream (north) side of the town. There is a huge roadside turnout just past the bridge. On the extreme upstream end of the turnout, look for a narrow dirt road that leads to a concrete ramp. This is the best launch site for this float. As an alternative, you can launch by the Riverside restaurant, and trim 3 miles from the trip, but you'll miss an exciting ride through the man-made whitewater bypass at the new diversion dam.

Shuttle: Drive west on Idaho 52 toward Emmett to drop a vehicle at the Montour Bridge, or at another road-side pullout of your choice. It is 9.3 miles from the junction of Idaho 55 and Idaho 52 in Horseshoe Bend to Montour Road. Watch for the turn on the left after the Montour Country Store. Proceed to the Montour wildlife refuge about one mile to the bridge. There's a good pullout on the south and downstream side of the bridge where you can park your rig.

The Float: This section of the Payette offers a relaxing family float trip with a few exciting drops under the bridges on both ends of Horseshoe Bend and two other small drops farther downstream. Skilled canoeists will have no problem with this reach at any float level. At higher flows (above 4,000 cfs), large waves could swamp and flip an open tandem canoe. Families with kids may want to bring a raft for safety and convenience at high water. During low flows, this section could be done with a myriad of crafts.

Less than a quarter-mile below the put-in, you'll approach a rapid that begins just before the upper bridge. The river bends

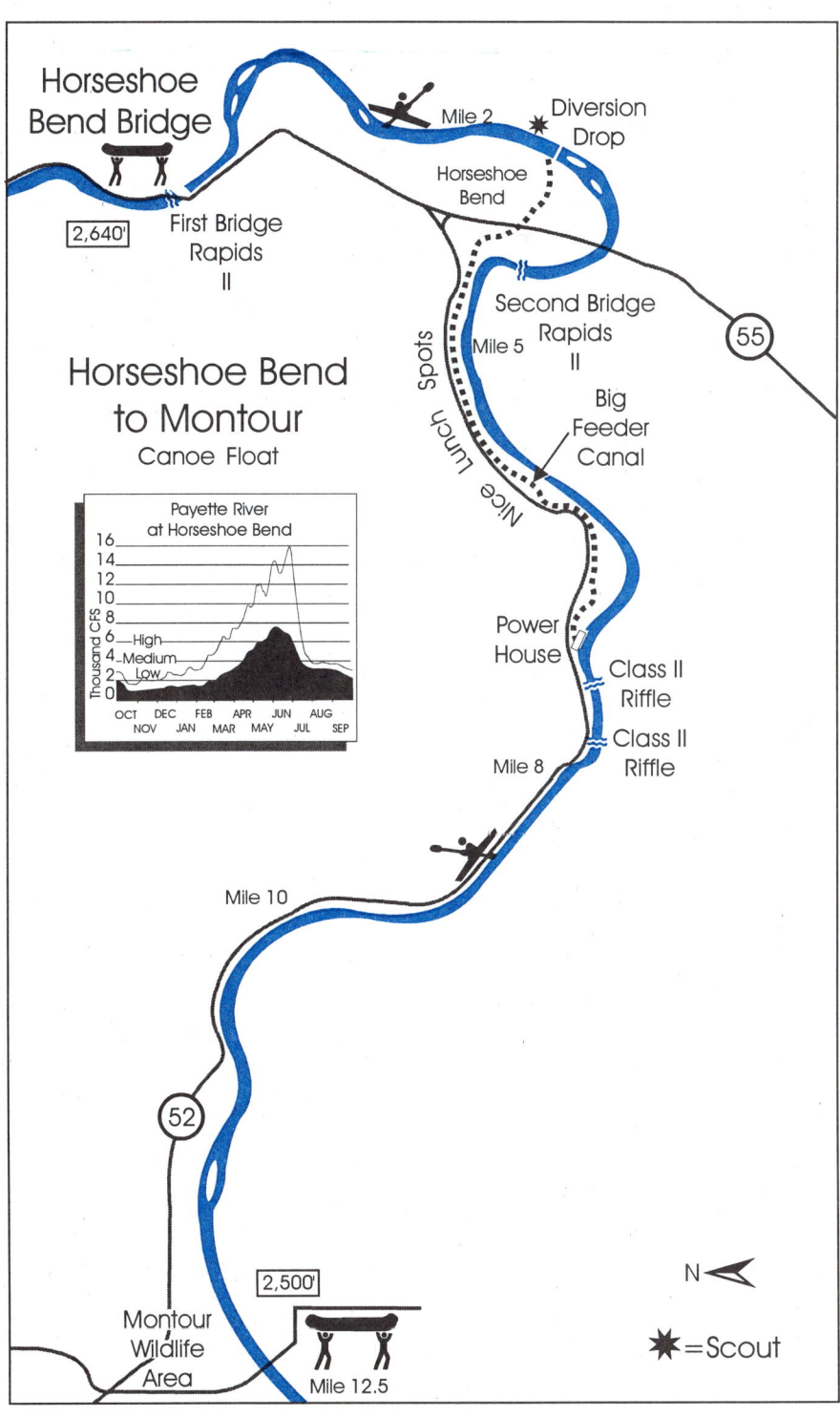

left, and then drops in a fairly gentle descent under the bridge. At high water, this drop can be run on the left or right sides. At low water, the left side is usually preferred. Watch out for the bridge pilings.

Below the bridge, enjoy a leisurely tour of rural Horseshoe Bend. Dense vegetation adorns the riverbank, providing good habitat for birds and other critters. Watch for herons, kingfishers, ducks, otters, beavers and mink in this reach.

A reflective moment near Horseshoe Bend.

Interpretive notes: The first name attached to this quaint old logging town was "Warrinersville," named for Benjamin L. Warriner, who built the first post office in Oct. 6, 1865. Previous to that time, settlers referred to this giant, graceful bend in the river as "The Big Bend" or "The Bend." The town's name was changed to Horse Shoe Bend (it was always three words in pioneer times) on Sept. 11, 1867, by John A. Douglas, the new postmaster. At the time, the Bend was a tiny town. It had a handful of settlers who ranched in the valley and built a small sawmill at the mouth of Shafer Creek. During the winter, miners from the Boise Basin apparently liked to escape deep snow and cold in the Bend (elevation 2,800 feet) and did not have snow most of the year. As a result, it was referred to as the "Arcadia of Idaho."

Apparently miners liked to leave their stock with ranchers in the Horseshoe Bend area and then headed up the trail to Placerville by way of the old Harris Creek toll road. Most of the time, historians say, the livestock was stolen. "It was easy to drive the stolen stock at night, skirt around the town and have them safe in the brush across the Boise River, near the present Broadway bridge, before daylight," wrote Nellie Mills in "All Along the River."

In 1872, Frank R. Starr, city editor for the San Francisco Chronicle, visited the town. He reported that about 300 people lived there. "The town is regularly layed out having a hotel, church, sawmill, schoolhouse, blacksmith shop, etc., etc.... The finest horses and cattle in the world are raised at Horse Shoe Bend and fattened on the luxurious hills. Extensive fishing is carried on here at certain times of the year." Starr also made note of seeing "red fish" (sockeye and kokanee salmon) in Payette Lake.

In 1866, Mr. G. Miner built the first bridge across the Payette River, the only way for many Lower Payette pioneers to cross the river during high runoff. The first school in Boise County, a smart-looking white one-room school house, was established at the Bend in about 1870. School kids used to ride horseback to school and leave their stock in a barn, offered to the kids by the Clark family.

After about two miles, the river begins to back up in a small reservoir behind the diversion dam. Work toward the left bank so you can scout the whitewater bypass on the extreme left side of the dam. DO NOT ATTEMPT TO RUN THE DAM IN THE MIDDLE OR THE RIGHT. THERE IS NO WAY THROUGH.

There are several places on the left bank to pull out before the dam for portaging or scouting.

Below the diversion, you'll notice that the river flow has shrunk markedly — by as much as 2,000 cfs. The river bends to the right and floaters will complete the giant horseshoe bend around the town. As the river bends toward the railroad bridge, you'll approach several small rapids above and below the bridge. This area is a popular swimming and rope-swinging spot for locals. Watch out for flying bodies.

Whitewater bypass, Horseshoe Bend

Below the RR bridge rapids, the river flattens out for the next two miles. The river flow picks up again below the powerhouse on the right. Not far below this point, the river drops into a Class I-Class II rapids. A half-mile later, there's another similar drop. Canoeists may want to sneak down the left or right side to avoid swamping in the main wave trains. After this drop, it's a tranquil paddle to Montour with no rapids of consequence. The take-out at Montour is unmistakable — it's the first concrete bridge you've seen for miles.

MONTOUR — BLACK CANYON

Difficulty: First-timers & up (easy flat water)
Put-Ins: Montour Bridge
Types of craft: Best for canoes, sea kayaks, duckies and rafts
Distance: 3.5 miles
Float time: 1.5-3 hours
Take-out: Upper end of Black Canyon Reservoir
Steepness: 2 feet per mile
Season: April-October

Getting there: Drive to Horseshoe Bend on Idaho 55 and turn east on Idaho 52 on the north edge of town. Drive about 9.5 miles to the Montour Road on the left. It's about three miles to a bridge spanning the Payette River. The best put-in is accessed by a dirt road on the southwest (downstream) side of the bridge. The river bottoms here are protected as a public wildlife area in compensation for wildlife habitat that was inundated by Black Canyon Reservoir.

Shuttle: Drop a vehicle or bicycle (it's an easy bike shuttle) at a small park on the upper end of Black Canyon Reservoir. The park is about three miles from Montour Road. This is the takeout for the Montour flat-water paddle. Note that vehicles can not park for more than 24 hours at this site.

The Float: The Montour flat-water paddle is a perfect place for families, beginning canoeists and others to enjoy a low-key scenic float down this unsung part of the Payette River. It's even possible for a parent to take one or two kids in a canoe on this reach — as long as it's not too windy because only one person will be paddling with any power. I know some families that load up their rafts with kids and float this section. It features a wide river course, a number of large cottonwood-forested islands, big sandy beaches, and occasional jet skiers from Black Canyon Reservoir. The only real hazard on this reach is getting stuck on a sandbar. The river is coated with sand and sediment in this reach. But the worst thing that can happen is you'll have to get out and drag your boat to deeper water. **As you pull away from the bridge,** you'll notice a

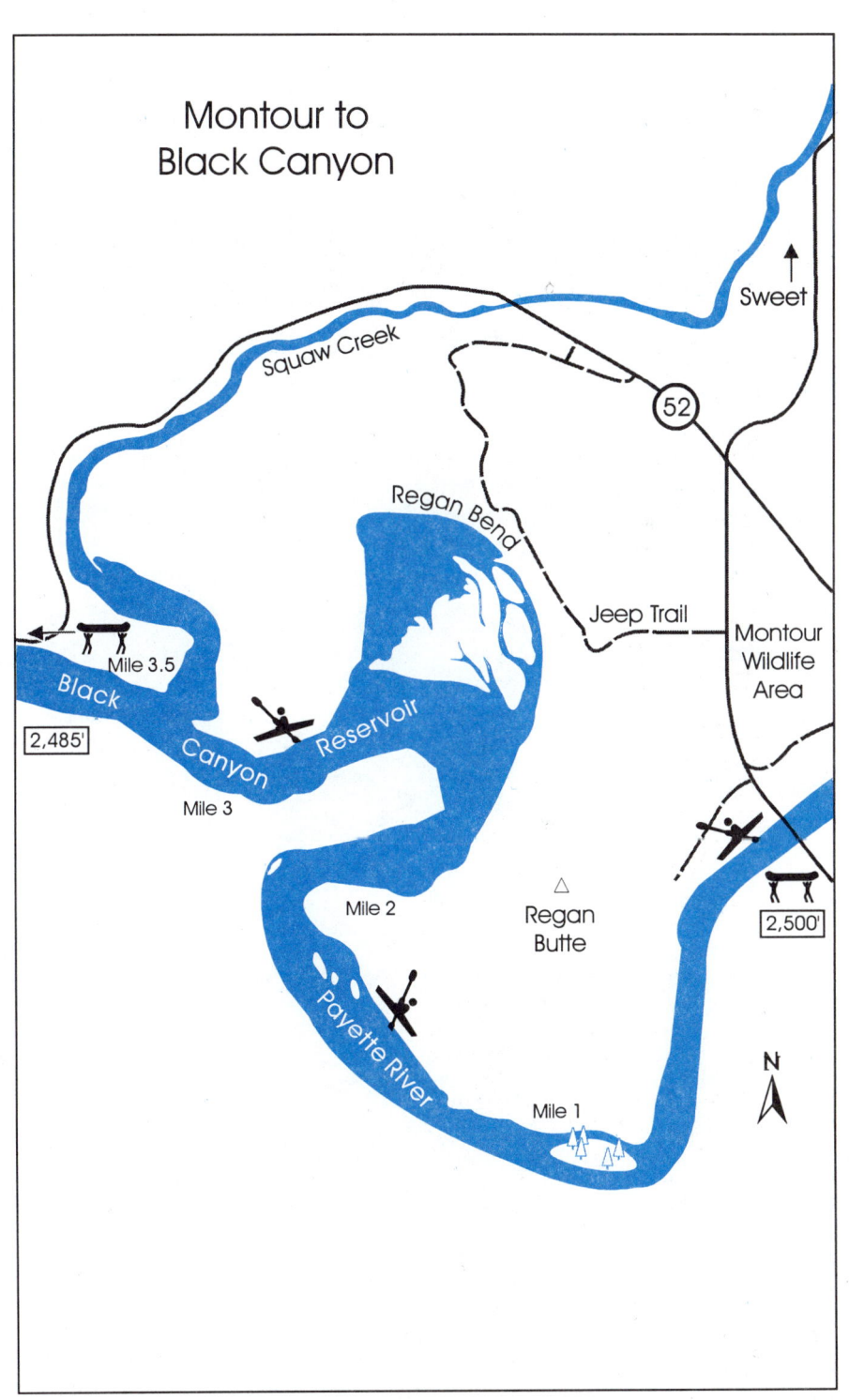

Big sandy beaches are plentiful in the Montour reach of the Payette.

bunch of old tires and cars in the river bottom. In the sunlight, one can see the flash of mica. A half-mile or so downriver, a nice sandbar and cottonwood grove appears on the right — a cool place to explore. A mile downstream, a larger island and sandy beach comes up on the right. This is a nice place to explore or have lunch. On your walk, it's fun for the kids to look at animal tracks. Watch for kingfishers, herons, ducks and geese, among other birds in the forest.

The first prominent land feature on this float is Regan Butte, a conical hill with an elevation of 3,300 feet (about 800 feet above the river). After floaters drift around a large bend in the river, the massive form of Squaw Butte comes into view. The Butte, a defining land feature in this area, is

Montour is a perfect place for families, beginning canoeists and others to enjoy a low-key scenic float.

a popular livestock grazing area and upland bird hunting area. Although it's quite steep on its east-facing flank — the one you see from here — the Butte is the headwaters for upper Squaw Creek and several other streams on its western flank. In the next mile, the river makes another big bend around a series of small islands. This is called Regan Bend. Local legend has it that before the advent of dams, when people drowned in the Payette River, the bodies had a tendency to wash up on one of the small islands in Regan Bend.

Often times, it was the kids playing out in the river that found the corpses. What a dreadful thought.

To avoid getting stuck in sand bars between the islands in Regan Bend, the deepest river course will be on the left side. In a half-mile, Squaw Creek will drain into the Payette on the right. It's a short distance now to the take-out. Floaters will notice the current ending and the reservoir beginning about here. If there's a stiff upstream breeze, it's best to stick to the right shoreline in your final approach to the take-out.

Bureau of Reclamation

Tons of sediment settles into the Payette River in the Montour reach, creating large sandbars.

BLACK CANYON-LETHA

Difficulty: Novice-Intermediate
Put-Ins: Wild Rose Park (below Black Canyon Dam); Plaza Road Bridge.
Types of craft: Canoes, open kayaks, duckies
Distance: 13 miles
Float time: 2-4 hours
Take-out: Emmett bridge; public access at Seven Mile Slough, Letha Bridge.
Steepness: 3 feet per mile
Season: April-September

Getting there: From Boise, drive west on State Street (Idaho 44), past Eagle, to Idaho 16. Turn right and follow the highway over Freezeout Pass to Emmett. At the junction of Idaho 52 and 16, turn right toward the city of Emmett and follow Idaho 52 through town about seven miles to Wild Rose Park, on the downstream side of Black Canyon Dam. From McCall, follow Idaho 55 to Horseshoe Bend. Turn right on Idaho 52 to Wild Rose Park, just below Black Canyon Dam. To launch your craft, follow a dirt trail next to the historical sign to the river.

Alternative put-ins: About two miles below the dam, watch for a Sportsmen's Access sign for Plaza Road Bridge. Floaters who put in here can avoid portaging a rocky diversion dam upstream of the bridge.

Shuttle: Leave a vehicle or bicycle at the Emmett Bridge, the public access for Seven Mile Slough, off of Cascade Road, or at Letha Bridge. To reach Cascade Road, drive 4.7 miles west of Emmett on Idaho 52. Turn right on Cascade Road. Follow the road for a mile to the riverside access. To reach Letha Bridge, follow Idaho 52 toward New Plymouth and watch for Vanderdasson Road on the right. It's a short-cut to the Letha Bridge.
    Note: During high runoff in the spring, floaters will have enough water to float to Letha Bridge, about five miles below Seven Mile Slough. During the summer, irrigators may dry up the Payette below Seven Mile Slough.

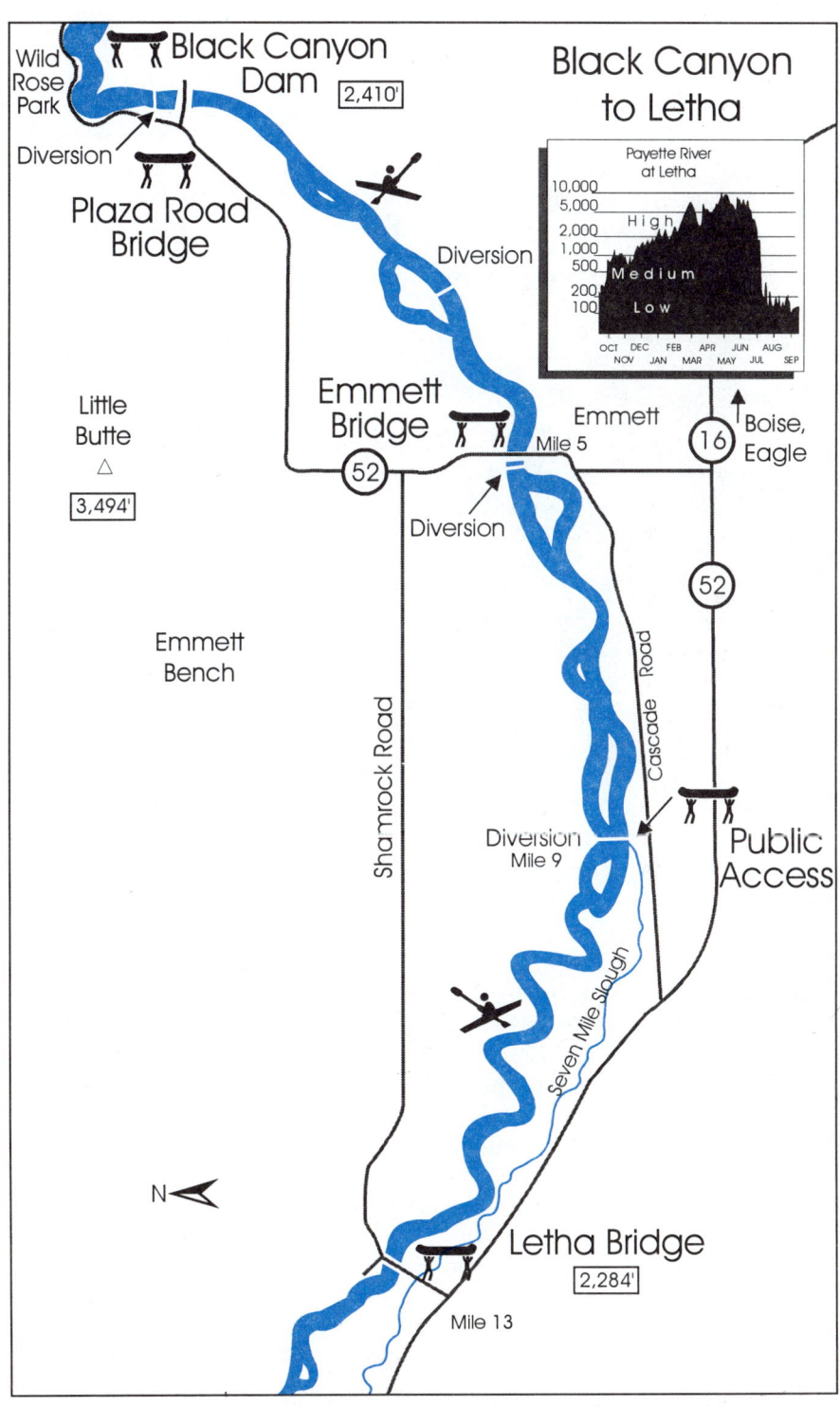

The Float: The Black Canyon-Letha section is an interesting flatwater tour through the Emmett Valley. In many areas, the river is braided by islands, requiring quick decisions and maneuvers to follow the preferred channel. Due to the number of diversion drops peppered on the river, boaters should exercise caution, particularly in high water. Watch for horizon lines and take a second to pull over and look at the drops before attempting them. You may need to portage. Trout-fishing can be good in the first five miles or so, and farther downstream, small-mouth bass fishing and carp fishing can be productive.

After launching at Black Canyon, the river winds toward the Plaza Road Bridge. This is the first diversion drop, and it's a big one. Fishing below the drop may be productive. Proceeding on downriver, boaters will notice a number of osprey-nesting platforms on river left on the top of telephone poles and power poles. This was a cooperative project between Fish and Game, Idaho Power Co. and the phone company. Even though the Payette River gets increasingly diverted for agricultural use on this reach, the upper portion is obviously productive for ospreys, herons, kingfishers and waterfowl, all of which are numerous. Just upstream of Emmett, the river begins to braid by Fuller and Ross islands. Try to stay with the channel where the water is deepest. It's about five miles to paddle into Emmett from Black Canyon, which may be plenty long enough for some folks, particularly at low flows. The take-out is on river right, just underneath the Emmett Bridge before a large diversion for the Boise Cascade plywood mill.

Below here, the river will have less water and current as it proceeds into the agricultural valley. Downstream from Emmett, boaters will get an up-close-and-personal tour of the backside of

Bureau of Reclamation

Black Canyon Canal serves over 50,000 acres of farmland.

the plywood mill, including a view of old rip rap of all kinds on the south bank. Floaters also will see lots of gulls flying around, due to the presence of sewage lagoons on river left. Adjacent to the lagoons, the river braids again around a number of small islands. Try to anticipate the corners and angle for your preferred channel to avoid getting swept or flipped into brush.

About three miles below Emmett, boaters will approach a large rocky diversion dam for Seven Mile Slough. A bulldozer parked on river left helps explain what goes on here. As the river level drops, the bulldozer pushes the gravel into a position to intercept most, if not all of the Payette River and send it into the slough, a key conduit for farms and irrigation. Sadly, there is no established minimum flow in the river here to ensure season-long maintenance flows for cold-water aquatic species. Someday that may change as farmers work to improve the water-quality of the lower Payette River. A recent water-quality lawsuit has made the lower Payette one of the four top priority streams for cleanup action in southwest Idaho. Citizen committees will help set priorities for cleanup. If the river is nearly dry when you float through here, it's best to takeout upstream of the diversion. At higher flows continue on to Letha Bridge. It's another four miles to Letha. The river will braid around several small islands in this reach.

Payette River dries up in mid-summer at the diversion for Seven Mile Slough.

Interpretive notes: The Lower Payette Valley was homesteaded by Idaho pioneers in the late 1800s. In 1870, Thomas Cahalan was named post master of the old town of Martinville, and Cahalan renamed the post office "Emmettsville" after his son, Emmett, the first white child born in the area. The name was trimmed to Emmett in 1885. Letha was named for the daughter of W.W. Wilton, Letha Wilton. Black Canyon Dam, 183 feet high, was completed in 1925 by the Bureau of Reclamation.

LETHA TO PAYETTE/SNAKE RIVER

Difficulty: Novice-Intermediate (diversion dams)
Put-Ins: Letha Bridge, Falk Bridge, Black's Bridge
Types of craft: Canoes, open kayaks, duckies
Distance: 11-25 miles
Float time: You make the call
Take-out: Kiwanis Park in Payette or Snake River
Steepness: 2 feet per mile
Season: March-November

Getting there: From Boise, drive west on State Street (Idaho 44), past Eagle, to Idaho 16. Turn right and follow the highway over Freezeout Pass to Emmett. Proceed west on Idaho 52, and put-in at either Letha Bridge, Falk Bridge, or Black's Bridge. Many combinations are possible in the Lower Payette, depending on river flows. In general, during the summer months, there will be more water in the river below Black's Bridge. In the spring and late fall (after irrigation season), there should be enough water to float from Letha to Payette. Floaters would be well-advised to check out river flow from any one of the bridge locations and select your preferred put-in accordingly. The Letha turnoff is about nine miles west of the Emmett Junction (Idaho 16 & 52), and eight miles from the New Plymouth junction (Idaho 72 & 52). Falk Bridge, called Vickery Sportsmen's Access, is 13 miles from the Emmett Junction and four miles from New Plymouth on Idaho 52. Turn north on Freemont Road, bear left and drive 1.5 miles to Falk Bridge. The next access downstream is Black's Bridge, which is three miles from New Plymouth and 9.5 miles from the city of Payette on the south side of Idaho 52. It is marked by a Sportmen's Access sign. Black's Bridge is the last public access to the river before the city of Payette.

Shuttle: Leave a vehicle or bicycle at Kiwanis Park in the city of Payette. This is the best takeout if Payette is your destination. An alternative is to leave a vehicle at the Snake River bridge, about 1 mile downriver from Kiwanis Park. The problem with taking out on the Snake is that you'll have to paddle a short ways on the massive river, whose currents and eddy lines could flip novice can-

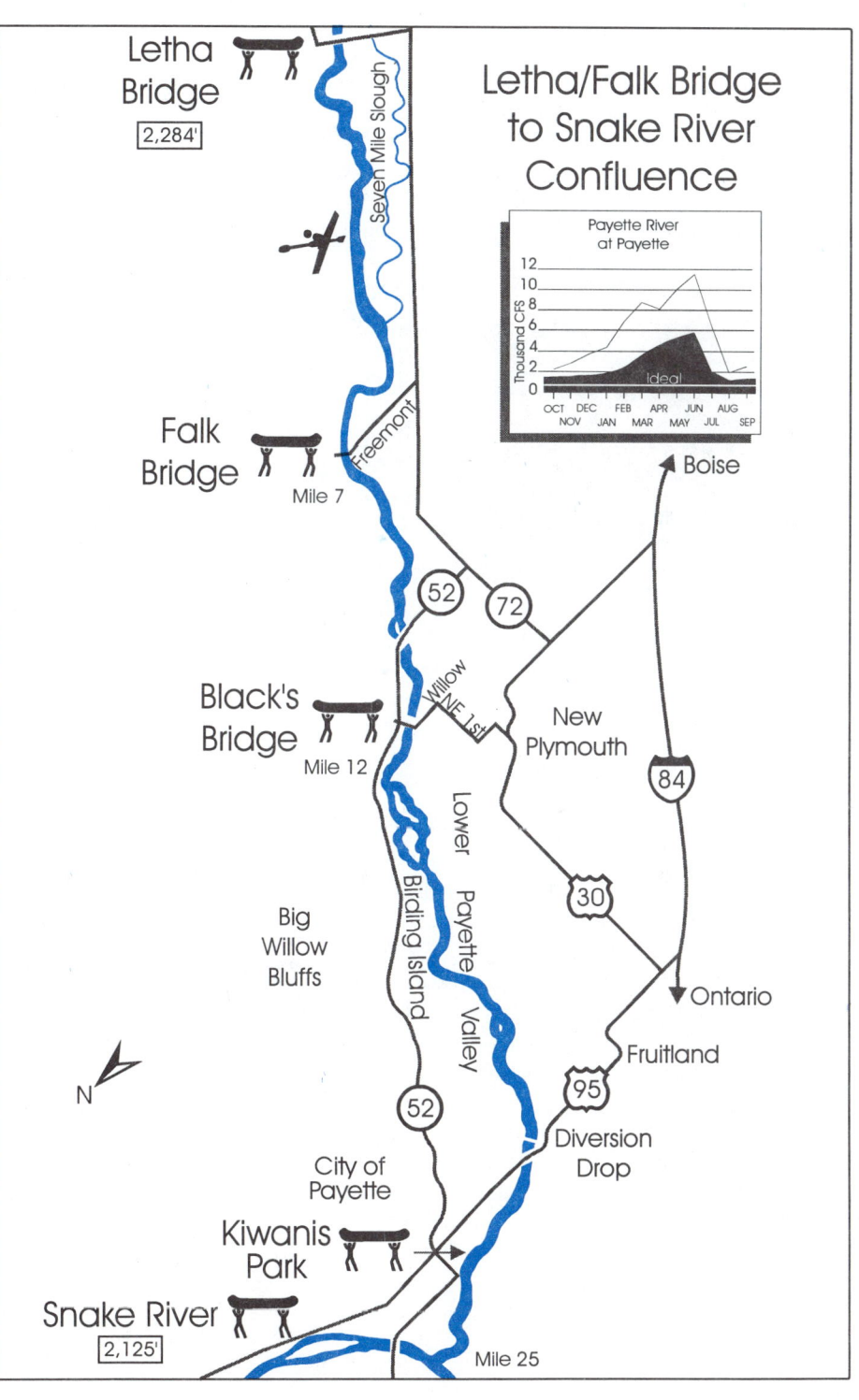

oeists. There are take-outs on both sides of the river.

The Float: The Lower Payette River flows through a well-forested corridor and natural island complex between Letha and the city of Payette. In general, the Lower Payette is known for good bass and carp fishing, productive pheasant and duck hunting in the fall, and a scenic flat-water tour of the Lower Payette agricultural valley for canoes or open kayaks. Families with kids may want to stop on river islands to explore, identify birds and look for other wildlife. From Letha, the river winds through a cottonwood-lined corridor and series of islands for seven miles to Falk Bridge. Throughout this reach, the river drops very gradually, about eight feet per mile. Five miles below Letha Bridge, Seven Mile Slough, a large irrigation ditch, replenishes the river with return flows from agricultural fields. For some boaters, the seven-mile Letha-Falk Bridge float trip will suffice.

Marty Morache
A bounty of fowl in the good-old days on the Lower Payette.

Below Falk Bridge, the river continues to wind in a northwesterly direction toward Payette. One and one-half miles below Falk Bridge, a large canal diverts water on river-right toward Big Willow Creek. The river proceeds downriver by several small islands, and in two miles, it passes under Idaho 52, a good vantage point for determining flows and river depth. Stay left in the widest and deepest portion of the river below the bridge. Boaters will pass by several more islands in the next 1.5 miles to the Black's Bridge put-in. This is the closest access to New Plymouth. Below Black's Bridge, boaters will encounter a rich and extensive island and wildlife habitat area known as Birding Island. It's a little tricky here to stay with the river channel that's deepest to avoid dragging your canoe

Genuine Idaho rip-rap

through gravel bars. But in general, the deepest water is in the right-side channels. Below this area, the river grows wide and follows a single corridor for several miles. River flow increases eight miles above the Snake River confluence when Big Willow Creek pours in from the right. It's a steady cruise now for the city of Payette. Three miles below Big Willow, boaters will pass under the U.S. 95 bridge, two miles north of Fruitland. Locals may want to take out here, on river right. It is not as easy to carry a canoe out of the river here as it is adjacent to Kiwanis Park in Payette. It's about two miles from here to the park take-out. About a mile after the U.S. 95 bridge, boaters will confront a sizeable river-wide diversion. Use caution here. Scouting may be necessary. Boaters will pass by one more island before a highway bridge, which signals the Kiwanis Park take-out on river right. There is a historical sign about Francois Payette in the park. Below the park, the Payette descends 1.5 miles to the Snake River. It's a half-mile to the Idaho 52 bridge over the Snake River. Take-out on river right.

The scene on the Lower Payette near Big Willow bluffs.

Interpretive notes: Letha was named for the daughter of early Payette Valley pioneer W.W. Wilton, Letha Wilton. A post office was established in the little farming hamlet in 1912 and remains to this day. Between Falk Bridge and Black's Bridge, boaters will pass by New Plymouth to the south. Though it's not directly visible from the river, the planned irrigation community of New Plymouth is laid out in the shape of a perfect arch. It was formed with the aid of the National Irrigation Congress in 1894. "The purpose was to promote irrigation projects and to prove the feasibility of making small farming communities in arid regions," according to *Idaho Place Names* by Lalia Boone. "Enthusiastic people from Boston and the Midwest banded together and secured 250 heads of families who came west in 1895 and established New Plymouth. It is a thriving close-knit farming community to this day."

As boaters float into Payette, think about logs floating nearly

100 miles or more during the turn-of-the-century log drives.

Although Francois Payette named the Payette River in 1818, the city of Payette wasn't established until 1864 during the gold rush era. The Payette County seat was established in the city of Payette in 1917. Previously it was part of Ada and Canyon counties.

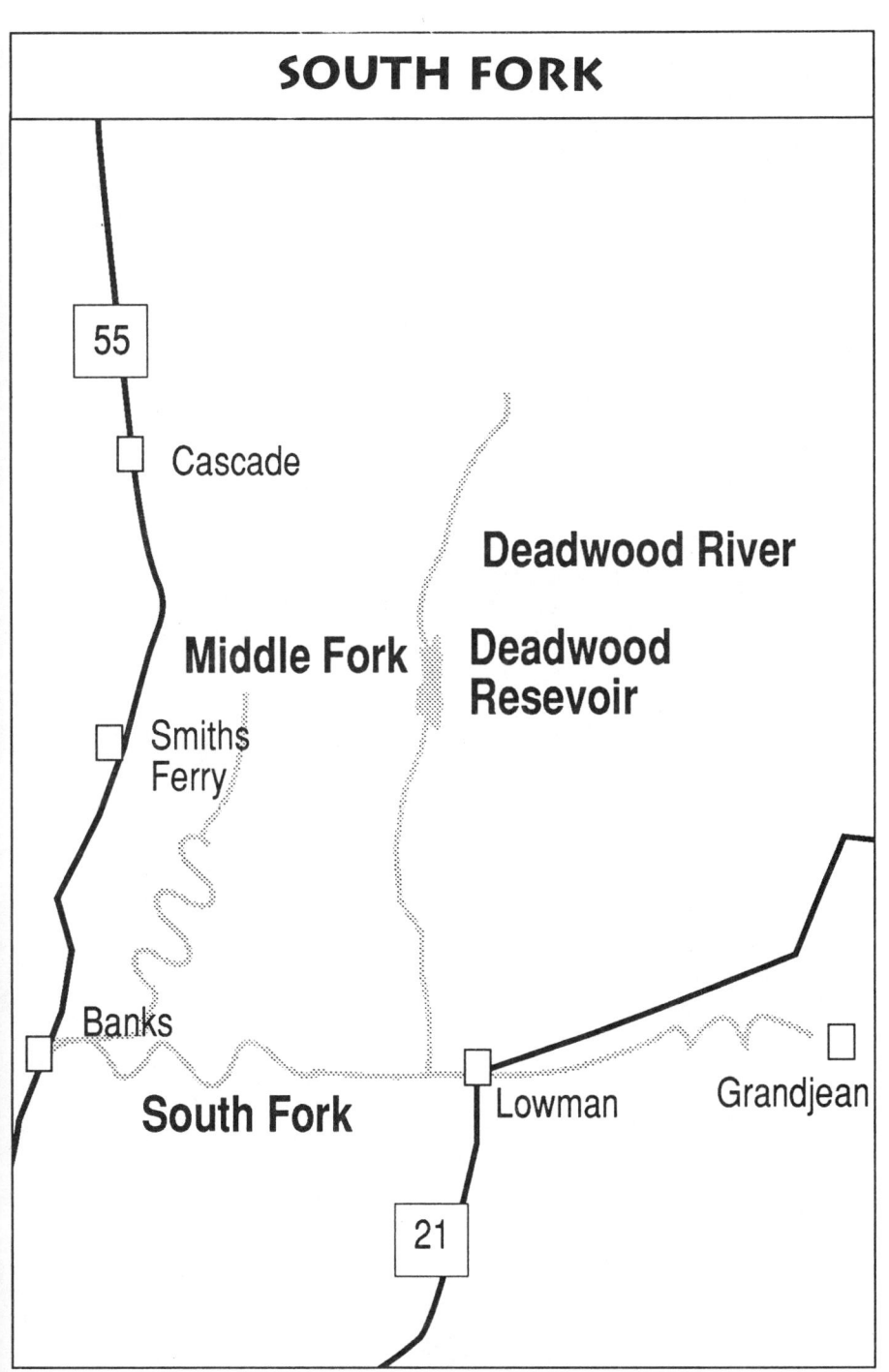

BONNEVILLE HOT SPRINGS — LOWMAN

Difficulty: Intermediate-Advanced
Put-Ins: Bonneville Hot Springs, Helende.
Types of craft: Kayaks, rafts, canoes, duckies
Distance: 22 miles
Float time: 2-6 hours
Take-out: Kirkham or Lowman
Steepness: 39 feet per mile
Season: April-July

Getting there: Drive to Lowman on the Banks-Lowman highway or Idaho 21. It is 70 miles from Boise to Lowman. Head east on Idaho 21 about 17 miles to Bonneville Campground and hot springs. Boaters can launch into Warm Springs Creek or put-in on the South Fork at a roadside pull-out about a half mile downriver from Bonneville. For a shorter run, alternative put-ins include the Tenmile trailhead, Eightmile road-side pull-out or Helende Campground. It used to be possible to put-in along the road to Grand Jean (several miles upstream of Bonneville) but a number of logs have plugged the river between Grand Jean and Bonneville. Below Bonneville, the river was clear of log jams in 1995. **Be aware that this section is prone to log jams. Every spring new logs may block the river or create new hazards.**

Special note for canoes: Canoeists can bypass Class III rapids at the upper end of this float and put-in at Eightmile for a scenic float with a fairly gradual Class I and Class II gradient to Helende Campground. Be sure to takeout at Helende or you'll wash into Class III and Class IV rapids below it.

Shuttle: Plant a vehicle at the takeout of your choice. Whitewater boaters may prefer to take out after Kirkham Rapids at the campground. It's a steep climb carrying rafts to the parking lot (heavier crafts should takeout at Lowman), but it's a nice spot to hang out while your friends drive the shuttle. After planting your vehicle, you can scout Kirkham, Wangdoodle, Pinball and Emma Creek rapids from the road on your way to the put-in..

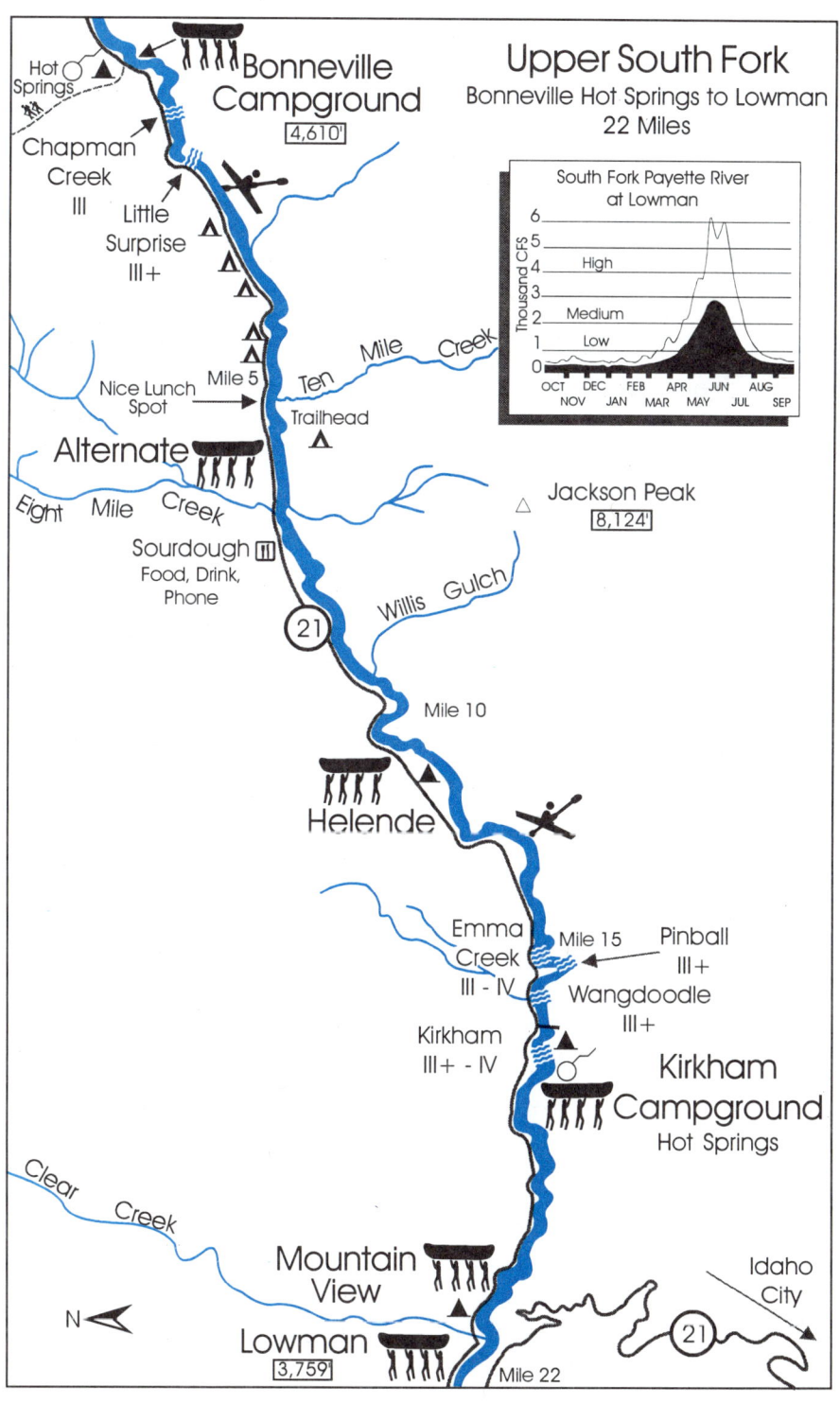

The Float: The Upper South Fork of the Payette River is practically a wilderness float trip because most whitewater boaters ignore it, and the river course runs away from the highway. Because this run is a little farther afield for McCall and Boise boaters, it's frequently overlooked. But it's a great alternative for Stanley boaters and it's an excellent place to get away from the crowds on the Lower South Fork, Main Payette or Cabarton. The Upper South Fork also is a very scenic canyon with gorgeous emerald water flowing out of the headwaters in the Sawtooth Wilderness. The whitewater run can be pushy with several tough Class III and Class IV rapids, so this is no place for beginners.

Payette Visions

Kayaker pops an endo in Chapman Creek Rapids.

To begin, launch at Bonneville or the roadside put-in. The river drops into Class II chop immediately and marches toward Chapman Creek, the first Class III rapids. Chapman is marked by a big right-hand bend, crossing under the highway, and then a left-hand bend right before the drop. It's possible to pull over on a river-left beach to scout Chapman Creek. At flows above 2,000 cfs, the run is typically down the middle. Below 1,500 cfs, rocks begin showing in the middle and the run is more technical. Once you're past Chapman, get ready for "Little Surprise," named so because of a frothing hole in the bottom of this rocky rapid. Little Surprise, a Class III-plus, is marked by a sharp left-hand bend in the river. Try to grab an eddy for a river-level scout. The run is normally right to left, with a final punch through the hole in the bottom. There is a nice recovery pool below if paddlers get ejected from the boat or kayakers swim.

After Little Surprise, the South Fork settles into a more gentle descent through the upper Lowman Valley. Mixed pine-fir forests form a dense carpet of green in the upper end, later giving way to a more open valley with tall ponderosa pine trees on south slopes and Douglas-fir on north slopes. The river, meanwhile, winds around sharp corner after sharp corner, leaving floaters wondering what's around the next bend. At mile 5, paddlers will see a major creek pouring in from the left. This is **Tenmile Creek,** a nice lunch spot and alternative put-in. There is a trail up Tenmile Creek if floaters want to take a side-hike. Tenmile, a pristine roadless area, is a candidate for an addition to the adjacent Sawtooth Wilderness. Eightmile Creek comes up in another mile or so. Watch for the Sourdough Lodge another mile downriver if you're low on drinks or food.

Two miles downstream from Sourdough, **Willis Gulch Creek** flows in from the left. A lightning-caused fire burned about 25,000 acres (double-check) in this area in 1988. It was quickly suppressed, despite the rugged unroaded terrain, in about two weeks. Helicopter-assisted salvage logging followed.

Helende Campground, an alternative put-in or take-out, will appear on river-right about 11 miles below Bonneville. There is a nice gravel bar on the right for a lunch stop. Helende is an excellent place to put-in if whitewater boaters wish to cut the float short and focus on the three major rapids below. It is about seven miles from Helende to Kirkham.

Helende was named by the first supervisor of the Boise National Forest, **Emil Grandjean.** A professional forester from Denmark, Grandjean arrived in Idaho in 1883 to mine, hunt and trap. In 1890, he built a cabin below Grandjean Peak, a site later occupied by the Grandjean Ranger Station. In 1905, President Theodore Roosevelt created a system of forest preserves throughout the nation and placed conservationist Gifford Pinchot in

Hot soothing water awaits chilled boaters at Bonneville Hot Springs.

charge. The present-day Boise National Forest started out as the west branch of the Sawtooth National Forest and a portion of the Payette National Forest, but in July 1908, it became an official forest unto its own, consisting of 1.14 million acres. After a number of boundary changes, the BNF grew to 2.6 million acres — one of the largest national forests in America. Grandjean oversaw early timbering, mining, grazing and recreation on the BNF until his retirement in 1922.

The South Fork continues to wind down the canyon in a gradual but consistent descent for about 3.5 miles below Helende until a sharp left-hand bend signals the beginning of **Emma Creek Rapids,** a Class III-IV drop, depending on flow. The river squeezes into a narrow chute for the big drop. This rapid also is known as "Wake Up" — named so by truckers because it is the sharpest bend in Idaho 21 between Banner Summit and Lowman. Emma Creek is named for **Emma Edwards,** a talented artist who fashioned Idaho's state seal as an 18-year-old. Edwards married John G. Green, a Boise Basin miner, in 1906. They lived along the South Fork for many summers. She included syringa, Idaho's state flower, in the seal. Syringa flowers can be seen on the banks of the South Fork by Emma Creek and other areas. Immediately after Emma Creek Rapids, a second, steeper drop awaits, called **Pinball**, an aptly named Class III-plus squeezebox that will toss your boat around like a Pinball in a slot machine. Cascade Raft guides named that one.

Payette Visions
Kirkham Rapids zooms around a tight corner before the hot springs.

There is a short break — just less than a mile — between Emma Creek and the next cataract, **Wangdoodle Rapids**, a Class III-plus drop. Wangdoodle is named for the creek of the same name, but it's an appropriate name for the move required at the entrance of this rapids. At high flows, a monster standing wave forms at the entrance of Wangdoodle. Boaters can either try to punch it head-on or "noodle" around it on the left bank. It's a tricky move. Once past the entrance wave, several smaller holes and waves finish off that thrilling rapid.

Do a quick paddle salute and get ready for **Kirkham Rapids**, a Class IV, which comes right up after the river cruises around a sharp corner, passes under the Kirkham Bridge, and a series of five or six stair-step drops begins. It's normally best to enter this drop in left-center position for the breaking waves leading into the corner sluicebox and final drop. At high flows, it's possible to flip off the right wall in the final drop if you're not in proper position. If you're planning to take-out at Kirkham, catch a left-side eddy immediately below the rapids.

From Kirkham to Lowman, the river descends at a more gentle pace but it continues to wrap around sharp corners. Floaters will notice fire-scarred mountainsides and toothpick-like snags on the river banks here, and farther upstream, all of which are the remains of the 1989 **Lowman Firestorm**. The fire was hot and intense when it erupted with a fury on July 29, a 90-degree day. It started as a lightning strike but when a lethal combination of tinder-dry drought-ridden forests mixed with stiff winds and hot temperatures, the fire blew up into a vicious beast, reaching 40,000 acres in size. While hundreds of firefighters tried to protect structures in the Lowman area, the fire raced through the lowlands and claimed more than 25 homes. Rock chimneys from incinerated cabins still stand as reminders of that horrifying event.

In the fall of 1989, the Boise National Forest moved rapidly into a fire-recovery project to keep the scorched mountainsides in place. After the firestorm, the mountain slopes above Lowman looked like towering mounds of raw dirt. Forest officials feared that heavy rains would cause enormous erosion events and cause the mountain faces to tumble into the South Fork. Fortunately, a $3 million seeding, tree-planting and haybale-stabilization project and nature's own resilience kept the mountains in place.

T. Glenn/NIFC/BLM

When the Lowman firestorm erupted, it looked as if a nuclear bomb had exploded.

It will take years, however, for the countryside to heal and the forest to rebuild.

CANYON RUN

Difficulty: Advanced, Class IV rapids; Class VI portage
Put-In: Deadwood Campground
Types of craft: Kayaks, rafts, expert duckies
Distance: 12 miles
Float time: 3-6 hours
Take-out: Below Surprise (kayakers & duckies only); Danskin Ramp.
Steepness: 35 feet per mile
Season: April-September

Getting there: Drive east on the Banks-Lowman Highway to the Deadwood Campground at the confluence of the Deadwood River and the South Fork of the Payette River. The campground is about 25 miles east of Banks, and five miles west of Lowman. If you're coming from Stanley, drive to Lowman on Idaho 21. Turn right on the Banks-Lowman highway and head for the put-in next to Deadwood Campground.

Shuttle: Rafters should drop a vehicle at the Danskin Ramp and Rest Area, about 10 miles from the Deadwood Campground. Kayakers who want to skip the four miles of the trip should leave a vehicle at the highway pullout below Surprise Rapids (see map on facing page).

The Float: The South Fork "Canyon" is the most challenging Class IV section of the Payette River Basin and one of the highest-quality whitewater day trips imaginable. It features six Class IV rapids, lots of smaller drops, soothing hot springs at Pine Flats, a scenic lunch spot at the Big Falls portage, and a gorgeous river canyon. One of my rafting friends suggests that the South Fork Canyon is analogous to all running all 102 miles of the Middle Fork of the Salmon River compressed into a single day. **Boaters should not attempt the Canyon until they feel comfortable on the Lower South Fork — the river here is very pushy, it's packed full of rapids, and flips, pins and swims are imminently possible. Boaters should be prepared for the worst and be experienced with river rescue skills and techniques.** Rafters should carry a minimum of

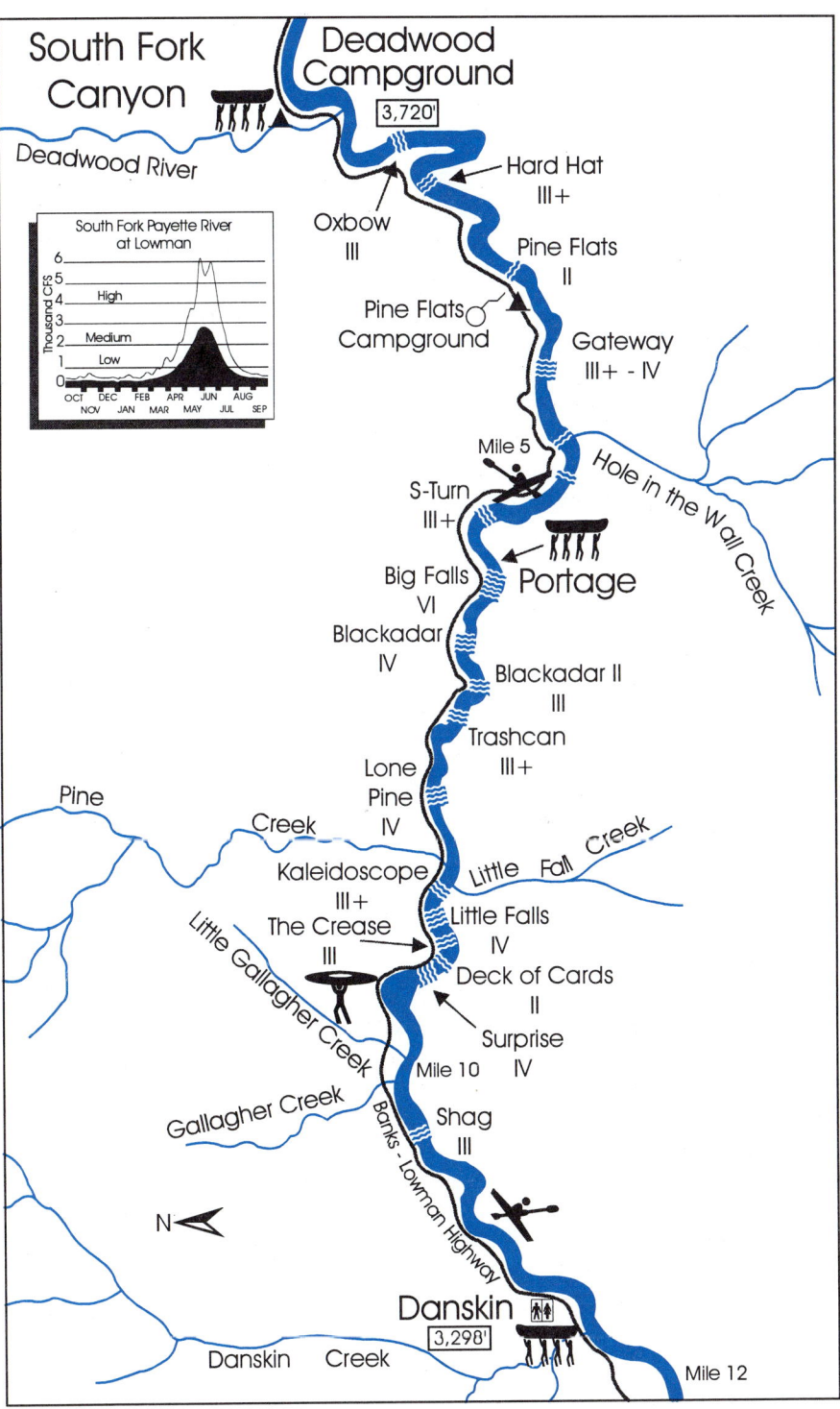

100 feet of rope with them on this run for portaging boats around the falls.

To begin, head out of the Deadwood put-in and use the first mile to practice paddle strokes with the raft crew — if you have a paddle boat — and get warmed up for the first set of rapids. After about one mile, the river takes a sharp left-hand bend and romps toward **Oxbow Rapids**, the first Class III drop. The run here is normally in the center as the current pushes boats to the right around the corner. A series of about three center drops ensues as the river wraps around the Oxbow. Kayakers should line up to surf these drops if they're so inclined — they're nice smooth waves. The Oxbow Bend was the site of a Golden Treasure Mining Co. in 1903. The project was unique in placer-mining operations due to the use of an underground tunnel through the oxbow.

Mark Lisk

The South Fork canyon.

After spring runoff, miners sluiced the center of the river channel for gold. Miners diverted the south fork through a quarter-mile tunnel, which began at the beginning of the Oxbow Bend and exited at the end. The tunnel portals can still be seen at both the entrance and exit points. A small 3-megawatt hydroelectric project was proposed for the Oxbow Bend in the mid-1980s by former Twin Falls engineer Mark Auth, who had hoped to take advantage of the tunnel works for the hydro project. The protection of the South Fork as a scenic and recreational river by the 1991 Legislature prohibited the development.

After the tail-end of the Oxbow Bend, the river bends to the left and drops into **Hard Hat Rapids**, a Class III. This drop is fairly smooth with tall stack waves and assorted holes at high water, but it becomes increasingly rocky and technical at lower flows (below 2,000 cfs). It's usually a rock dodge maze with no obvious run at low flows. The rapid was named "Hart Hat" due to rocks and concrete Jersey barriers that were dropped into the river during the paving of the Banks-Lowman Road.

The South Fork flattens out for a mile after Hard Hat. Take a moment to relax and soak in the magnificent canyon, the springs and the beautiful turquoise water. There are two Class II drops between here and Pine Flats Hot Springs. The first one is an island rapids: the left channel is usually best. Kayakers can find some play spots here. The second drop is pretty straightforward with a little rock- and hole-dodging. The take-out for **Pine Flats Hot Springs** is a large gravel bar on river right, a half-mile past the first signs of the campground on the right bank. Take a minute to stop and soak if you're so inclined.

Mark Torf

Hard Hat Rapids was named for concrete barriers that cartwheeled into the river during construction.

The river is narrow, deep and slow as it cuts toward **Gateway Rapids**, the first Class IV of the run. The horizon line above Gate-

Pine Flats Hot Springs is a required stop.

115

way and the roar of whitewater signals the rapids ahead. At high water, a right-center run is fairly smooth through tall stack waves as the main current whips toward the right wall for the final drop. At low flows, more rocks and holes form, and the run is either far right or far left with lots of quick moves. A rock and hole blocks the center route at low flow. Cascade Raft Co.'s guides named this drop because it signifies the beginning of more serious rapids in the steep forested granite canyon. Boaters will cruise through a number of splashy drops flanked by steep canyon walls in the next mile or so. Watch for a tall granite spires and a tall snag on river-left right before a sharp left-hand bend. This is the run into **S-Turn Rapids**, a Class III-plus to IV-minus, depending on flows. The trick here is to be ready to paddle like the dickens for the left-side of this sharp turn. Lazy and ill-prepared paddlers who don't pay attention to this corner will get washing into a horrible log jam and rock garden on river-right. It's possible to pull out in an eddy on river-right before the sharp corner to scout this drop. Be prepared to dodge holes and rocks to make the left-hand corner. Once you make the cut, the rest of the run is a fairly straightforward wave train. At high water, there is no discernible end to this rapids as the stack waves continue and the river bolts for **Big Falls**, a Class VI 25-foot waterfall. Two successive red signs on ponderosa pine trees on river-right provide a warning to the falls ahead, but don't count on them.

Payette Visions

Boaters can count on Gateway Rapids for a challenging, but thrilling ride.

> Ill-prepared paddlers who don't pay attention to this corner will get washed into a horrible log jam and rock garden on river-right.

Tall snags lying on the left-side rocky shoreline and several groups of shrubs indicate that it's time to pull over in an eddy and get ready to portage the falls. If you're unfamiliar with the canyon, it's a good idea to pull over in a left-side eddy high above the falls and then eddy-hop to a point where you can carry your boat around the falls. The last eddy above the brink of the falls on the left side is the final chance to land.

Portage etiquette: If you see a number of rafts pulled over ahead of you, it's best to eddy out and let them work their way through first. On weekends, the portage take-out area can get congested with outfitted boats, private boats and a bunch of people. Please be courteous and wait your turn.

Payette Visions
Portaging boats around Big Falls is a fun part of a canyon experience.

Outfitters have developed a cool method for portaging rafts around the falls, a method that most private boaters mimic. The idea is to unload your rafts at the portage take-out, have your passengers carry paddles, coolers, dry bags and other gear to the staging area below the falls, and then carry your rafts to a rock outcropping just below the last drop of the falls. Tie a rope around the pinnacle point below the falls, and run a rope back to the rafts

Mark Lisk
A perfect toss to a boater below the falls.

117

waiting to be tossed off the edge (see photo). It's best to position three people with the rafts, one person on the pinnacle, and a person in between. Once the rope is secured on the point and on the raft, toss it off the cliff while the point man pulls on the line and ferries the boat around the corner to the eddy below. Make every attempt to keep boats away from the nasty reversal at the bottom of the falls, it may flip your raft. Once all the boats have been ferried around the corner and tied up, it's time for lunch. Whew!

It's a good idea to warn your passengers that they shouldn't eat or drink too much at Big Falls because the toughest rapids of the whole trip still lie ahead. Seconds after shoving off from Big Falls, boaters will plunge into a playful wave flush, and then the river flattens out for a second before **Blackadar Rapids**, a Class IV. This is the site where Salmon, Idaho paddling legend Walt Blackadar got pinned and drowned under a sweeper log on the left side of the drop in 1978.

It immediately became known as Blackadar Rapids. The Blackadar run is typically a center-to-right move with powerful hydraulics. At lower flows (below 1,600 cfs), a large boulder becomes visible in the left-center portion

Payette Visions

A major "stopper" curling wave forms a crown in Blackadar Rapids at high water.

of the drop. At these flows, it's important to veer to the right of the boulder with the main current. At high water, it's best to cut towards the far-right side of the drop, and holding on through steep drops and tall waves as you fly by the canyon walls. If anyone swims or falls out of a boat here, it's critical to rescue quickly because **Lower Blackadar or Blackadar II Rapids** comes up immediately at the next corner. The river continues to march downriver toward a frothing hydraulic on the left wall, known as **"Trash Can."** It looks ugly but it almost always spits you out in good shape. After Trash Can, it's a good idea to catch an eddy to rest a second

Trash Can Rapids gets big and frothy at high water.
Payette Visions

and enjoy the narrow canyon. Boaters get a small break in the action in the next mile before **Lone Pine Rapids**, a Class IV which is marked by a large gravel bar on the left and a lone pine tree on river-right. Long-time Payette boater Rob Lesser named Lone Pine after the lonely tree in the mid-'70s and it stuck. The entrance to Lone Pine is always from the right side, tucked in between the roundish rock in river center and the right bank. It's important to scoot quickly through this slot, work center for the main drop and hang on. At high water, strong laterals on the right side will flip rafts faster than you can say "Oh Shit!" The run is easier for kayaks at high water because the center rock is buried and kayaks can run it down the middle.

Below Lone Pine, floaters will have to dodge holes and rocks on their way through **Kaleidoscope** as they make the final approach to **Little Falls**, a Class IV rapids. Be sure to take a look at Little Falls on your way to the put-in. At high water, Little Falls is run on the far right. At low water, there is a nice glassy chute about five feet off the left wall for rafts. Expert kayakers like to ski jump off a pancake-like ledge against the left wall. The main issue in Little Falls is to avoid a huge hole in river center. This frothing snowcone can be a keeper,

Little Falls at high water.
Steve Jones

and it's most definitely a flipper. I remember running the canyon a few years ago, and ran into a father and son in a raft. They didn't wear life jackets, they didn't tie anything down on their raft, and they flipped us off when we told them to put on their lifejackets. Almost happily, when we approached Little Falls, we saw their raft frame sticking up vertically in the center hole, their flipped raft against the shore, and the two idiots running down the road, shouting, "Pick up our cooler and gear!" We picked up their stuff littered all over the river but we never saw them again, robbing us of the chance to say, "I told you so."

> We picked up their stuff littered all over the river but we never saw them again, robbing us of the chance to say, "I told you so."

Immediately after Little Falls, the river streamrolls toward **"The Crease,"** a sharp, angular Class III rapids that gets tougher at lower flows. The most thrilling route is to run left and follow the fan wave that catapults your boat into the center of the corkscrew hydraulic. It's possible for kayaks to sneak this on the right. Right after the Crease, there a series of waves and holes. Some outfitters call this **"Deck of Cards"** because the waves kind of shuffle together here, emulating the quick hands of Las Vegas blackjack dealer. At higher flows, Deck of Cards forms a big hole in the center that's easily avoided if you're paying attention.

First-time canyon boaters often mistake Deck of Cards of the final and steepest drop of the run, **"Surprise,"** a Class IV with a nasty hole at the bottom. Lesser is credited with naming this one, too. Legend has it he frequently took kayakers through here for the first time, bluffed them that the run was done after Little Falls, and then, when they came to the horizon line he turned around and said, "Surprise!" grinning ear-to-ear. It's important to line up for a right-center drop into Surprise. The waves push you directly toward the giant hole, so it's wise to begin making a cut to the left or right as you're flying through the wave train. At lower flows, kayaks can grab an eddy on river right just above the final ledge to catch your breath and decide what to do next. At high flows (above 3,500 cfs), the Surprise hole washes out. Below Surprise — way to go, you survived! — kayakers should watch for a quick take-out on river right. It's a steep walk up to the road, but you avoid the last three-four miles of relaxing flatwater leading up to the Danskin Ramp.

Payette Visions
Paddlers make the left cut in Surprise Rapids.

If you go on, watch out for the holes on river-right in **Shag**, about 1.5 miles below Surprise, and cut left in the eddy above. From there, it's a low-key float to the Danskin Ramp.

As you're lolly-gagging along in the flatwater, ponder **the story of Lee Paw**, a Chinese mining boss who drowned near Gallagher Creek in 1880. Paw, who supervised mining operations at Deadwood and the Boise Basin, was returning over the old Scott Trail from Deadwood with a heavy sack of gold. Apparently he was anxious to return to the Boise Basin, but the Scott Bridge near Danskin Creek and the Harrison Bridge near Gallagher Creek had been blown out by high water. So Lee Paw pressed John Galligher to take him across the river in a boat. Soon after they shoved off, the boat flipped and the two swam for their lives. Galligher survived but Lee Paw and his sack of gold sank to the bottom of the river. When word reached Idaho City, a group of Chinamen traveled to the South Fork to search for their boss man's body. They camped at the Carpentier place, a few miles downriver, and explored the river bottom for Lee Paw, without success. They put up a $100 reward, attracting a well-known vegetable peddler, **Yank Ladd**, a Garden Valley resident, to collect the reward. In *All Along the River*, author Nellie Mills said Ladd insisted on collecting the money before he informed the Chinese of Lee Paw's location. "Lee Paw was cooling off until the full hundred dollars was paid," she wrote. Yank Ladd had fooled the Chinese.

SWIRLY CANYON

Difficulty: Intermediate-Advanced (Class III-plus in high water)
Put-In: Danskin Ramp
Types of craft: Kayaks, rafts, canoes, duckies
Distance: 5-8 miles
Float time: 1-3 hours
Take-out: Hot Springs; Alder Creek Bridge
Steepness: 20 feet per mile
Season: April-September

Getting there: Take the Banks-Lowman Highway to the Danskin Rest Area and Boat Ramp. Danskin is about 18 miles east of Banks, and about 17 miles west of Lowman.

Shuttle: Plant a vehicle at the take-out across from Hot Springs Campground or at the Alder Creek Bridge, near Garden Valley.

The Float: Swirly Canyon is another one of those overlooked, unsung reaches of the South Fork. It is getting more popular as time goes on, however. The canyon features less challenging water than the Lower South Fork or the South Fork "Canyon." But the "Swirly" river experience is unique unto itself due to the canyon's own peculiar river dynamics, history and scenery. Swirly is popular among solo canoeists, kayakers of all kinds, and ardent anglers. At higher flows, the rapids in Swirly can be quite challenging and cause experienced kayakers some grief.

To begin, head downriver from Danskin and soak up the scenery. It's about a mile or so to the official entrance of Swirly Canyon. In the first mile or so, the river is wide, with several small surf waves available for beginning kayakers to get a feel for grabbing waves and pointing the bow upstream in a non-threatening environment. But the test is yet to come. The South Fork bends hard to the right at the entrance to the canyon, and a series of Class III to Class II rapids follows for the next couple miles. As boaters negotiate this section, they will see how the canyon got its name — the eddy swirls can be powerful and the waves in rapids seem to shuffle and overlap, creating tricky circumstances for kayakers and canoeists. John Wasson, a Class V kayaker who has lived on

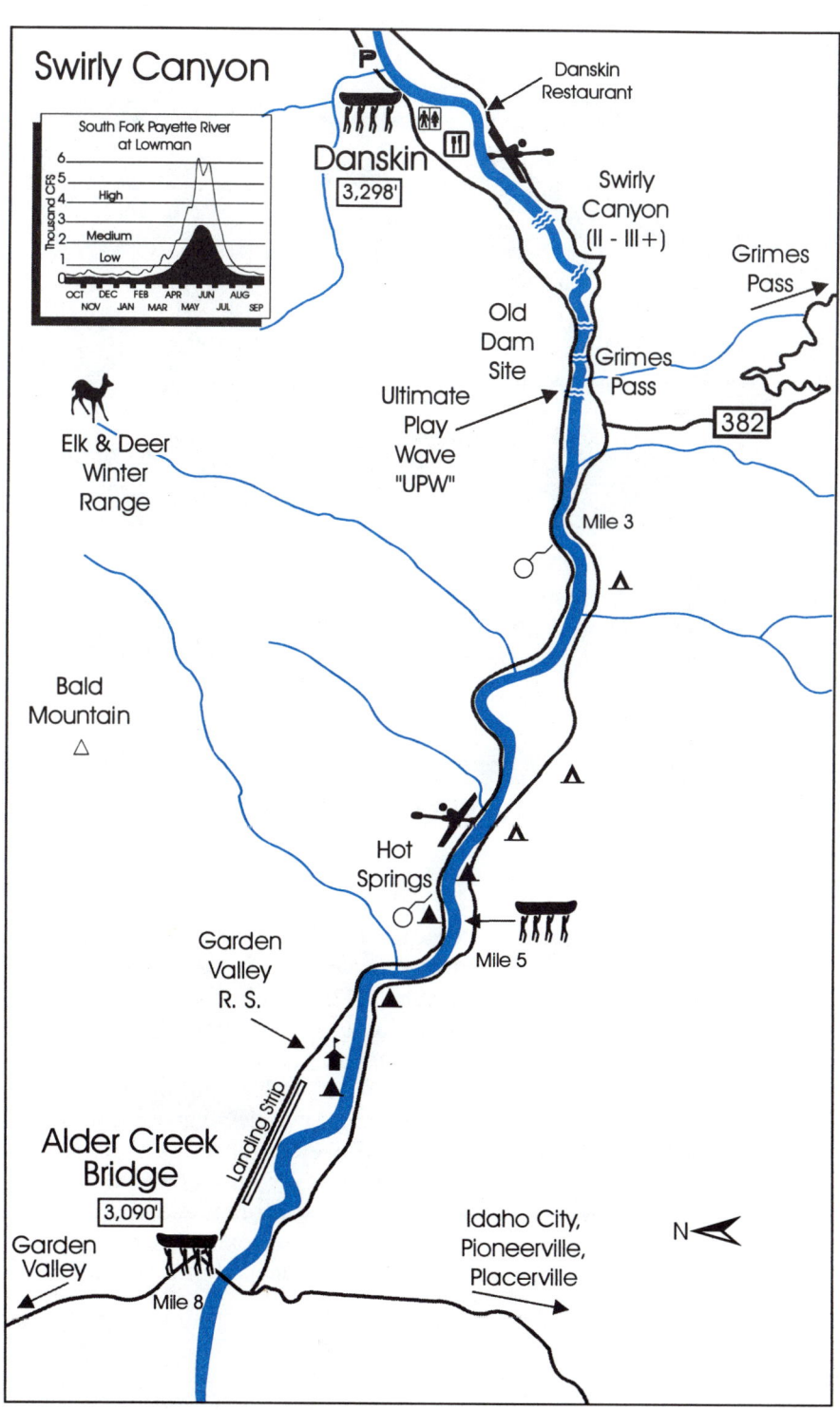

Grimes Pass Dam, circa 1910
Idaho State Historical Society

the edge of Swirly since 1980, named Swirly Canyon afer its rigid eddy lines and unique river dynamics. "It's really only in the last few years that I've discovered Swirly Canyon," Wasson says. "The run from here to Alder Creek is just beautiful — there's a whole bunch of kind of cool little nooks and cliffs."

A SWIRLY SWIM

OK, it's time for the author to fess up about one of his own close-calls. I got spanked in Swirly last summer on a seemingly beautiful day at relatively low water. I got flipped while surfing an innocuous two-foot wave, with no air. I was getting whirled around and couldn't get my paddle on the surface. I missed my roll and swam. As I got swept around the corner-rapids at the entrance of Swirly, I cried out to my incredulous friends that I needed to be rescued. Right at the corner, I saw a way to leap out on the left cliff and landed safely. But my boat and paddle whipped downstream. My buddy and his girlfriend peeled out to chase them, and I was stuck on the wrong side of the river without a boat or a paddle. So I spy a slow eddy 50 feet downstream and think to myself, OK, I'll float on my back through the next drop and then swim like hell for the right shore. Right. I leaped into the river, floated along and then cut for shore. I stroked into a void that wouldn't let me through. I had underestimated Swirly's rigid eddy fences. I hadn't even considered that possibility. So as my energy was getting zapped by the cold water (I was paddling with just a life jacket that day) I swim back into the current and stroked for the left wall. I see a bead of current heading right for it. I get there and reach up for the wall. I get a grip with my fingertips on a crevace and pull myself out. Whew! I'm still on the left side of the river without a boat or paddle, though, and my friends are no where in sight. A tow is out of the question. So I look up at the cliff. I see a route ... but it looks really steep on the final approach, a nip-and-tuck climb through a couple of overhanging pines and, oh my god, a huge patch of poison ivy. I was literally up a creek without a paddle. I climbed the cliff, gingerly making my way through the poison ivy, and then had a couple of close calls — agonizing cliff-slippage on moss— before I reached the top. A road! Much to my amazement, there was a dirt road up there right on the edge of the canyon. I ran down it until I saw my buddies pulled over in an eddy above the "Ultimate Play Wave." They had my boat, but no paddle. I was done for the day. They ferried me across and I walked back upriver to look for my paddle and run our shuttle. No paddle.

John Wasson in his front yard on the South Fork.

In this case, the river taketh and spanketh me. It's always a good lesson. But the moral is: Don't underestimate the Swirlys in the Swirly Canyon. John Wasson, a veteran Class V boater who lives above the UPW, says that people frequently seek assistance. He grabs his kayak and rescue gear and bolts for the river, just down the trail from his house. "I pretty much take everything with me — my kayak, a throw-rope and whatever because a lot of times I have to jump in and go after people or equipment."

At the tail end of Swirly Canyon is a sweet scoop-shaped wave, dubbed the UPW "Ultimate Play Wave" by Wasson and fellow 'yakers in the late '70s. The wave is all that remains from the old Grimes Dam, which powered dredge mines in the Boise Basin from 1907 to 1927. In the early 1940s, high water took it down. The dam sort of "mushed," Wasson says, when the timber-crib structure blew out. Today, the dam's remains provide a perfect surfing and play wave — one that was even better in the late '70s and early '80s. Then, the wave had a foaming back crest that provided a perfect cushion for somersaults, front and back endos. In a "Great American Sportsman" episode from the early '80s, Wasson, Lesser and a couple boating buddies took turns doing flips, spins and pirouettes on the wave. "This is just pure good times," Wasson says as he performs twirls on the wave for the TV cameras. "It's a combination wave-pull. You can do enders forwards and backwards, you can play without a paddle; it's just pure good times." Since the mid-1980s, though, the wave has turned more glassy and it's not quite the platform for a wide variety of tricks like it used to be.

Below the UPW, the river slows down and winds through a box canyon of sorts, although not as tall and abrupt as the Swirly Canyon itself. Boaters will notice numerous hot springs and cool water springs emerging on the left and right as they drift through this swift, flat section. Old remains of Chinese placer-mining work appears on both the left and right bank below that.

Interpretive notes: On the gentle plateau above the UPW, on river left, was the site of a thriving community during the early 1900s. It was called Grimes Pass, not to be mistaken with the actual mountain pass several miles above. The site was first homesteaded by the Calderwood family in the 1880s. William H. Estabrook, a wealthy gold tycoon, took over the property at the turn of the century and built a spacious, innovative log-chalet, known widely as "Estabrook's Castle." The multi-stored log "castle" featured broad eves, a fenced deck surrounding the house, and a tall stone foundation. The castle's biggest whiz-bang feature were electric beds, mounted on railroad tracks, that wheeled from inside bedrooms to sleeping porches with the flick of a switch. Visitors said Estabrook had a rich wine cellar unlike any in Boise County, as well as a billiard table. Beyond Estabrook's chalet, the Grimes Pass community consisted of a barn, some houses and cabins for the workers, a post office and a school house. "It was quite a little community," Wasson says. Grimes Dam was a key part of the town's existence. The dam had twin turbo generators that powered Estabrook's gold-dredge on Elk Creek, about a half mile above Idaho City, and of course, provided electricity to his "Pinetop" home. The dredge operated until 1917, scooping up untold amounts of gold. Unfortunately, the Estabrook Chalet burned in March 1918. Ever the opportunist, Estabrook went on to make another mining fortune on the Trinity River in California. Grimes Pass, as a community, fell into obscurity after the dam failed. The name Grimes comes from George Grimes, whose party struck gold in upper Grimes Creek in August 1862. Grimes was killed by Indians soon after. Wasson bought four acres in the old townsite in 1980, the first whitewater boater to take up permanent roots on the Payette River. By 1995, a year after Wasson had directed river logistics for "The River Wild" movie with Meryl Streep, he had acquired 140 acres on the banks of the south fork — pretty much the whole townsite.

As boaters approach Hot Springs take-out, they'll notice a Good Sam campground on river left. This is a deluxe campsite, complete with a swingset, for families with kids. A dirt pathway and a hot springs tub mark the Hot Springs takeout on river right. If you continue on to Alder Creek Bridge, the river winds along in a small rimmed canyon with nice eddies and structure for fishing and enough gradient to glide along with little to no effort. Enjoy the float to Alder Creek Bridge.

Camping restrictions: The Boise National Forest has established some new camping restrictions for primitive campsites on the south side of Swirly Canyon. To prevent forest fires, all campfires must be burned in fire pans. Human waste is supposed to be packed out as well. Be sure to respect private property along the canyon — many of these folks don't want to be bothered by boaters.

GARDEN VALLEY SCENIC TOUR

Difficulty: Beginners-Intermediate (Class I-II)
Put-In: Alder Creek Bridge
Types of craft: Canoes, duckies, kayaks, rafts
Distance: 4 miles
Float time: 1-2 hours
Take-out: Middle Fork confluence, Deer Creek, Lower South Fork put-in.
Steepness: 5 feet per mile (flatwater)
Season: April-October

Getting there: Drive east on the Banks-Lowman Highway to the Alder Creek Bridge, located about 10 miles east of Banks and a mile east of Garden Valley. Put-in here.

Shuttle: Drop a vehicle or bicycle on your way up the canyon at the Lower South Fork put-in, Deer Creek put-in (old bridge pilings stand in the river by the creek) or Middle Fork confluence. Canoeists who wish to avoid running any rapids should take-out at the Middle Fork confluence (the old Worm Farm).

The Float: The Garden Valley reach of the South Fork is a nice relaxing float trip through the pastoral valley. Cattle ranches adjoin the river here — as do livestock at times — as well as a number of summer cabins. This reach is popular with hobby gold-dredgers. You'll see them in wet suits and scuba gear working the bottom gravels along the edges of the river, while their family hangs out by the river fishing or whatever. As boaters float along, they'll see Charters Mountain on the left, a large rounded mountain which burned in the 1930s. Charters Mountain is named for a family that homestead on that side of Garden Valley in 1866. Heavy brush growth following the fire has precluded timber from re-establishing on parts of the mountain. Proceeding on, floaters will cruise through the valley to a point where the river narrows and begins to bend to the left. The Middle Fork flows in on the right at this point. This is your sign to paddle to the right shore and take-out if you want to avoid about two miles of Class I and Class II rapids below. The Deer Creek take-out is marked by concrete pilings in

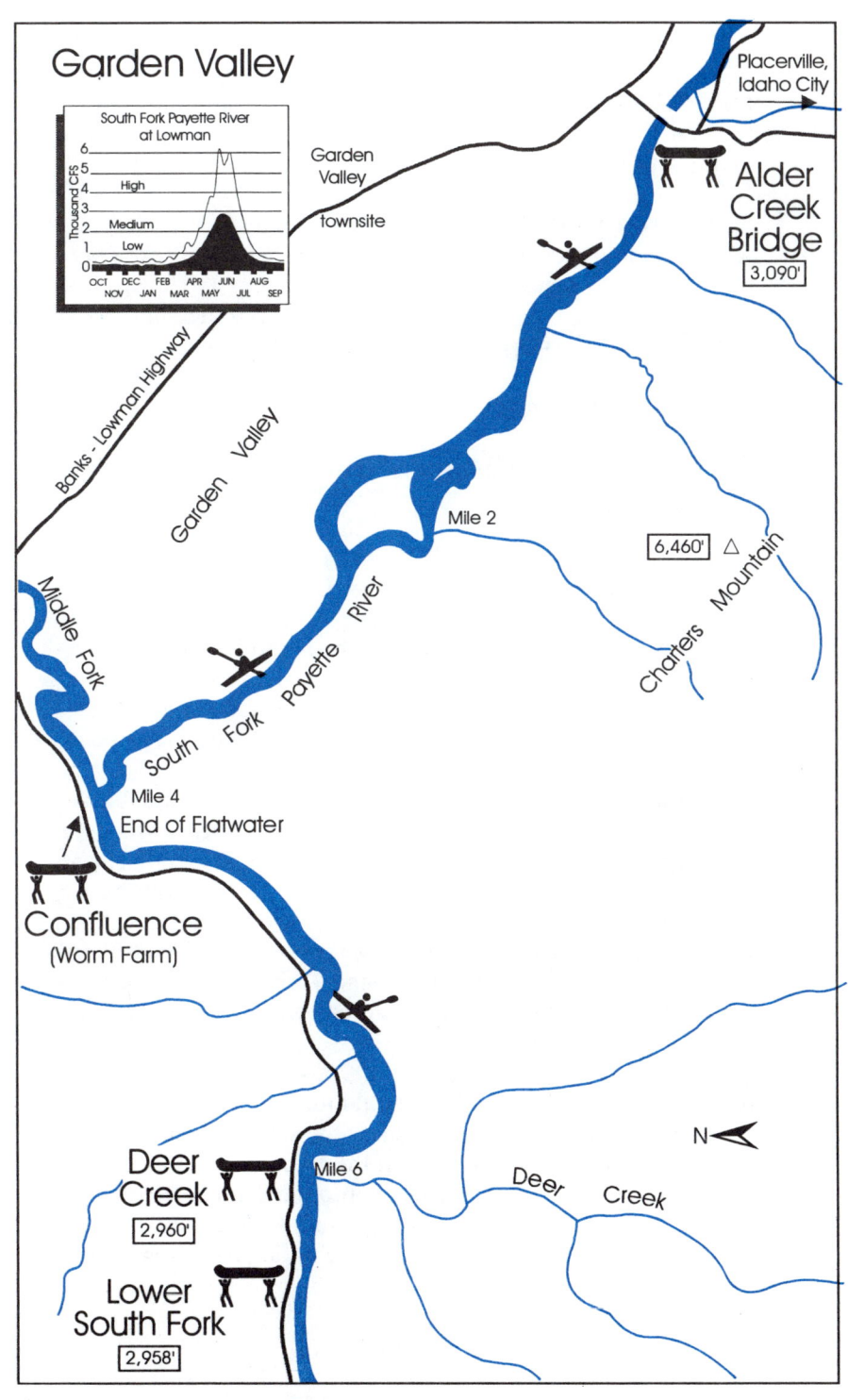

the center of the river. The Lower South Fork take-out is marked by a small beach and eddy on the right and a cliff and rope swing on the left.

Interpretive remarks: Garden Valley's name dates back to the 1870s when a smattering of settlers homesteaded there, and eeked out a living growing vegetables for Boise Basin miners and raising livestock. Several families, including Donald and Margaret McBridge, raised dairy cows to produce dairy products for miners. Yank Ladd, a skilled trapper and fisherman, settled at the confluence of the Middle Fork and set up a fish trap for chinook salmon. A.S. Abbott, the son of another early Garden Valley settler, Bill Abbott, reminisced about the early days in a column printed in the Idaho Statesman in September 1928. Abbott writes that Ladd "marketed immense quantities of the delicious fellows (salmon) to the miners and others of the basin ... and also from which the farmers of the valley stocked their larders."

> Yank Ladd "marketed immense quantities of the delicious fellows (salmon) to the miners...."

Before there was a road from Banks to Crouch and Garden Valley, pioneers had to reach the valley via the Boise Basin, literally following Indian trails. Bill Abbott, Alex Sifers and hired hands built the first dirt road into Garden Valley from Placerville by way of Alder Creek. They built a bridge near the present-day Alder Creek Bridge, and established the new route as a toll road. Abbott's success won him election to the Idaho Territorial Legislature in 1866. The toll road was soon transfered to Boise County and became a public thoroughfare.

During the Indian uprising of 1878, several historians make note that Garden Valley pioneers hid in the brush by the South Fork for fear of being slaughtered. Some settlers even moved to Placerville for the time being. But the Indians never killed anyone in Garden Valley as they raced into the Salmon River country, with the U.S. Cavalry in close pursuit. Further settlement in Crouch and Garden Valley didn't come until a road was built up the South Fork of the Payette from Banks in 1915. The road, which required blasting in the lower canyon by Staircase Rapids, Slalom and Bronco Billy rapids, was one of the first built by Morrison Knudsen. The job was done with hand and team labor, and many Garden Valley residents contributed. Once the road was completed, Garden Valley established a daily mail stop and a sure-fire route to the new railroad line at Banks.

Garden Valley pioneers hid in the brush by the South Fork for fear of being slaughtered

LOWER SOUTH FORK — STAIRCASE

Difficulty: Advanced-Expert (Class IV-plus in high water)
Put-Ins: Middle Fork confluence; Deer Creek; Lower South Fork put-in; Below-Staircase put-in.
Types of craft: Kayaks, rafts, solo canoes, duckies
Distance: 5 miles (from Deer Creek)
Float time: 30 minutes-1.5 hours
Take-out: Banks or Beehive Bend (South Fork-Main Payette take-out)
Steepness: 35.5 feet per mile
Season: Early April-late August

Getting there: Drive to Banks, at the junction of the South Fork and North Fork of the Payette, on Idaho 55. It is 35 miles to Banks from Boise, and 70 miles to Banks from McCall. Just after Banks, the Banks-Lowman highway turns off to the east. Take that two-lane highway to your desired put-in — Middle Fork confluence, Deer Creek, lower South Fork or below Staircase.

Shuttle: Drop a vehicle where you wish to take-out — either at Banks or Beehive Bend on the Main Payette (seven miles south of Banks).

A word about flow: At high water, river hydraulics in Staircase get very pushy. At flows below 1,000 cfs Staircase becomes extremely rocky.

The Float: The Lower South Fork run is the place where boaters of all kinds test their mettle. For boaters who feel they have conquered the Main Payette, Cabarton and Upper South Fork run, the Lower South Fork is the next reach to try out. But even after you've "conquered" **Staircase Rapids** — the biggest nemesis on this run — there's every chance that you'll get munched the next time. In short, many experienced boaters have a hearty amount of respect for Staircase. By virtue of its steep drop (35 feet per mile), the Lower South Fork is narrow, pushy and requires the boating skills necessary to make mid-rapid maneuvers to miss holes, rocks and logs in several rapids. The Lower South Fork also features a

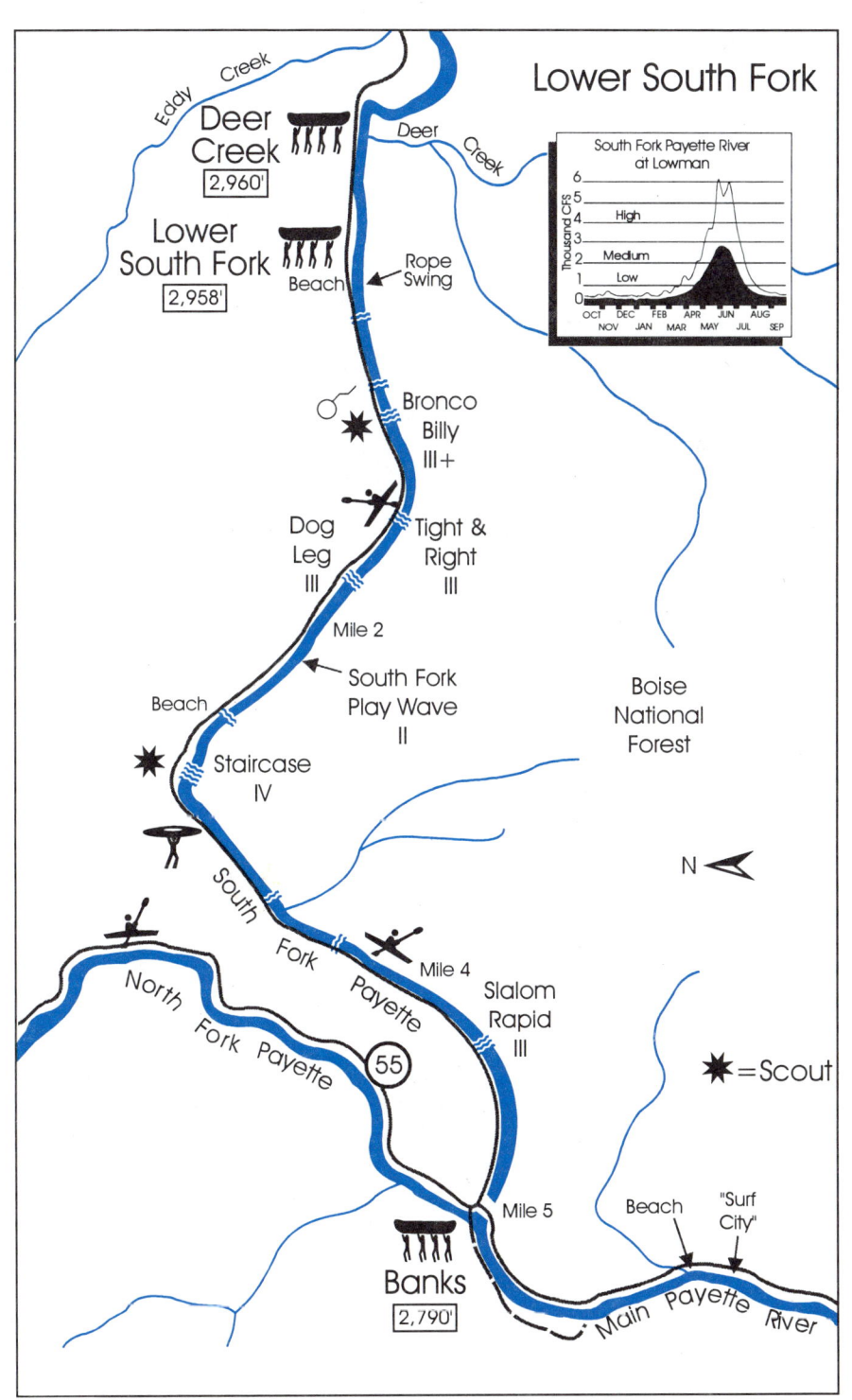

number of playing opportunities for kayakers, especially the South Fork Play Wave, located conviently about half way down.

The Float: Below Deer Creek, the first rapids on the Lower South Fork is a Class II riffle, typically run on the left side. Cascade guides call this rapids Nose Drop after the nose-shaped rock in the middle of the drop. After a short break, a series of Class II drops (and good play spots) leads into the beginning of **Bronco Billy Rapids,** a Class III-plus drop. The optimum run for rafts here is a classic S-turn: Begin the run in center position, negotiating a series of stack waves, and then as the river bends left, make a move to the left to miss a major hole on the right, and then make a move back toward center to miss a hole on the bottom left. Of course, as luck would have it, the rapids push you into the hole on the right. Many rafts have flipped in this hole, and many a kayaker has gotten window-shaded in here. At higher flows, the lower holes in Bronco Billy tend to wash out, and it's just a raging torrent through there.

Above: Young boaters tackle Bronco Billy in the National Junior Championships. Left: The rapid is named for Boisean Dick Knapp.

Rob Lesser

Early kayakers called this rapids Dog Leg, but as time has gone on, that name has been applied to a Dog Leg farther downriver. Roger Rosentreter, a Class V kayaker and a Ph.D. botonist/naturalist, named Bronco Billy after a paddling buddy, Dick Knapp, in the late 1970s. "Dick is your classic Clark Kent Superman type," Rosentreter says. "He's an accountant, and he's got these thick black glasses, and looks like a real nerd, but when he gets into his kayak, he turns into a different person. Dick used to love to play in that hole in Bronco Billy (the hole on the bottom left) — he'd just get bounced around in there like a guy riding a bucking bronco. Dick would just hold onto the front rim of his cockpit and hang on for the ride." Knapp was a Class V boater as well; he ran the North Fork with the "big boys" like Mike Lyons and Rob Lesser in those same black glasses.

Rosentreter warns kayakers that if they plan on dropping into Knapp's hole, beware that at certain flows, it gets real "sticky" and 'yakers end up swimming to get out.

Below Bronco Billy, the river bends hard right and enters **Dog Leg Rapids**, a Class III. The run is usually on the far river-right side. Follow the tongue of the river around the corner and be ready to dodge rocks or holes. **Tight and Right Rapids** comes up next after a short calm pool. It's best to position for the right side of the river. The main run here is to skirt a hole at the top, work center and then avoid a rock or hole at the bottom.

The South Fork play wave features a slick scoop wave and pop-up hole for simultaneous action.

You can coast a bit below here and gear up for the **South Fork Play Wave**. This most gorgeous slick wave, combined with an ender hole on river left, has got to be one of the finest surf spots on the planet. The wave is pretty gnarly and tough to catch at flows above 4,000 cfs. But after the high-water season and the flows drop to 3,000 or less, the wave becomes river central for hot-shot 'yakers. At flows between 1,500 and 2,000 cfs, the wave becomes super slick and smooth — it's easy to catch for front, back and side-surfs, and the adjacent pop-up hole provides automatic front and back endos. To give an idea of how low-key the wave gets at lower flows, kayakers have put dogs on their boat and surfed the wave, and Boise solo canoeist Phil Lansing has locked into the wave with his red Whitesell (check) canoe, stood up and dropped his shorts while he surfed there on the wave. Yep, it's a place for 'yakers and solo canoeists to play to your heart's content.

Play wave etiquette: Kayakers should be sure to surf out of the way when rafts come whizzing by the wave, but rafters should be aware that it's best to steer clear of kayakers if the 'yaker happens to be off in the clouds somewhere and doesn't pay attention. Get rolled over by a raft in a kayak is not a fun experience. Below the Play Wave, the river flows by a number of small riffles in the final approach to **Staircase Rapids**.

Top: Paddle crew with oarsman crashes through curling wave in Staircase at high water. Above: Swimming Staircase is nasty: Get to shore quickly.

Early Payette River Outfitter Steve Guinn used to tack a colored T-shirt on a road-side power pole to signal the start of Staircase. The easiest way to spot the rapids well upstream is to notice how the roadbed drops down very close to river level as the river bends to the left. There is also a small drop just above Staircase around a large split granite boulder. There are a number of eddies boaters can catch to scout Staircase. Many locals prefer to scout it on the way to the put-in. Be ready for a big gallery — on weekends there's always a bunch of people hanging out in lawn chairs, hoping to see someone get munched.

The run through Staircase changes at many flow levels, but for rafts it's a safe bet to stay to the right side of the **Whale Rock**,

At low water (flows below 1,200 cfs), the "fang" rock in the middle of the run becomes a pointy nemesis to rafters.

a large hunk of granite in the left-center side of the main drop. Many boaters scout their run based on how the river hydraulics form just to the right side of the rock. Expert kayakers like to run to the left side of the Whale Rock for kicks, but in 1995, there was a nasty log jammed in there that could kill somebody. Be sure to take a good look. The main thing to avoid in Staircase is swimming. "Anyone who has ever swam it has gotten totally beaten up," notes Tullio Celano, a Payette kayak pioneer and Boise urologist who named Staircase. Paddle raft passengers should make sure that their feet are well wedged and keep their center of gravity toward the center of the boat, if possible. Big holes in Staircase have a tendency to "stop" rafts dead in their tracks, causing paddlers or passengers to vault skyward ass-over-tea-kettle.

Tullio was the first modern boater to call the rapids "Staircase." He named it after he ran the first modern descent in August 1970. "I had to go to bathroom three times before I did it, but I made it without any problems," Celano says. The whole rapid "is just kind of like a staircase," he says. "With each little drop, the river just kind of drops like a set of stairsteps."

Early log-drivers who boated the Lower South Fork to shepherd logs downriver from Garden Valley apparently called the rapids "Hells Half-Acre" after at least a half-dozen men who died there. Early woodsmen who drove logs down the North Fork apparently called the Class V reach "The Stairs."

For kayakers, the big trick in Staircase is to stay in your boat and roll if you get flipped in Staircase. The only problem is, once

Payette Visions

If the "fang" rock doesn't get you, a stopper hole may launch paddlers.

you're flipped over, the powerful hydraulics spin you around and make the task difficult at best. Linda Olson, a Boise veteran kayaker, recalls that Staircase had a huge reputation in the mid-1970s. "Staircase had such a mystique that everyone was afraid of it," she recalls. "Everyone was really psyched out about it." She includes herself in that camp. One of the problems was that early 'yakers used to put-in just above Staircase; no warm up, just launch into the madness. "I thought that was pretty stupid thing to do," Rosentreter says.

Olson recalls that she swam Staircase at least 10 times before she finally stayed in her boat and made a roll in there. It took a near-death experience to acquire the mental toughness to stay in her boat. "The last time I swam Staircause, I got stuck in a hole toward the bottom and my foot got wedged between two rocks in the bottom of the river," she says. "I felt like I was a goner. I yanked on my foot and yanked on it and I couldn't get it loose. Then a thought flashed through my mind that I learned swimming as a little girl in Minnesota. They always told you, if your feet get stuck

138

in the weeds, relax your legs. So I relaxed my legs and my foot came loose. Man, that was really a close call." The next time she ran Staircase, she tipped over again. "I remember I held inside my boat and I tried to roll eight times before I got up. I thought, swimming is stupid. I'm a lot safer in my boat."

Boaters should remember to scout the whole Staircase run, around the corner, because there are some nasty holes down there in high water. It's important, for instance, to move toward the center after the first part of Staircase to avoid a big thundering hole on river-right at flows above 6,000 cfs. The runout of Staircase is always rough and rocky, and the final drop is huge fun because you made it!

Below Staircase, there is a road-side put-in for floaters who prefer to bypass the Class IV drop. Below here, floaters will encounter a number of smaller Class II drops (and some nice surfing possibilities) for a mile or before running the final drop, **Slalom Rapids**, a Class III. Slalom was named so after kayak slalom races were held there. It's a suitable name for the S-turn shape of the rapids as boaters start out on the right and have to slalom around rocks and holes. This is a long, two-part rapid. In the upper half, the run is typically down the middle to begin with and then move to the right to avoid a large pointy rock or hole in river-center. At high water, it's tough to see the holes because the waves in here get so high. In the lower half of Slalom, watch for a cliff wall on the left and follow the current toward the wall for the final runout. At low water, several routes are possible in this section.

Below Slalom, the South Fork flattens out for a quarter mile before the rapids under the Banks bridge at the confluence with the North Fork. Take-out at the beach on the right or continue downriver as you like.

MIDDLE FORK PAYETTE — TIE CREEK

Difficulty: Novice-Intermediate
Put-In: Tie Creek Campground
Types of craft: Canoes, duckies, open kayaks, kayaks, innertubes
Distance: 8 miles
Float time: 2-3 hours
Take-out: Crouch
Steepness: 8 feet per mile
Season: May-August (depending on flows)

Getting there: Follow the Banks-Lowman highway about 10 miles east of Banks to the left-hand turnoff for Crouch and Terrace Lakes. Proceed about 10 miles on the Middle Fork road to Tie Creek Campground, on the right, just after the Forest Service boundary. Pull into the fee campground and park. The float starts here.

Shuttle: Leave a vehicle or bicycle in Crouch. Park next to the river, across from the Crouch Merc.

The Float: The Middle Fork offers a low-key pleasant refuge from the adrenaline-charged whitewater experience on the south fork. Floaters won't find this reach to be intimidating at all — the river is mostly flat, with small riffles, as it winds through a scenic pastoral valley. Wildlife viewing opportunities include herons, kingfishers and occasional ospreys, not to mention red-tailed hawks, mule deer, maybe even a small group of elk. Fishing in this reach is usually quite slow. Fish and Game stocks catchable rainbows in the Middle Fork several times each summer.

Beginning kayakers should consider the Tie Creek run as an excellent alternative to the lower main Payette "warm up" run below Beehive Bend. On the Middle Fork, kayakers can practice maneuvers, rolls and eddy turns in a non-threatening setting.

Canoeists, duckies and open kayakers will enjoy a peaceful float down the Middle Fork.

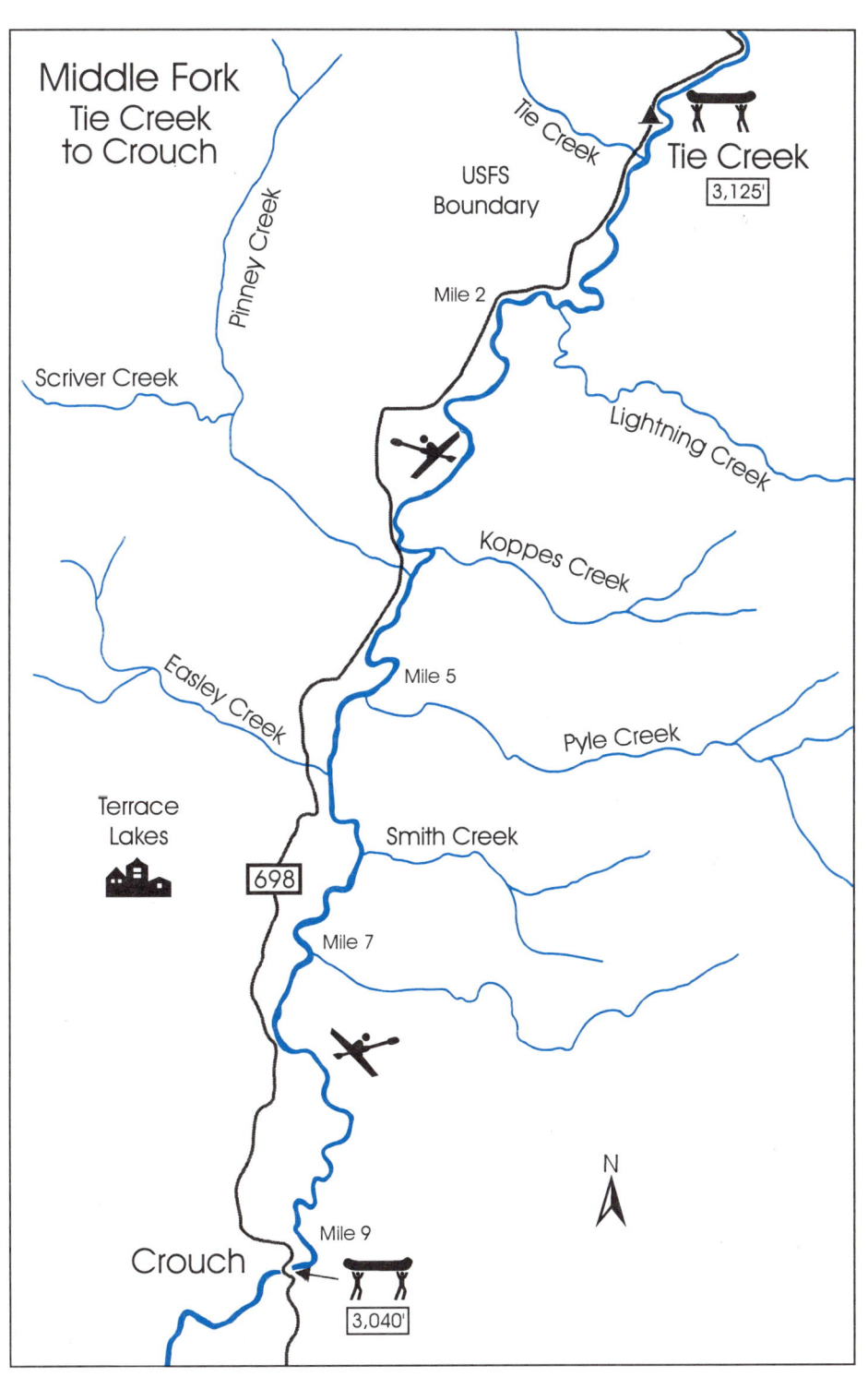

DEADWOOD RESERVOIR

Launch sites: Riverside Campground on the lake's north end, Barney's Park Campground and Homer's Campground on the east shoreline, or Cozy Cove Campground on the south end.
Types of craft: Canoe, open kayak, ducky, drift boat.
Maximum width: 6 miles
Maximum Depth: 137 feet
Average Depth: 54 feet
Float time: You make the call
Season: May-October
Elevation: 5,311

Getting there: It's a relatively long haul to reach Deadwood Reservoir. The most direct way to reach the lake is by driving the Banks-Lowman highway to a left-hand turnoff for Scott Mountain and Deadwood Reservoir. This turn is about 25 miles east of Banks and nine miles west of Lowman. Follow the washboard-prone STEEP dirt road about 26 miles to the bottom of Deadwood Dam. It's another couple miles to the reservoir. Once there, survey the campgrounds for your desired put-in and launch. As an alternative, it's possible to reach Deadwood Reservoir from Stanley via the Stanley-Landmark Road or from Cascade, via the Warm Lake and Landmark. See a Boise National Forest map for directions.

Shuttle: Since there's a dirt road on the east side of the lake, it's possible to spot a bicycle or vehicle on the opposite end of the lake if you wish.

The Float: Because of its remote location, Deadwood Reservoir is normally an off-beat place to paddle, meaning you're likely to have a secluded, quiet time. There may be a few fishermen motoring around the lake in search of rainbow trout or kokanee. The fishing here can be quite good. When the reservoir is full in June, there are a number of coves and small bays to check out as you paddle around the reservoir. It takes a couple hours to paddle the length of the lake, which is about six miles across, north to south. Due to the possibility of high winds in the afternoon, it's best to paddle the lake in the morning or evening. However, paddlers may

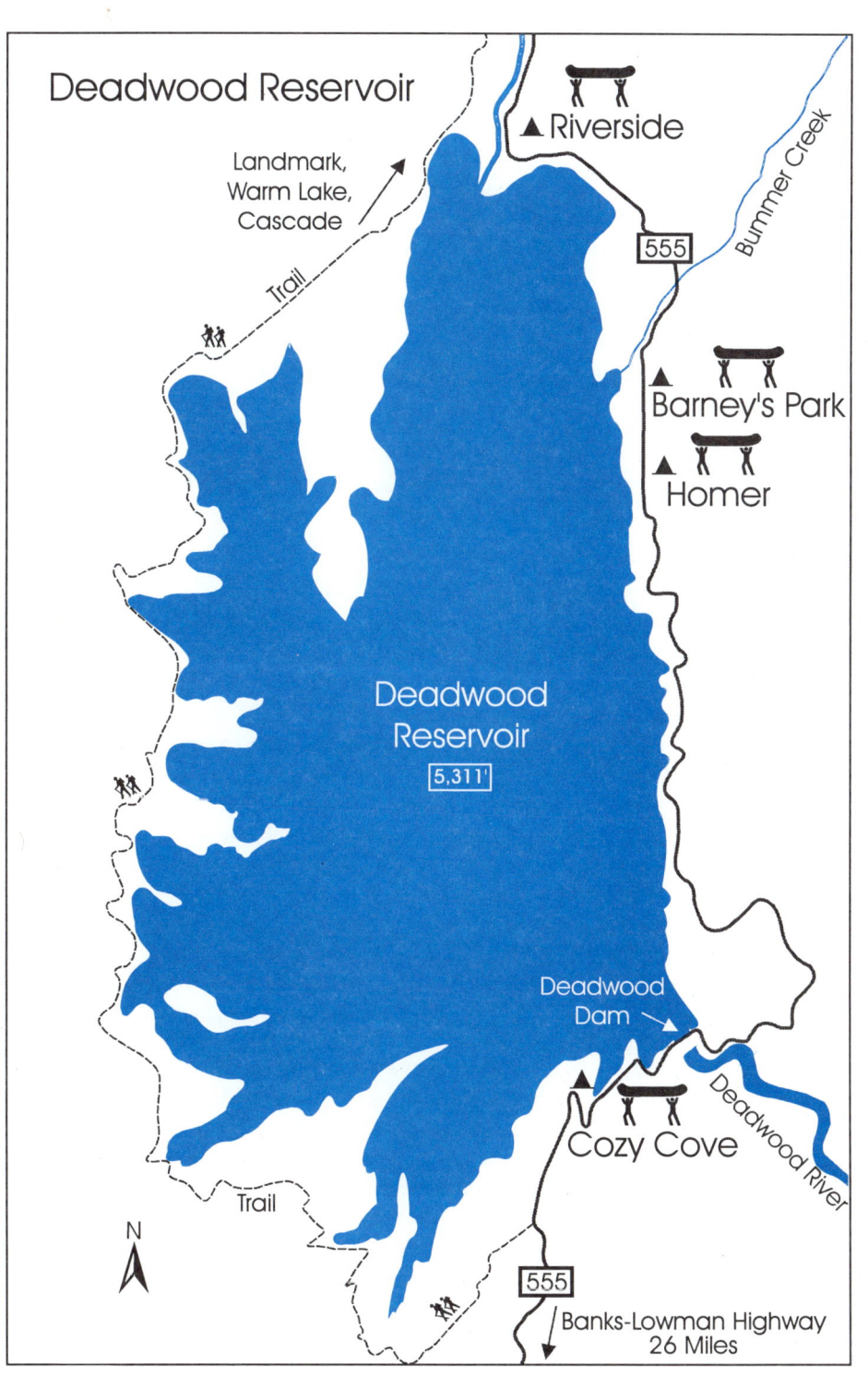

Paddlers enjoy the solitude of Deadwood Reservoir.

luck out and experience no wind at all. Group outings to Deadwood Reservoir are normally held once a year by the Southwest Idaho Canoe Club (correct).

Interpretive remarks: Deadwood Reservoir is a man-made lake. The 170-foot-tall structure was completed on Nov. 7, 1930, just before winter set in. The dam was built by Morrison Knudsen Co. and Utah Construction Co. for the U.S. Bureau of Reclamation and Lower Payette Valley farmers, orchardists and ranchers. It has a maximum capacity of 164,000 acre-feet. At full pool, it covers 3,055 surface acres. As part of the contract, construction crews had to fell thousands of lodgepole pine trees with cross-cut saws. When the reservoir was filled, it buried the old gold-mining towns of "Bummer" and Deadwood City. Bummer Creek flows into the reservoir near Barney's Park Campground. Deadwood City became a ghost town by 1876.

Water from Deadwood Reservoir is typically released for flood-control in April and May, and then stored until natural runoff recedes in early to mid-July. Then the flows pick up and the lake's level drops until late August or September. At this time, the Bureau typically satisfies irrigation requirements with water from Cascade Reservoir and it holds storage water in Deadwood, "banking it" for the following season. The upshot: paddlers should expect to find the lake partially drained (and stumps showing on the north, upstream end) in August and September.

Potential sidetrips: A fine single-track trail on the lake's west side makes for a nice hike or mountain bike ride. If you're interested in doing some more paddling, consider traveling toward Stanley to Elk Creek and Bear Valley Creek on the Stanley-Landmark Road. Those two streams are deep and flat, and the surrounding country is teeming with wildlife. If you're planning to return home via the Banks-Lowman highway, consider a side hike or mountain bike ride to Scott Mountain Lookout. The jeep trail junction for the lookout is near the summit of the dirt road pass. It's five miles one-way to the lookout from the junction. The views from the top are totally fetching.

Bureau of Reclamation

Bureau of Reclamation

Top: The dam site just as construction got under way. Above: Deadwood Dam was built in the early 1930s; loggers had to fell thousands of skinny lodgepole pine trees by hand.

UPPER DEADWOOD

Difficulty: Expert, Class IV-plus to Class V
Put-In: Below Deadwood Dam
Types of craft: Kayaks, catarafts
Distance: 14.5-22 miles
Float time: Full day
Take-out: Julie Creek Road or Deadwood Campground.
Steepness: 80 feet per mile
Season: April-September

Getting there: The most popular route to the upper Deadwood is the Scott Mountain Road, which connects to the Banks-Lowman road just above Little Falls on the South Fork Payette. It's about 26 miles on the steep, washboard-prone dirt road to the launch site below Deadwood Dam. Alternate routes to the put-in are the Clear Creek road from Idaho 21 north of Lowman, the Warm Lake road and Landmark-Stanley road from Cascade or Stanley. Year-round access is NOT maintained to Deadwood Reservoir. Therefore, all of these routes may be blocked by snow until mid-summer. Road conditions are available from the Lowman District of the Boise National Forest.

Shuttle: Leave a vehicle at the end of the Julie Creek Road or at Deadwood Campground. Due to the length of the shuttle (47 miles), a shuttle driver or an early start are highly recommended.

Warning: The Deadwood River was named the "Deadwood" for a reason. Boaters should watch for logs blocking the river channel throughout the Deadwood River section. Portaging may be necessary.

The Float: The upper Deadwood combines several factors which increase the difficulty beyond that encountered on other class IV whitewater runs in the Payette Basin. These factors include a long, inaccessible canyon, very cold water, log strainers, continuous rapids, and a long shuttle. A mishap on this run can turn your day trip into a memorable hike or self-support overnighter. There is no trail or road which can be seen or reached from the river without

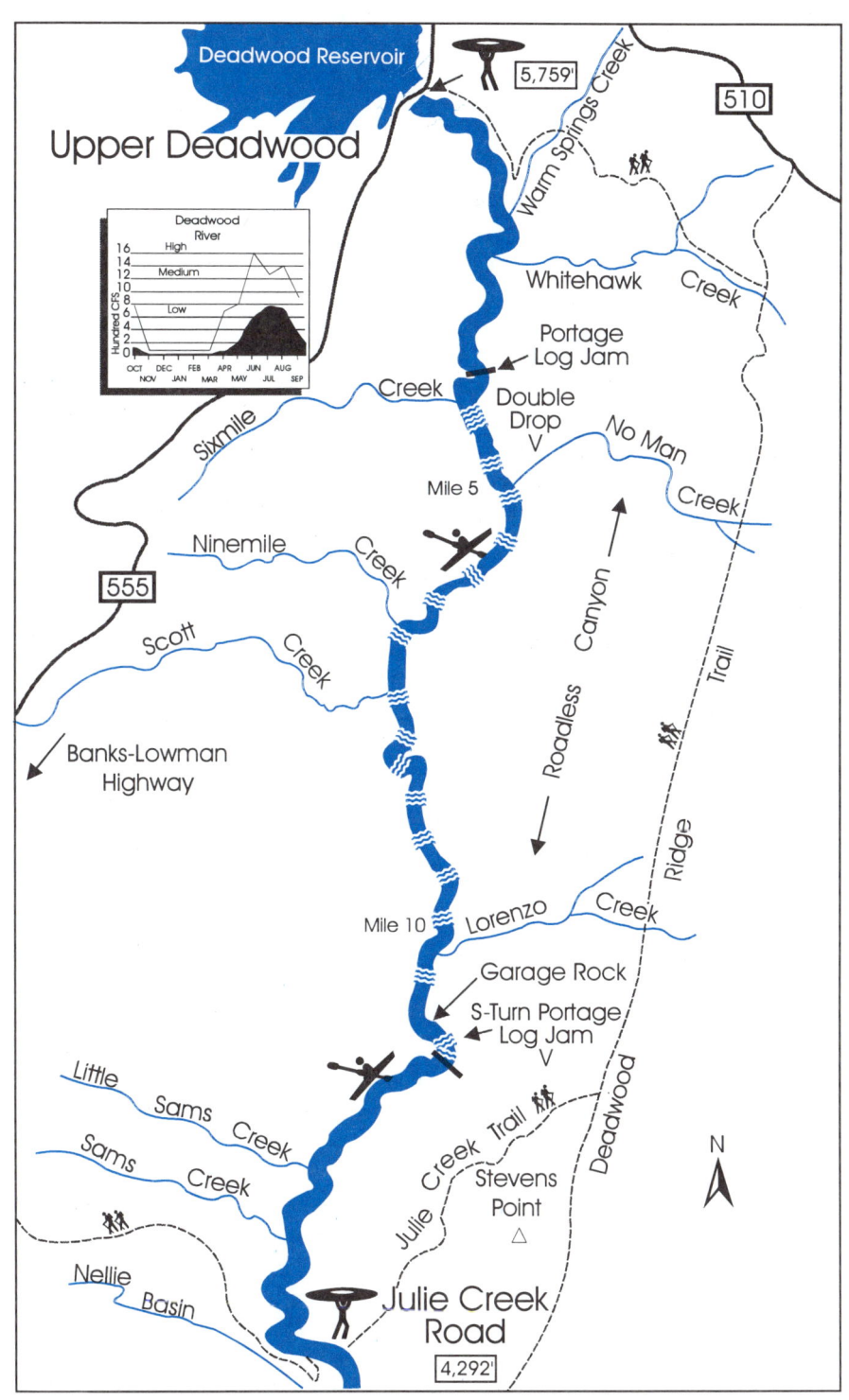

extreme difficulty. Plan accordingly.

The float trip starts downstream of Deadwood Dam, beginning with three miles of swift Class I and Class II water. Sometimes it's necessary to portage around downed trees spanning the river. A mile below the put-in, the Deadwood Ridge trail leaves the river corridor and climbs Warm Springs Creek on river left. The remainder of the run has no trail at river level until the end of the road at the Julie Creek trailhead.

Real whitewater starts around mile three. The river gradually steepens, then turns sharply right into a class III jumble for a quarter mile before a hard turn back to the left. There is a significant ledge just below this left turn. The runout gradually fades to flat water.

A pool above a horizon line marks the first mandatory PORTAGE. This would be a good drop to run if it wasn't blocked by logs. The logs blocking this drop are not visible from above. Portage on the right.

Rob Lesser

A rare relaxing moment in the Upper Deadwood.

The next horizon line marks the top of Double Drop, a closely spaced pair of ledges that most paddlers should scout from the right. Below here, there is some easier whitewater in a steep-walled granite canyon. The whitewater fades out into a long stretch of class I-II water. Look for a nice lunch stop at the mouth of Nine Mile and Scott Creeks.

A huge garage-sized rock in the middle of the river marks the return to whitewater. Both sides of the rock are usually runnable, but the passages are narrow and tend to collect logs. A scout is prudent for paddlers not extremely confident at maneuvering and catching tiny eddies.

A huge garage-sized rock in the middle of the river marks the return to whitewater.

148

Just below the garage-rock a mandatory PORTAGE on the right for nearly everyone. The river funnels to the right and drops over a seven-foot ledge where it is immediately blocked by logs. Most of the river sweeps left around the logs. This route has been run both intentionally and accidentally. Fifty yards below the logs, the river turns hard right into a long, rocky class IV rapid with several logs. Most paddlers will wish to make a short portage around the ledge and logjam; a longer portage that avoids the whole rapid is possible by making a ferry just past the right turn and continuing the portage on river left.

From here to the end of the road is about three miles of whitewater of diminishing intensity. Take out at the campground at the Julie Creek trailhead, visible on river left just upstream of the bridge.

Rob Lesser

Boaters can expect at least two portages on Upper Deadwood.

— Scott Smay

LOWER DEADWOOD

Difficulty: Advanced-expert, Class IV-plus
Put-In: End of Julie Creek Road
Types of craft: Kayaks, catarafts, solo canoes
Distance: 9 miles
Float time: 1.5-2 hours
Take-out: Deadwood Campground or Danskin
Steepness: 67 feet per mile
Season: Totally dependent on dam releases; typical season is for a few weeks in May, July and August.

Getting there: Follow the Banks-Lowman highway about 25 miles to Deadwood River bridge, just before Deadwood Campground. Turn left on the Julie Creek Road, a dirt road that proceeds 7 miles to a dead-end. Put in on river left, just below the bridge.

Shuttle: Leave a vehicle either at Deadwood Campground or at the Danskin Rest Stop and boat launch, if you're planning to run the Lower Deadwood and South Fork Payette canyon for a totally long and awesome day.

The Float: The Lower Deadwood features continuous whitewater, potential log jams, and potential rock-pin situations for nine miles below the Julie Creek put-in. Therefore, it's essential that kayakers who attempt this stretch should have a dependable roll and a solid brace on both sides. A swim in this reach could be deadly.

To begin, launch below the bridge and watch for a log on river-left. At low flow, kayakers can pass under the log but at higher flows, kayakers must flip over to pass under the log and then roll up below it. After that, it's continuous paddling through one drop after the next on the way to the South Fork confluence. Please be cautious in this reach for log jams. The Deadwood received its name for a reason. The rapids in the Lower Deadwood get more difficult with flow. There is a substantial difference in difficulty between 2,000 and 1,000 cfs.

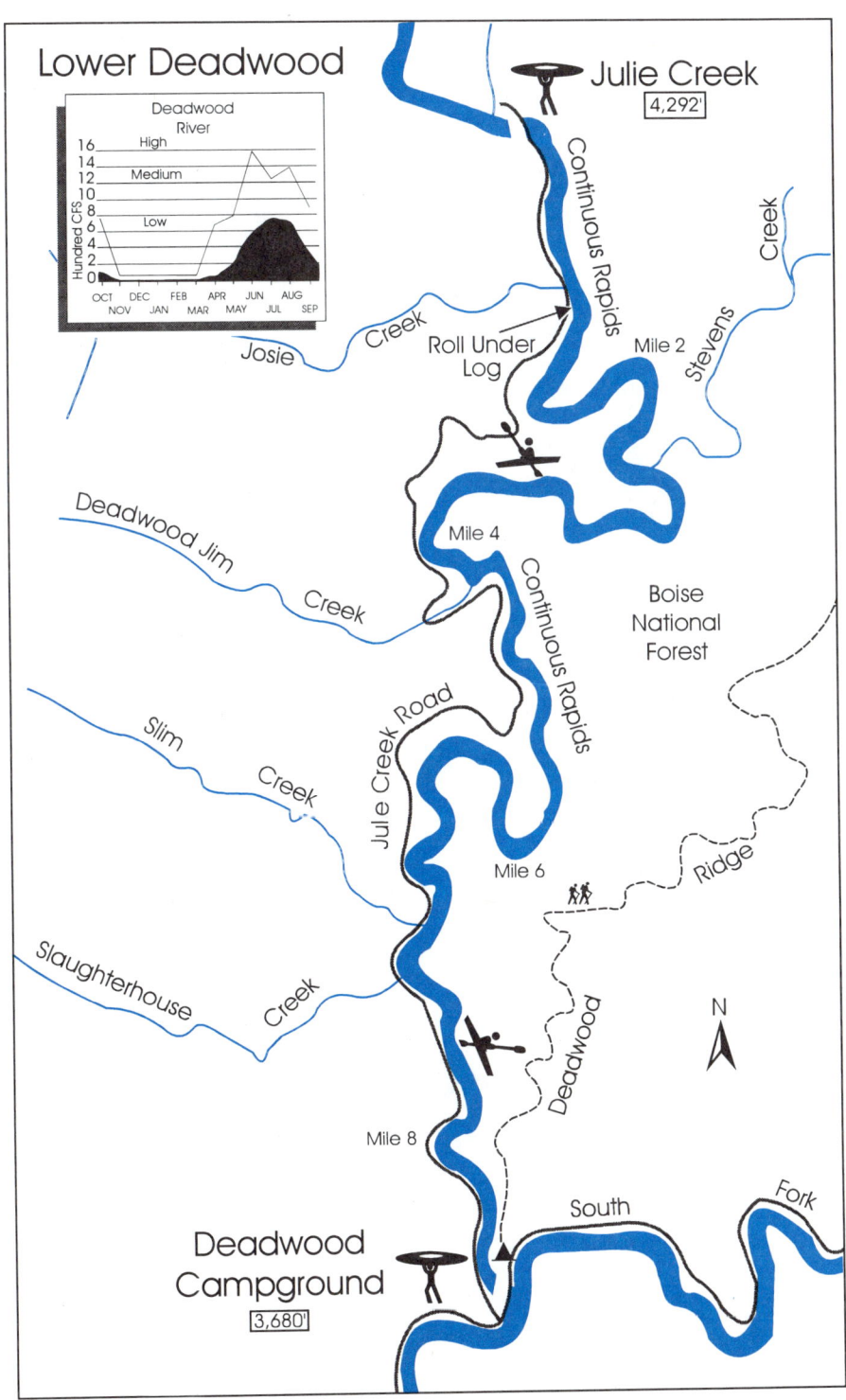

WHITEWATER FOLLIES

Mark Lisk

Payette Visions

Payette Visions

Clockwise from top left: Greg Ramp and Tim Schultz get rear-endoed in Jacob's Ladder; Headwaters' guide is launched in Gateway; Rear-endo on North Fork; Paddle crew flips in Surprise.

Payette Visions

Boaters who miss the cut in Surprise get to run the big hole in the bottom. It's always risky to hit the hole, but there's a good recovery pool below.

Payette Visions

Payette Visions

Payette Visions

Expert boater Phil Lansing doesn't get trashed very often, so when he does, we've got to make it public. Here he gets flipped in a hole in the South Fork Canyon.

Payette Visions

Payette Visions

Lone Pine Rapids flipped rafts routinely at high water in 1995. Watch how Cascade's guide refuses to let gravity take her down.

Payette Visions

Payette Visions

Payette Visions

Payette Visions

Mark Lisk

Above: Paddlers in double-kayak pop an endo on the South Fork play wave.

Left and below: Keith Taylor tries to rescue his son, Steve, on the Lower South Fork but a hole grabs Keith and pops him out, leaving Steve behind.

Rob Lesser

Rob Lesser

Chad Long surfs the South Fork play wave with Jonesy's dog, Abby.

Kayaker gets launched and flipped on the play wave at high water.

Marty Morache

Marty Morache

Marty Morache got pushed sideways as he took Ernie Day through Little Falls, sending Ernie into the drink in the late 1970s.

Marty Morache

Marty Morache

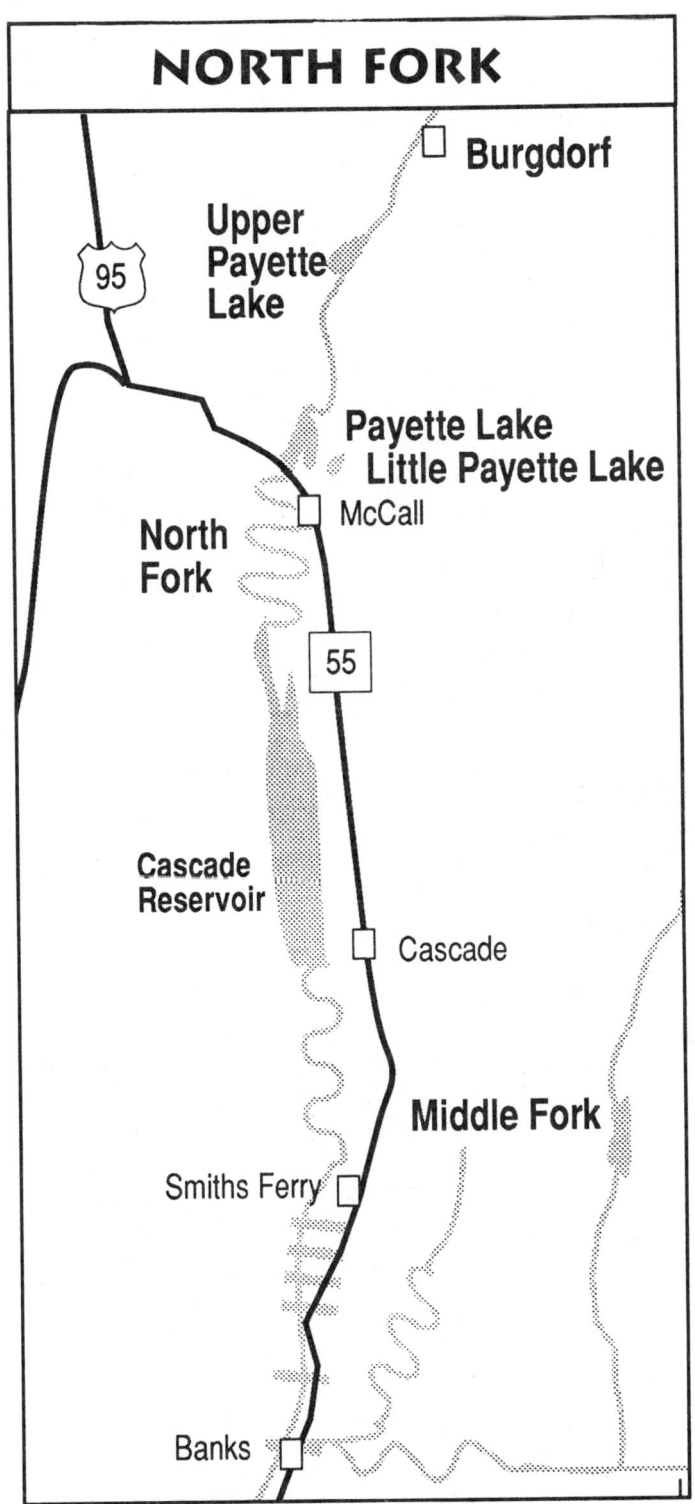

UPPER PAYETTE LAKE

Launch site: Upper Payette Lake campground
Types of craft: Canoe, open kayak, ducky, float tube.
Distance: 2 miles across the lake
Maximum width: .5 miles
Float time: You make the call
Season: May-October
Lake elevation: 5,555 feet

Getting there: Drive to McCall. Proceed through downtown, past the Shore Lodge, and then turn right on Warren Wagon Road. It's a well-marked turn just after Shore Lodge. Proceed on Warren Wagon Road along the west side of Big Payette Lake and continue toward Burgdorf to a left-hand turn for Upper Payette Lake campground. The turn is about 15 miles from the Warren Wagon turnoff. This is the only access to the lake.

The Float: Nestled in the white granite mountains and dense Douglas fir forest of the Payette National Forest, Upper Payette Lake is a small scenic lake and an off-beat place to paddle. Launch your craft at the campground and tour the lake. It's about two miles or so from one end of the lake to the other. Paddlers who like to fish can double-dip on this trip. Fish and Game stocks the lake with "catchable" rainbow trout. Ospreys and other birds of prey frequent the area, as well as an occasional moose, deer or elk. You may see smaller critters as well in the early morning or late evening. Adventurous paddlers may want to paddle Upper Payette Lake and the North Fork "meanders" on the same weekend.

Interpretive remarks: Upper Payette Lake is a natural glacial-fed lake that was enlarged by the Lakes Reservoir Co. in the mid-1920s with a concrete dam at the lake's outlet. Water from the lake is used for irrigation in the Lower Payette River Valley. The North Fork of the Payette River feeds the lake and emerges again below the dam. Due to the fact that the lake level fluctuates and drops several feet by late summer, paddlers may find the lake is more enjoyable to paddle — more aesthetically pleasing — in June and July.

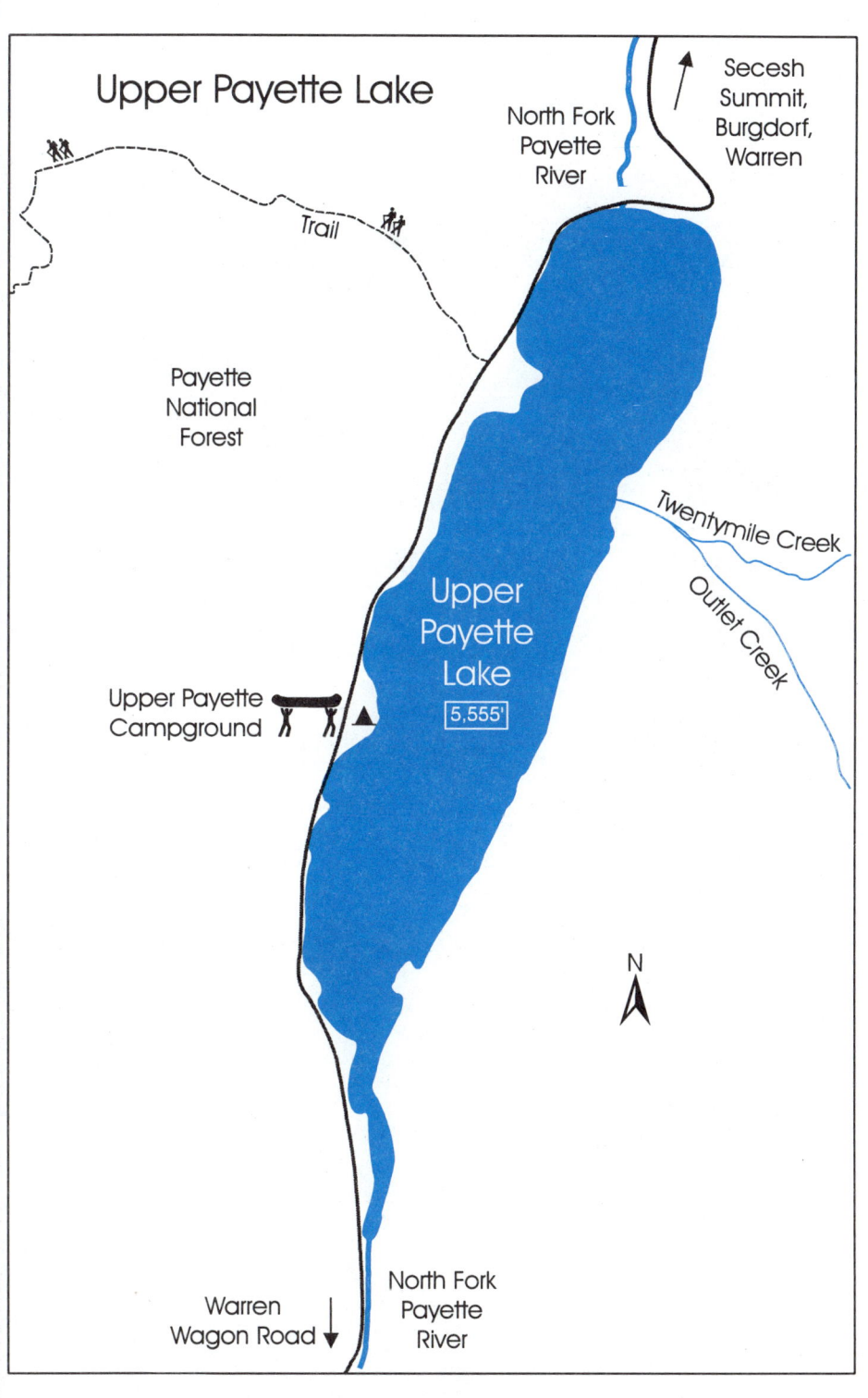

Paddlers will find solitude at Upper Payette Lake.

Side trips: Upper Payette Lake is located across from the 20-mile trailhead on Warren Wagon Road. The 20-mile trail is a nice place to go hiking and mountain biking. Experienced cyclists may want to try the Duck Lake-20-mile ride (see the Payette National Forest map). Ambitious hikers may want to check out the 20-mile lakes area. It's a steep climb to the lakes, but the fishing is excellent.

Anglers enjoy a peaceful morning on the North Fork "Meanders."

NORTH FORK MEANDERS

Difficulty: Novice (no current)
Put-Ins: North Beach on Payette Lake, Eastside Road Bridge, Fisher Creek confluence.
Types of craft: Canoes, open kayaks, kayaks, fishing boats
Distance: 4.5 miles
Float time: Up to 3 hours (up & back)
Take-out: Same as put-ins.
Steepness: None.
Season: June-October

Getting there: Take Idaho 55 to McCall, proceed through downtown, and watch for Warren Wagon Road on the right, just after Shore Lodge. Turn right and drive about six miles to the North Beach boat launch. It's on the right at the north end of Payette Lake. You can put-in here, or drive a little farther on Warren Wagon to the junction with the Eastside Road, turn right, and put-in at the bridge crossing the meanders. Or, drive another two miles on Warren Wagon Road to the Fisher Creek confluence and put in there. At Fisher Creek, the North Fork is a running stream for a tiny bit before it begins to slow down and meander through thick timber and meadows toward the lake.

Shuttle: You can plant a vehicle or bicycle at any one of the put-in points mentioned above if you're pressed for time. But the beauty of this stretch is you can paddle it both ways. Some floaters like to paddle from North Beach to the point where the current begins, turn around and paddle back to the lake. It's up to you.

The Float: The North Fork Meanders is a gorgeous piece of water. I'd venture to say it is one of the most stunning still-water paddling paradises in Idaho. On a still morning or evening, paddlers will feel as if they're paddling across a finely polished mirror. Double-images of tall Douglas-fir trees, golden aspens and white granite mountains appear before you in the water and on the land. Look around for wildlife: Watch for beaver criss-crossing the river in front of you — their heads poking out of the water and forming a wake as they swim across. Lately, there has been a moose family

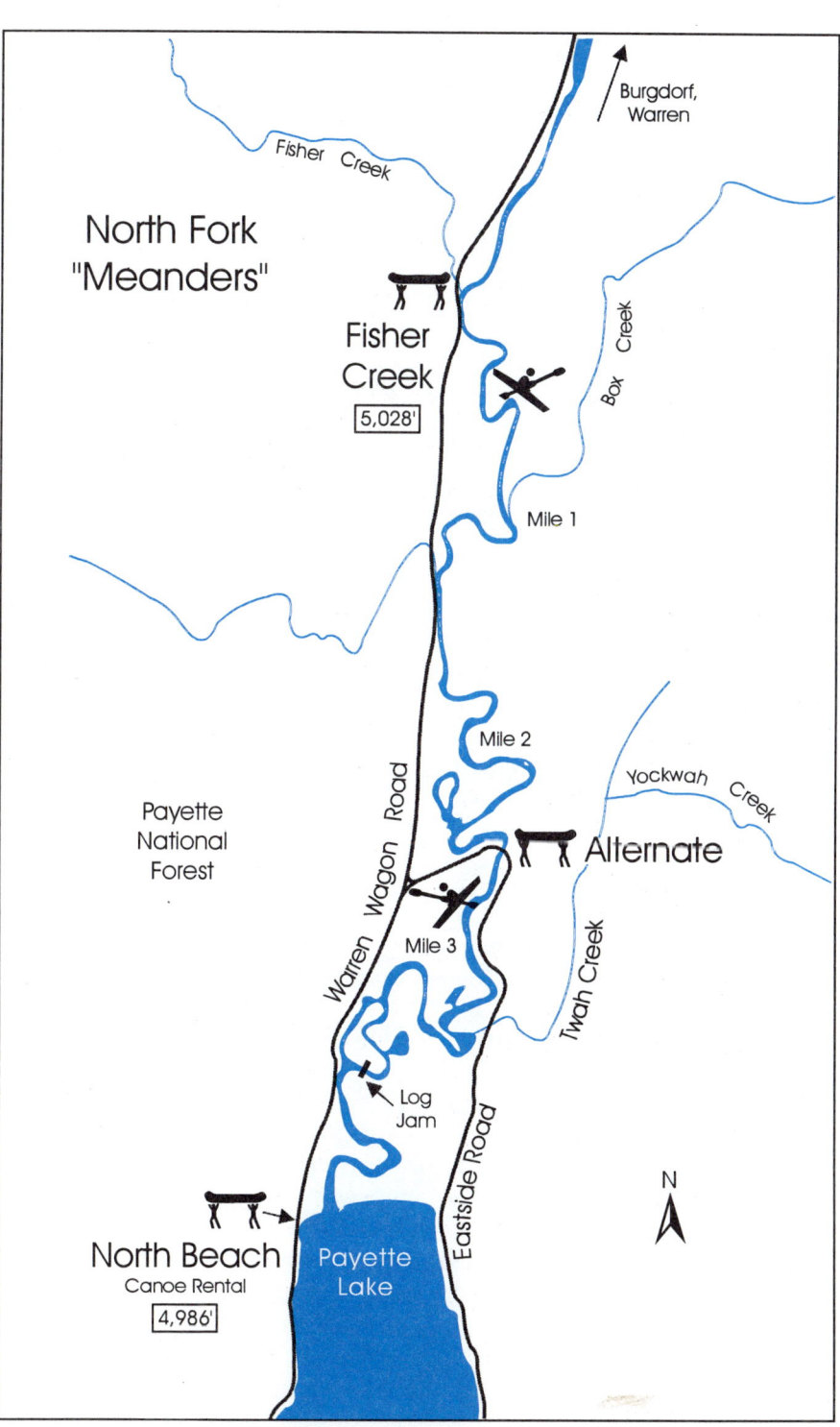

hanging out along the banks. Give them a wide berth. Ospreys will fly overhead as well as herons, hawks and eagles. Other wildlife include mink and muskrat. Fishing for rainbow trout can be good, and in the fall, when the kokanee are spawning, it's really cool to look down in the clear water and gaze at those crimson-colored fish.

Optimum times to paddle this reach are early morning and late evening — either before the jet skis and motorboats get revved up for the day or afterward. Early morning and late evening offer the best times to see wildlife, too. For a real bonus, bring along a bottle of champagne and float this reach during a full moon. I can't imagine a more romantic setting for outdoorsy paddlers.

It takes about an hour of slow paddling to reach the Eastside Road Bridge, and another hour to reach Fisher Creek, depending on how fast you're moving. The beauty of this reach is that you can float as far as you want, and simply turn around and go back when you need to leave.

The North Fork Meanders is one of the most stunning still-water paddling paradises in Idaho.

At press time, the meaders were classified as a "no wake zone," meaning motorized craft are allowed, but at closed throttle. There is still a problem of errant jet-skiers buzzing around on this reach in the middle of the day. The author encourages paddlers to write a letter to the Idaho Parks & Recreation Department and urge them to designate this as a non-motorized area to preserve its uniqueness.

Devoid of current, The Meanders resembles a finely polished mirror.

Canoe rental: Silver Pig rents canoes at North Beach. If you're hanging out in McCall for other activities and you didn't bring a canoe, this is the most convenient place to rent a boat. Gravity Sports in McCall rents solo open kayaks and canoes. Medley Sports in McCall rents canoes, too.

BIG PAYETTE LAKE

Launch sites: Rotary Park in downtown McCall (across from Hometown Sports), public boat launch on the southeast side of the lake (twin launch site for motor boats), Ponderosa State Park, North Beach.
Types of craft: Canoe, open kayak, ducky, drift boat.
Distance: Six miles, north to south
Maximum width: 2 miles
Maximum Depth: 300 feet
Float time: You make the call
Season: May-October
Lake elevation: 4,986 feet.

Getting there: Drive to McCall. To launch at Rotary Park, drive on Idaho 55 past downtown McCall and watch for a public park on the lake (north) side of the road. There is a public parking area, rest rooms and beach. It's easy to launch a canoe or small watercraft here. North Beach is accessed by turning north off Idaho 55 onto Warren Wagon Road across from Lardo's restaurant on the west side of McCall. Eastside Drive is another excellent launch point. You'll have to pay the camping fee ($9-$12 a day) at Ponderosa State Park if you launch there, but if you're planning to camp there anyway, it's a good place to put-in. Ponderosa Park is a large peninsula that bisects Payette Lake. It can be reached by turning off main street to the east next to Hotel McCall and following the signs to the park. The public motor boat launch on the southeast side of the lake is not recommended for non-motorized boats. It's busy and congested.

Shuttle: It's not a bad idea to plant a vehicle on the other side of the lake if you're planning to paddle across Payette Lake. By the time you reach the other side, it may be windy and congested on the lake — less than ideal conditions for the return trip.

The Float: Big Payette Lake is a gorgeous setting, indeed. The city of McCall has been called the "Switzerland of Idaho" because of its majestic scene — the sparkling clear lake, surrounded by white granite mountains and a dense carpet of coniferous trees. Even

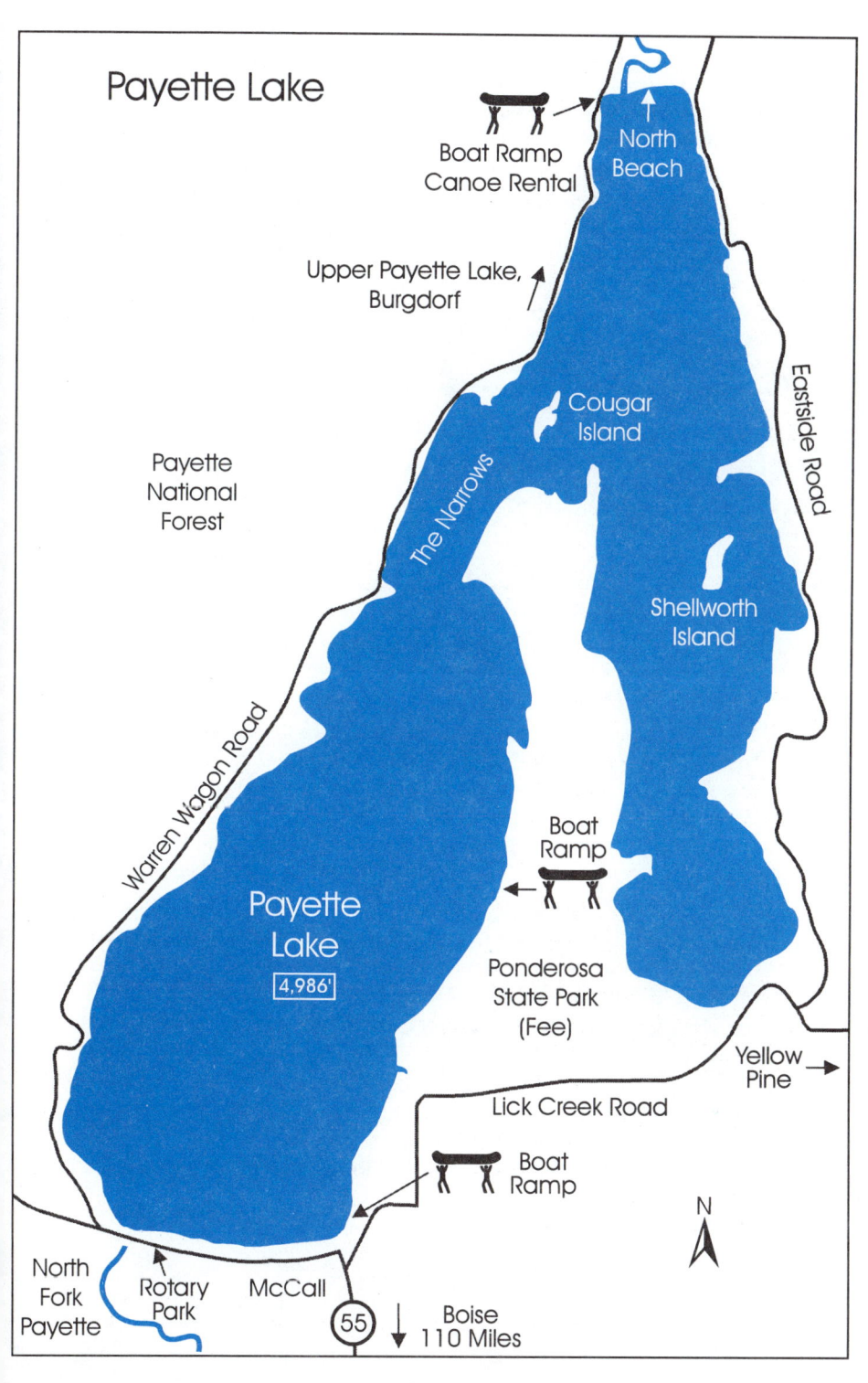

the big forest fires of 1994 are barely detectable when you drink in the scene.

As one might expect, paddling Payette Lake is best done in the early morning hours or late afternoon and evening, when the jet skis and motorboats are not present and the wind is calm. It's my opinion that the north end of the lake is the most enjoyable for paddling, from The Narrows, around Cougar Island, to North Beach, on the east arm of the lake. These are the less-traveled parts of the lake, depending on the crowds and activities of the day.

Idaho State Historical Society
Sunbathers lounge on shore, early 1900s.

Church camps and the University of Idaho McCall station dominate the east shoreline, by Paradise Point, Shellworth Island, Lucks Point and Pilgrim Cove. The west arm of Payette Lake is dominated by private homes, especially on the west shore, which are kind of cool to look at as you paddle by. Many of the homes represent the who's who of powerful, wealthy and successful political and business leaders in southern Idaho. J.R. Simplot has a place on the west shore. So does Gov. Phil Batt. As you're driving down Warren Wagon Road, take a look at the nameplates on the trees. You'll see what I mean.

Warning: Local paddlers report that some idiotic jet skiers have been buzzing canoe and kayak paddlers, apparently for an extra thrill. The worst situations occur when two jet skiers criss-cross in front of a canoe or kayak in an attempt to spook or swamp the paddlers. If you see a jet skier bearing down on you, get a good grip on your paddle and be ready to club these scoundrels if they get too close.

Interpretive remarks: White settlement came to Big Payette Lake early on — albeit temporarily — when Warren miners discovered gold in the North Fork of the Payette River above Upper Payette Lake. That led to the formation of "Lake City," as it was called then, in the 1860s. The town consisted of a couple log cabins, shacks and saloons. It didn't last long, however, as the gold discoveries were not substantial.

The Thomas and Louisa McCall family are credited with establishing the present-day town of McCall in the 1890. Nellie Mills wrote in *All Along the River*, that the McCalls traveled to Long Valley in two heavy wagons with all of their worldly possessions. They also had a small herd of cattle and horses. They headed out from Boise and rode to Emmett over Freezeout, up Squaw Creek to Ola, and then climbed to High Valley where they ran into several feet of snow. They were forced to make a temporary camp, along with several other eager-beaver families that were waiting to stake out new homes in Long Valley.

Instead of hanging out and waiting for the snow to melt, the eastern transplants forged on toward Payette Lake, making all of two miles a day. "Often at night they could see the smoke of the last night's camp," Mills said.

Once the family arrived at Payette Lake, things began to improve. "The boys were delighted with the lake, the fish, the timber, everything," Mills wrote. The first winter was harsh, however, as expected. All of their cattle died except for one cow. But they could travel to New Meadows for fresh supplies. The McCalls, ever the generous bunch, put up a destitute family in their home until spring.

The first post office in the area was established at "Lardo," near the present site of the popular McCall eatery and bar. Lardo didn't last long, however. Eventually, Tom McCall built his own post office, a school, a hotel and a sawmill, which prospered and was later sold to the Brown family.

Idaho State Historical Society
Lyda was the first steamship on Payette Lake.

171

LITTLE PAYETTE LAKE

Launch site: North side of lake, off Lick Creek Road.
Types of craft: Canoe, open kayak, ducky, drift boat, float tube
Distance: 2-4 miles around the lake
Maximum width: 2 miles
Float time: You make the call
Season: May-October
Lake elevation: 5,119 feet

Getting there: Drive to McCall. On the main drag through town, watch for a corner-intersection in front of the Hotel McCall. Turn right (east) and follow the main road past the public beach and Gravity Sports to a red flashing light. Turn left and proceed toward Ponderosa State Park. At the intersection of Davis Road and Lick Creek Road, turn right on Lick Creek and head for Little Payette Lake; it's 2.5 miles away. Bear right at the junction with Eastside Drive and stay on Lick Creek Road. Less than one-half mile after the pavement ends, watch for a right-hand turn into the Little Payette Lake access ramp.

The Float: Little Payette Lake is mainly a hangout for float-tubing fly anglers who come here in search of big trout. But it's also an off-the-beaten-path spot for some low-key paddling. Of course, there's nothing wrong with fly fishing from your canoe, either. Perhaps the biggest draw here is that on a busy day on Big Payette Lake, Little Payette Lake offers a nice quiet refuge from jet skis and water skiers. In late summer, floaters will find the level of Little Payette Lake several feet below full, exposing hundreds of old tree stumps.

Interpretive remarks: Little Payette Lake was a smaller, glacial-fed lake with an original size of 485 acres before the Lake Reservoir Co. more than tripled its size with an augmentation dam on the Lake Fork outlet in 1926. In 1987, Fish and Game poisoned the lake to get rid of "trash fish" and clear the way for a trophy rainbow trout fishery. Regulations as of 1995 allow anglers to take up to two fish over 20 inches a day. Artificial flies and lures and single barbless hooks only.

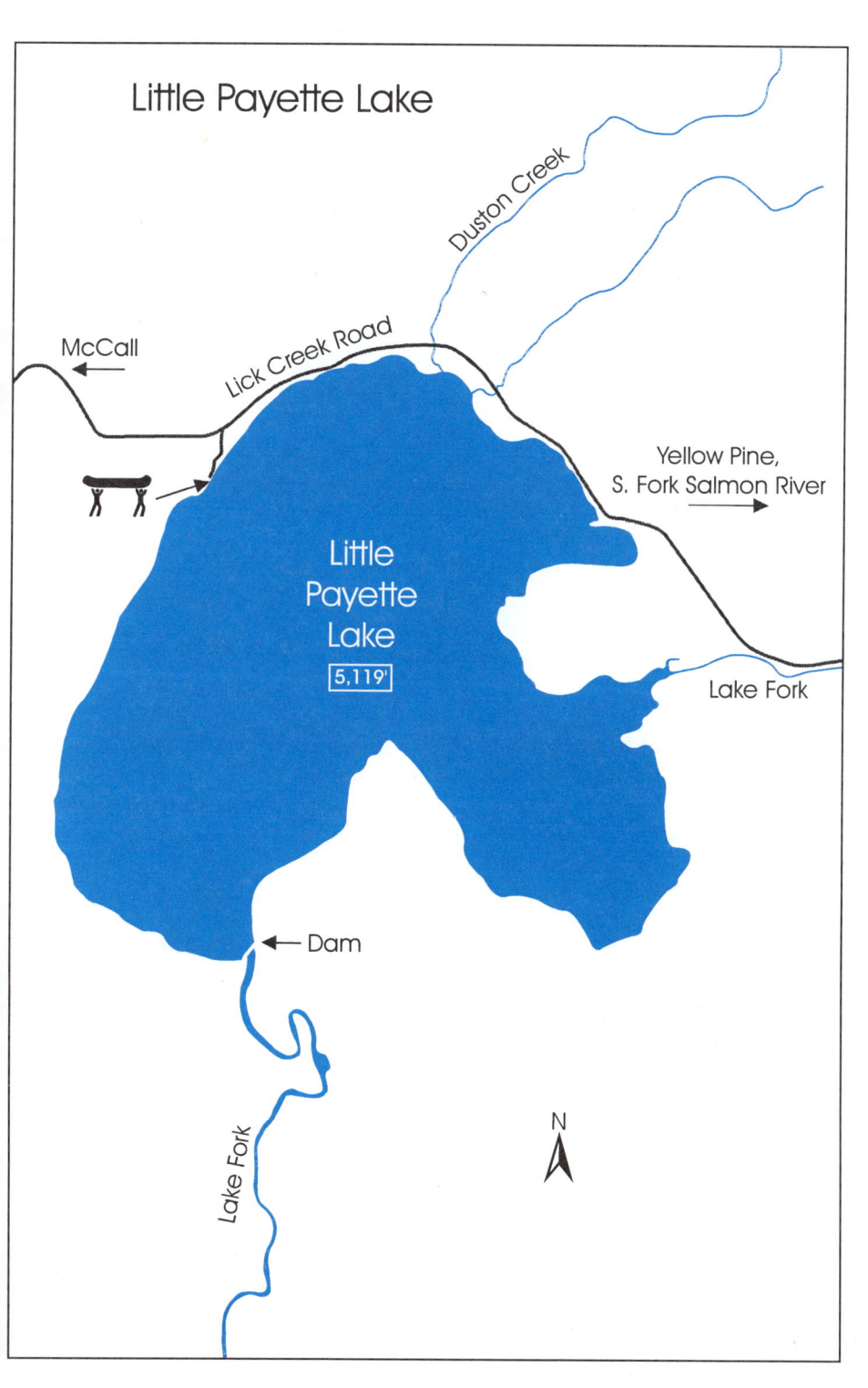

SHEEP BRIDGE TO HARTSELL BRIDGE

Difficulty: Intermediate
Put-In: Sheep Bridge (west of the Smokejumper Base)
Types of craft: Canoe, open kayak, ducky.
Distance: 9 miles
Float time: 4-6 hours
Take-Out: Hartsell Bridge
Steepness: 2 feet per mile
Season: Early May-early October

Getting there: Drive to McCall on Idaho 55. At the south end of town, there is a flashing yellow light at the junction of Dienhard Lane and Idaho 55, next to the McCall Airport. Turn left on Dienhard and proceed about a half mile to Mission Street. Turn left. The Smokejumper Base is straight ahead. Off to your right, you'll see the North Fork of the Payette River flowing in the valley below and the old Sheep Bridge. Head for the bridge on one of several gravel roads that drops into the giant gravel pit area on the right. Launch your craft below the bridge.

Shuttle: Drop a vehicle or a bicycle (be ready for a 10-mile ride back to McCall) at the Hartsell Bridge takeout. The best access is on the west and upstream side of the bridge. To reach Hartsell Bridge, turn west on Smylie Lane, about four miles north of Donnelly, off of Idaho 55. It's about three miles from Idaho 55 to the bridge. Bike shuttlers may want to take West Mountain Road, a single-lane dirt road, back to McCall to avoid riding on Idaho 55. To reach West Mountain Road, continue west past Hartsell Bridge on Smylie Lane. Smylie ties into West Mountain Road in about a mile.

The Float: This reach of the North Fork is one of the premiere slow-water paddling reaches in the Payette Basin. The water is unmistakably clean and clear. The riparian area is lush and bordered by trees. Dozens of pairs of ospreys and herons frequent this reach. At last count in the fall of 1995, there were 69 pairs of ospreys that nested between Upper Payette Lake and Cascade Lake, according to Fish and Game. The river winds back and forth

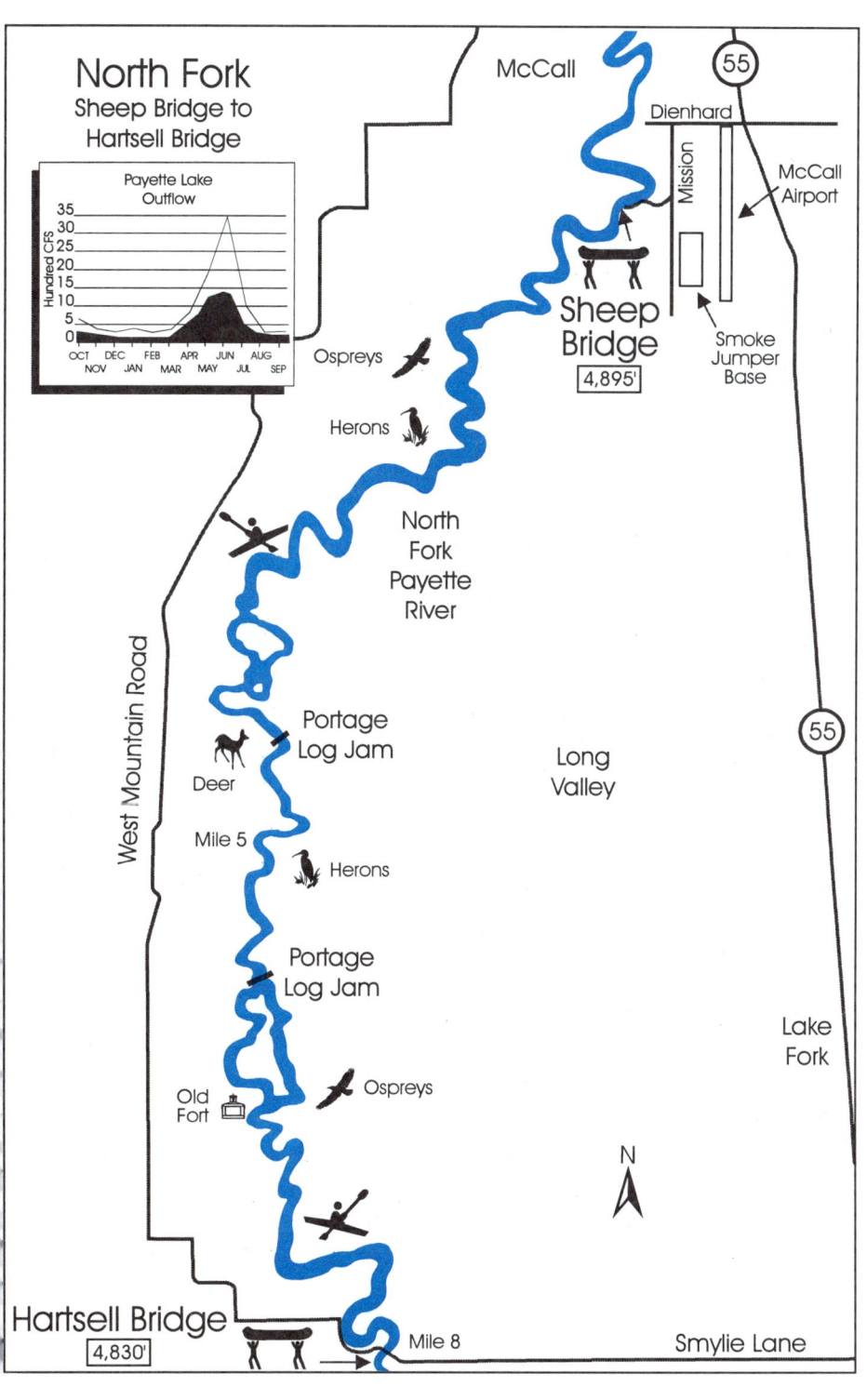

across a lush valley, so this float is time-consuming and long, depending on float craft and paddling skills. Be sure to allow most of the day if you float this reach. Fishing for rainbow trout can be productive on this section, depending on river flow and temperature.

From Sheep Bridge downstream to Hartzell Bridge, there are a couple of obstacles of note. At low flows, canoeists should pay attention to find the deepest channel through small riffles. This can be a challenge. But if you make the wrong call, it's no big deal to get out and walk through the riffle to the next pool. Most of the time, the river is deep and slow, allowing folks to just drift along and enjoy the scenery.

A typical tranquil scene on the North Fork south of McCall.

There are two river-wide logjams in this reach. The first one is about six miles downriver. It is marked by a big left-bend in the stream. There is a faint portage trail on river left around the jackstrawed logs blocking the river. The second log-jam is about a mile below the first one. It is easily portaged on the right.

Floaters will notice that there are a number of places where one could camp overnight along this reach. I recommend that folks

Boaters may want to bring a fly rod to catch trout on this reach.

float through this reach at least once before bringing your camping gear. Be sure to avoid any conflicts with private land.

Water levels for this reach are set by the Payette Lakes Reservoir Co. They installed the dam that raised Payette Lake by about seven feet, and they control the flow at the lake outlet. Call 642-3866 (weekdays) to obtain the latest information on water releases at the outlet. A flow of 200 cfs or higher is ideal for this reach.

Over 50 pairs of ospreys nest along the river.

CASCADE RESERVOIR

Launch sites: Cascade city ramp, Cabarton, Campbell Creek, French Creek, Poison Creek, Rainbow Point, Donnelly City Park.
Types of craft: Canoe, open kayak, ducky, drift boat.
Distance: 17 miles, north to south.
Maximum width: 4 miles
Maximum Depth: 65 feet
Average Depth: 25 feet
Float time: You make the call
Season: Early May-November

Getting there: Take Idaho 55 north of Boise 70 miles to the city of Cascade. Turn left on Old State Highway to reach the Cascade City Ramp, Lakeshore Drive or West Side Road. To access the lake from the north, proceed north on Idaho 55 to the city of Donnelly. Head for Donnelly City Park to tour the Lake Fork Arm (3.5 miles one way) or cruise to the Tamarack Falls junction and launch at one of several campgrounds on the North Fork Payette Arm, either Rainbow Point, Amanita, West Mountain north or south, or Poison Creek, the last campsite on the northwest side of the lake.

Shuttle: If you're planning to cross the lake, it'd be a good idea to plant a vehicle at one of the ramps on the lake's north or south end, depending on where you begin the journey.

The Float: Cascade Reservoir is so huge (17 miles long by four miles wide) that canoe and kayak paddlers have to be cautious about getting stuck in the middle of the lake in a big wind and, worse yet, big-time waves and heavy chop. Therefore, it's smart to paddle the lake in the early morning hours or evening, and in general, stay close to shore. I personally recommend paddling around the south shore, cruising around the Lake Fork arm or North Fork Arm, or dashing across to Sugarloaf Island or Sugarloaf Point. It's about 5.5 miles to Sugarloaf Point from the Cascade ramp; Sugarloaf Island is one mile beyond that. Fishing in Cascade Lake used to be legendary for rainbow trout, but after a major fish kill occurred in the sweltering summer of 1994, rainbow fishing is dic-

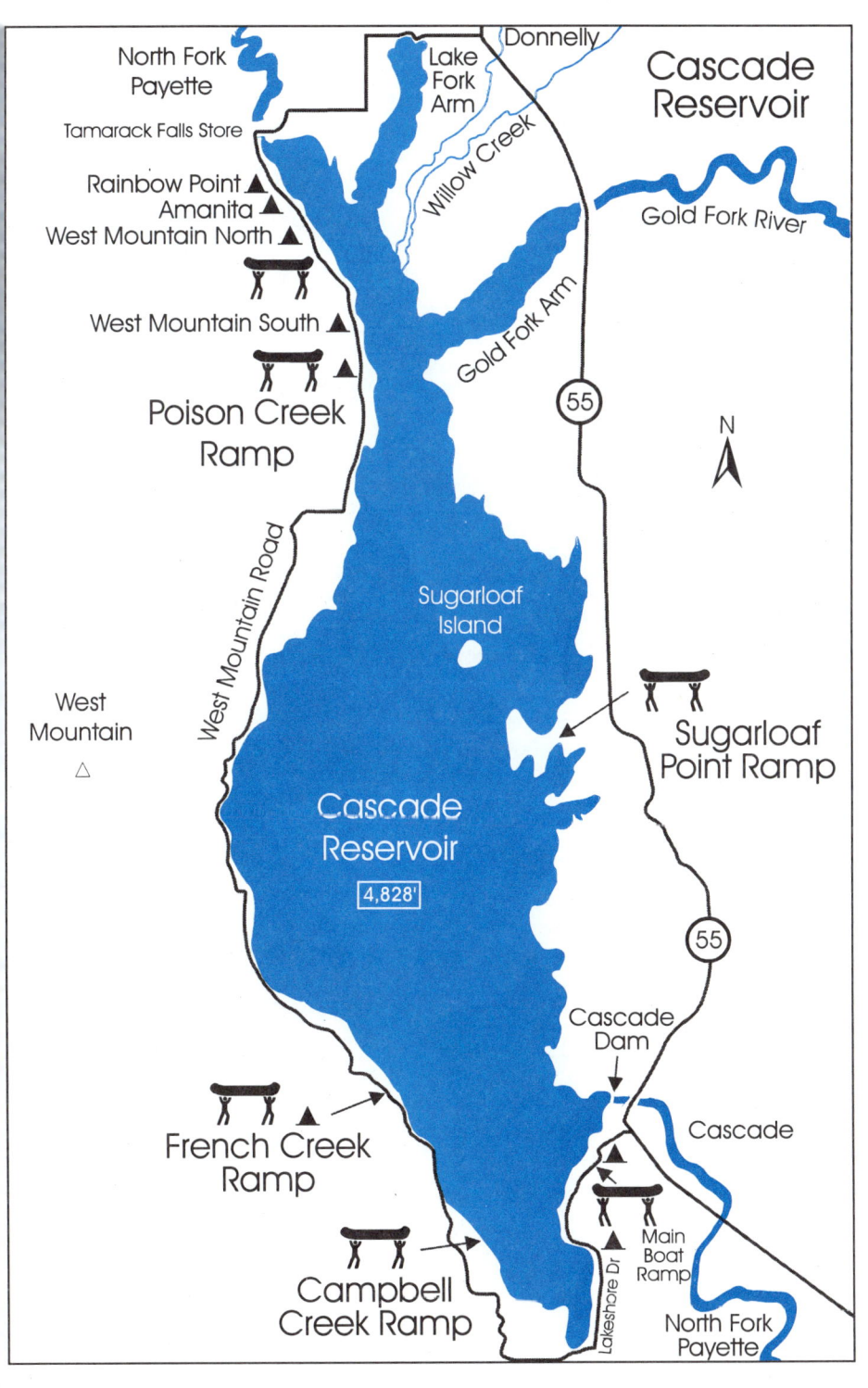

Bureau of Reclamation

Cascade Reservoir was once a large agricultural valley.

tated by the release of hatchery fish. Perch fishing is still good, however,. Idaho Fish and Game officials report in 1995 that the perch fishing, which runs in seven-year cycles, is nearing the peak of the cycle. That means the fish are getting as big as they're going to get — about 12-13 inches long or 1 pound. In a few years, the population will crash when the big perch eat all the young perch, and the cycle will begin again. Scores of waterfowl, ospreys and bald eagles hang out around Cascade Reservoir throughout the spring, summer and fall. The large mountain on the lake's west shore is called West Mountain. It runs the length of Long Valley.

Bureau of Reclamation

Paddlers have to be cautious about getting stuck in a big wind and serious chop.

Interpretive remarks: Cascade Reservoir, a U.S. Bureau of Reclamation project, was completed in 1948. It is backed up by a multi-

Bureau of Reclamation
Cascade Reservoir stores nearly 700,000 acre-feet of water.

purpose dam and provides storage water for Lower Payette Valley farmers, orchards and ranchers, electric power, recreation and flood-control. When the reservoir was filled, it flooded out the former town of Van Wyck and a number of Long Valley ranches, which were purchased by the bureau. There is no doubt that Cascade is immensely beneficial for Lower Payette agriculture, but it also provides late-season flows for whitewater boaters on the North Fork and Main Fork of the Payette. It's a nifty situation that gives whitewater boaters much higher water than they'd have otherwise in August and a longer season than any natural river would provide.

Water quality issues: Cascade Reservoir has been reeling from severe water-quality problems for more than a decade, resulting in the loss of a major rainbow trout fishery and tourism. The reservoir suffers from excessive sediment and nutrients from numerous sources, including septic tanks, the McCall Sewer Treatment Plant, valley farms, logging and cattle grazing. Local citizens are working diligently to rectify the problem.

CITY OF CASCADE TO CABARTON BRIDGE

Difficulty: Easy — Class I riffles (except for an abrupt, two-foot diversion drop)
Put-In: Below Cascade Dam on the north side of the city or the second bridge on the south side of town.
Types of craft: Canoe, open kayak, ducky, raft
Distance: 12 miles
Float time: 3-5 hours
Take-out: Cabarton Bridge
Steepness: 3 feet per mile
Season: Early May-early October

Getting there: Drive to the city of Cascade and put-in at the highway bridge east of Cascade Dam. If you'd like to avoid a couple diversion drops — the only excitement of the trip — put in at the bridge on the south side of Cascade, next to the ball fields.

Shuttle: Leave a vehicle at the Cabarton Bridge, the takeout for this run. To reach the bridge, watch for Cabarton Road on the west side of Idaho 55 across from the Clear Creek Inn. The road and Inn are about six miles north of Smith's Ferry.

The Float: This is a delightful, winding flat-water paddle that's suitable for beginning canoeists, open kayakers and inflatable kayakers. Like many low-key sections of the Payette, this run is commonly overlooked. The only crowds that you'll see on this trip will be at the Cabarton takeout.

To begin, launch your craft below Cascade Dam. Suitable roadside access exists on the downstream side of the Idaho 55 bridge as you head out of Cascade. Note how the ospreys, gulls and anglers flock to the area: this is your first clue that you might want to bring your fishing pole.

For the first mile, the river winds toward the east for a big gentle bend around the town of Cascade. Stay alert because very shortly, you'll come up on the first of two diversion drops. The first one is more of a riffle; the second one, the Boise Cascade sawmill diversion, is a larger, abrupt drop of about two feet. To be safe, you may want to portage or scout on the left bank. At higher

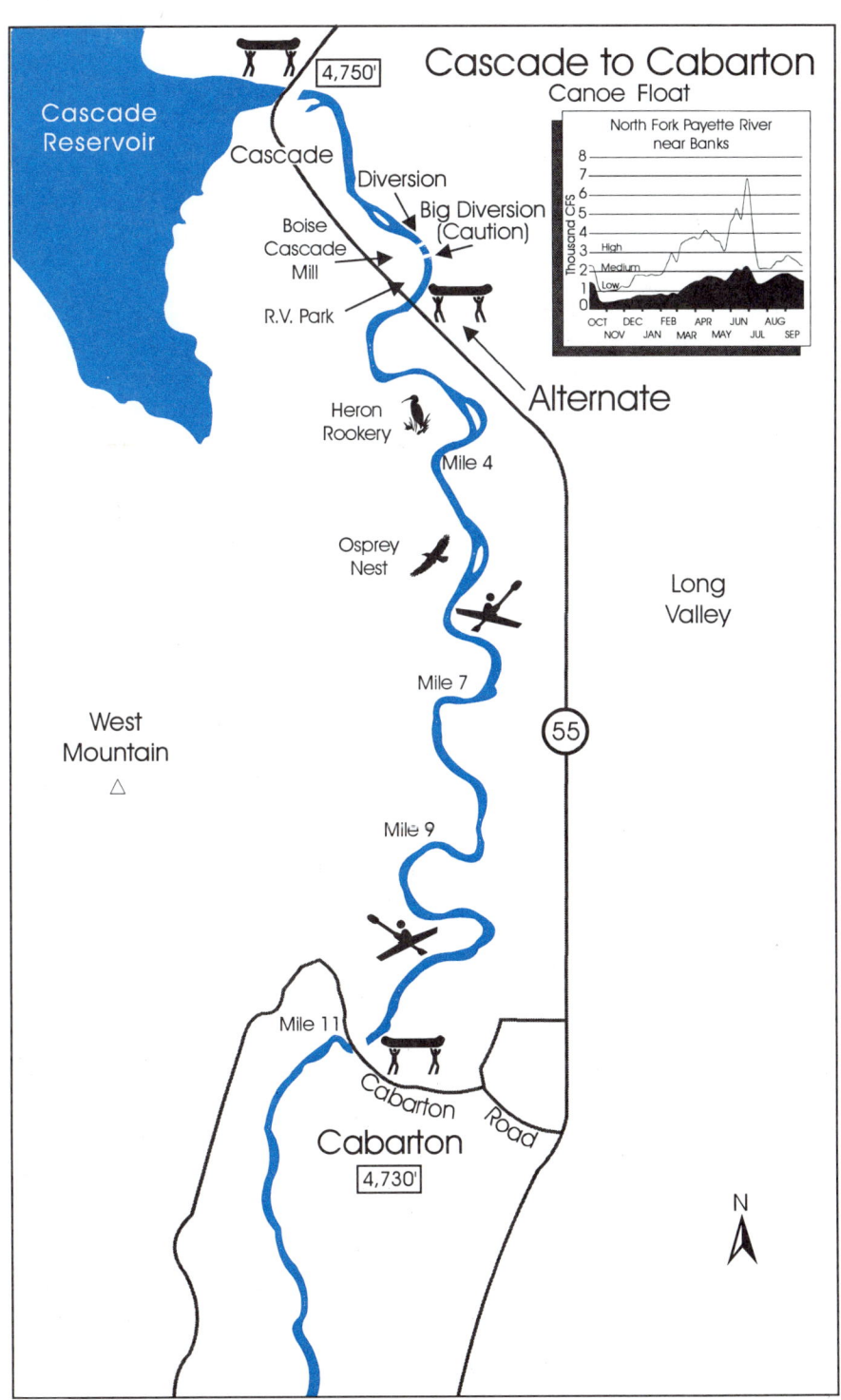

water (flows of 2,000 or more), this drop could swamp inexperienced tandem canoeists. After the second drop, however, there are no more big diversions to worry about.

Canoeists will enjoy fetching views of West Mountain on this trip.

As paddlers wind back toward second highway bridge, you'll approach a shooting range on the right bank. The second bridge is an alternative put-in. After passing under the bridge, there is a finely manicured lawn of an RV park and campground on river-right. A row of adorable birdhouses along the river frontage indicates that these folks enjoy wildlife. Paddling on downstream, floaters can expect to hear the rat-tat-tat chatter of kingfishers as the ring-necked birds fly from one bank to the other. Ospreys will soar in the breeze overhead, and herons may be seen perching in snags and tall cottonwoods, or cruising from one side of the river to the other.

In the next couple miles, paddlers will tour the backside of the Cascade airstrip — the site of nationally famous Arnold Aviation, the home of backcountry pilot and mail carrier Ray Arnold — and the old railroad stop for Alpha, one of the first post offices established in Long Valley in the late 1800s. Continuing on, paddlers will enjoy fetching views of West Mountain and pastoral Valley County ranches. Be sure to respect private property. After several miles, watch for a good place to eat lunch.

Floaters can expect to hear the rat-at-tat chatter of kingfishers

At about mile six or so, the river bends right and a large pine

Floaters are likely to see cows on the riverbank.

tree full of heron nests appears on the right bank. This is called a heron "rookery" due to all of the nests concentrated in one area. It's a little unusual in southern Idaho to see herons nesting in a pine tree, but hey, whatever turns them on, eh?

During higher flows (1,200 cfs and up), paddlers can kick back and let the current carry them downstream with little effort. At lower flows, paddlers will have to exert more effort to dodge sand bars and low spots in the wide river course. After paddling about half way downriver, floaters will notice that most of the river gravel and substrate is totally smothered with sand and sediment from riverbank erosion — the downside of overgrazing and river-flooding. It's a nice cruise in the final approach to Cabarton Bridge, as the river winds out of the valley and toward Boise Cascade's private forest. Fortunately, the company has been generous to public recreationists and provides free access to a nice boat ramp at the take-out. Don't miss the launch at the Cabarton Bridge because there's no way out for the next six miles. Class III rapids lie ahead.

CABARTON RUN OF THE NORTH FORK

Difficulty: Class II-Class III Intermediate
Put-In: Cabarton Bridge
Ideal craft: Kayaks, rafts, whitewater canoes
Distance: 8 miles
Take-out: Smith's Ferry
Float time: 2-4 hours
Steepness: 20 feet per mile
Season: May, early June, August, September

Getting there: From Boise, drive north on Idaho 55 about 65 miles to Smith's Ferry. Proceed north on Idaho 55 10 miles to Cabarton Road. Turn left. The turn is across from the Clear Creek Lodge. Proceed on Cabarton Road about 1.8 miles to the Cabarton Bridge. A gravel road on the left, just before the bridge, provides access to the river.

Shuttle: Drop a shuttle vehicle at one of two take-outs — the riverbank area behind Cougar Mountain Lodge in Smith's Ferry or at a highway pullout on the right, about a mile beyond the lodge.

Launch etiquette: On a hot sunny weekend day, particularly in August and September, the Cabarton run is a very popular destination for whitewater boaters of all kinds. As a result, the launch site can be crowded and congested. The key here is to provide an open lane for vehicles to unload rafts, kayaks, canoes and other craft. If you show up early enough to snag a parking spot around the launch area, be sure to park off to the side and DON'T BLOCK THE RAMP. After unloading and blowing up rafts, carry your boats down to the water and tie them up in the large eddy, leaving room for other boats to do the same. Many boaters leave their rafts in the middle of the ramp until they're loaded with all their gear, blocking everyone else. It's no big deal to simply tie up your boats in the water first, and leave the ramp free for other folks to do the same. Again, PLEASE DON'T BLOCK THE RAMP.

The Run: The Cabarton reach of the North Fork is a very pleasant day trip for boaters of all kinds. It features a number of Class

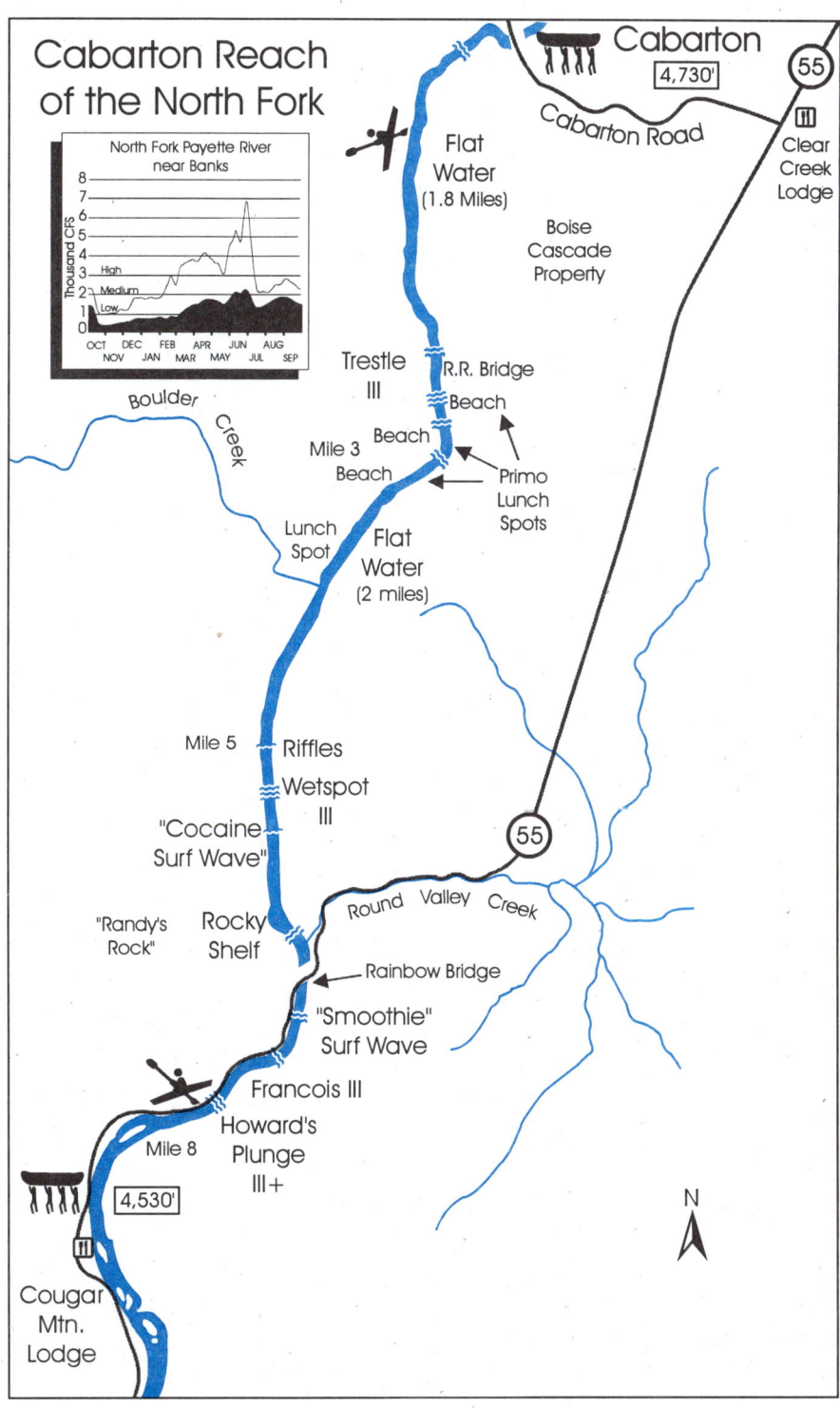

III rapids, two lengthy placid sections for swimming, gazing at wildlife and relaxation, several sandy beaches that make for ideal lunch stops, a number of play spots for kayakers, and fishing. All of the fun builds to a climax for the final Class III-plus monster drop at the end called "Howard's Plunge."

The river is wide and slow at the beginning of the run, providing a perfect area for paddle boaters to get synchronized and figure out their left- and right-hand turns. The river narrows quickly and bends to the left for a couple of small Class II drops. Rafters should watch out for hard-to-see doming rocks. Both of these drops feature mini play waves for kayaks. Catch an eddy and look for a ride.

Watch for a nice sandy beach for lunch.

After the second drop, the river gradient flattens out for the next 1.8 miles. A large campsite appears on river right if boaters need to pull over for an early or late lunch. Otherwise, relax and enjoy the scenery. Try fishing for big rainbow trout.

Interpretive remarks: Most of the Cabarton run cuts through Boise Cascade Corp. timberland. Just beyond the put-in is the site of the old logging camp of Cabarton. This site was owned and operated by the Boise-Payette Lumber Co., the predecessor to Boise Cascade. As you float downstream, you'll notice that the forest appears to be slightly thinned, with a number of large ponderosa pine, Douglas fir and Grand fir trees. The look of the forest is the result of "selective" cutting, taking a large tree here and there. Loggers call it "Pick and Pluck."

It's likely that floaters will see some ospreys — and possibly bald eagles — flying above on the float trip. There are several osprey territories (nesting sites) in this 10-mile reach. If the river's not too crowded and you're really lucky, you might even seen an osprey dive for a fish in the north fork. I was fortunate to witness that one time while kayaking on the Cabarton reach, a few miles from the launch. I was just drifting along, spinning around with the current when an osprey dove for a fish about 50 feet in front of my boat. The bird plunged into the river with characteristic vigor and emerged with a huge, squirming trout in the grasp of its feet. The osprey flapped its wings, rose about six feet over the water, and the big fish wiggled free. The osprey dropped its dinner! It whirled around and dove again, only to emerge with its talons empty. Although I felt for the osprey, I had to marvel at the strength and survival instincts of the large trout in this classic clash of predator and prey.

As you're lolly-gagging along on the flat water, watch for railroad tracks about 50 feet above the river on the right as you approach a sharp left-hand bend. This is your signal that **Trestle Rapids**, the first Class III drop, is coming up. Just after the corner, the river narrows and drops into a set of Class II down-the-middle rapids before the railroad spans the river over a black trestle. At flows above 1,000 cfs, several holes form behind large rocks under the bridge. The challenge for rafts — as you pass underneath the trestle — is to thread around the holes, and then follow the wave train around the corner for the final big drop — which typically consists of big rolling waves flying by strong laterals on the left and right side.

For kayakers, Trestle Rapids presents opportunities for mucho-playing. The first and second Class II drops are typically fine surf waves. Experienced play-hogs aim for the largest hole under the trestle in river center. I've seen people get launched out of that puppy quite handily. The following wave train contains some tight side eddies that can be caught to surf steep resonating waves in river center just past the RR bridge. This is not a move for novice kayakers, however, because if you've got a weak roll, you might be in for a rough swim for the next 150 yards.

> For kayakers, Trestle Rapids presents opportunities for mucho-playing.

Beginning tandem canoe paddlers testing their mettle frequently swamp and swim in Trestle Rapids. If you're unfamiliar with the river, canoeists are advised to scout the trestle holes and pick a route. The railroad can make for a good scouting platform, but watch out for trains (see "Run for Your Life" passage below).

Below Trestle, watch for prime lunch spots on river left and right. Spacious beaches are ripe for the picking here. During busy parts of the season — typically August and September — the prime beaches will be tough to snag at high noon.

After a few more riffles, the river flattens out for about 2.2 miles. Enjoy.

"RUN FOR YOUR LIFE"

Let me digress for a moment to suggest a new name for Trestle Rapid. Boise photographer Steve Bly was out on the trestle one day, shooting promotional shots for Cascade River Co. It was a clear sunny day. The light was perfect for a classic whitewater shot. Bly was seated on the bridge, hanging over the edge for a neat aerial shot, ready to snap the trigger.

Cascade's Owner Steve Jones was about to leap into his raft and paddle for the bridge when he heard a train coming. The whistle, then the train. He could feel the earth moving under his feet. Bly didn't hear or feel a thing. Jonesy yelled. His voice was drowned out by the roar of whitewater. Jonesy started motioning with his hands, frantically lifting his arms in an upward motion, yelling "GET UP! GET UP!" Finally, Bly, a former Idaho Parks & Recreation director, heard the train, got on his feet and galloped for the left bank. "I've never run so fast in all of my life," Bly says.

Jonesy thought, "Oh my God," as the train rolled across the bridge at what seemed to be 80 mph. Bly nearly bought it. The train licked his heels as he dove to the left just at the edge of the bridge. Bly hit the rocks hard: His camera and chest absorbed the fall — all at the same time. The impact crushed three ribs. It was such a close call that two years later, Bly says he still gets a gruesome feeling in his gut.

And so, I propose we rename the rapid "Run For Your Life." Let's see if it sticks.

A number of riffles and a gradual left-hand bend signal the end of flatwater and the lead-in to "Wet Spot," the next Class III rapid. As the river bends left, it comes to an abrupt drop. There's a pretty good cork screw in river center, but a smoother route in left-center. Jonesey named Wet Spot because the rapid is very dependable for big grins and wet faces — it always drenches paddle rafters no matter if it's low or high flow.

Kayakers should be attentive through this reach if they want to play — there's an abundance of pour-over waves and holes behind rocks and a number of excellent glassy waves in river center after Wet Spot. About one-quarter mile below Wet Spot, there's a fairly large and steep glassy wave in river center called "Cocaine." The wave gets bigger and harder to catch with higher flows. If you're fortunate enough to catch it, it's one beautiful ride.

Rainbow Bridge

After Cocaine, the river drops gradually for a mile and bends 90 degrees to the left for the approach to Rainbow Bridge. There's a rocky shoal upstream of the bridge that's kind of difficult to see and read. People with wooden dories should be careful here to find the groove through the rocks in right-center. For kayakers, there are a bunch of small play spots in here.

Cascade calls this rocky drop "Randy's Rock" after a customer named Randy who took a dive here when his raft hit a hole. Randy swam for a short distance and was yanked back into the raft.

Below Randy's Rock, there are a number of play opportunities for kayaks, including some small holes on river left. The river descends below Rainbow Bridge in classic pool-and-drop fashion. All of the Class II drops are easy-to-read center runs. Surf-happy kayakers should watch for a beautiful large glassy waves. It's an unmistakable ramp-like wave at the brink of a Class II drop, a wave that'll hold you as long as you want to stay. I remember the first time I caught that wave ... it was a thrill to ride, but when a raft came heading right for me, I tried to peel off left, then right, and the wave wouldn't let me go. The raft was right on top of me, and I somehow pulled over to the left bank long enough for the raft to pass by, but when I tried to peel out back into the current, the back of my kayak hit jagged rocks on the bank and flipped me next to shore — at the top of a steep drop! I put my head on the front deck for protection but I lost my paddle and had to swim. I surfaced in the wave train, got my feet downstream and fetched my boat and paddle in the pool below. Even though I swam, the thrill of surfing that wave was worth the crash and burn.

Below that golden surf wave, you'll see a horizon line ahead — the unmistakable sign for Francois, a Class III rapids named after the ebullient French Canadian trapper, Francois Payette (see page 4). This drop is typically run right-center, being careful to avoid a good-sized hole in left-center. At low flows, the hole becomes a large rock that's been known to wrap a few boats.

Raft party cruises through Francois Rapids.

Cascade's Mary Williams named Francois in 1986. "We had to name something after Payette," she said.

The river drops through one more wave train before pooling up for the final approach to Howard's Plunge, the final and steepest drop in the Cabarton reach. The run is typically on the left or left-center, depending on the flow. There is usually a large hole on river right that grows and dominates the rapid as flows increase above 5,000 cfs. In the spring of 1995, flows reached beyond that level and the hole in Howard's became a big-time stopper. Several kayakers I know got May-Tagged in there from bow to stern before they were pitched out. Wild stuff. There's a huge pool below for recovery. Many first-

192

Paddlers get a face full of water in the Plunge.

time boaters on Cabarton will scout the Plunge on their way to the put-in. As an alternative, you can pull out on either side of the river to scout it if you wish.

Takeout on river-right either below the rapids or a mile downriver at the Cougar Mountain Lodge.

THE NORTH FORK · CLASS V

Difficulty: Experts only — Continuous Class 5
Put-Ins: Lower Smith's Ferry; Big Eddy; Swinging Bridge (below Jacob's Ladder and Golf Course); Hound's Tooth.
Types of craft: Kayaks, catarafts, round boats
Distance: 15 miles
Float time: Several hours to a full day. You make the call
Take-outs: Big Eddy; upstream of Jacob's Ladder; Hound's Tooth; Bank.
Steepness: 125 feet per mile (average)
Season: Early May & June, August & September

Getting there: Access to the entire reach of the North Fork Class V run is very convenient with Idaho 55 running along its entire length. Beyond the put-ins and take-outs mentioned above, there are numerous highway pull-outs that provide other options. The uppermost launch point is just south of milepost 95, a dirt two-track that drops into a little flat next to a tranquil North Fork. It is the classic "calm before the storm." Big Eddy wayside is below the top three rapids near milepost 92. The Swinging Bridge pull-out provides a place to put-in below the steepest and most difficult rapids on the North Fork: Jacob's Ladder and Golf Course. The Hound's Tooth pull-out, about 4.5 miles north of Banks, is a large dirt pull-out next to the rapid itself.

Shuttle: Drop a vehicle at the take-out of your choice. Bicycle shuttles on narrow Idaho 55 are risky.

A word about flow: The North Fork is considered easier at 1,200 cfs, and increasingly difficult at 2,000 cfs on up. Top experts have run the North Fork up to 7,000 cfs, when it is considered Class V-plus. Swimming at this level is considered to be certain death.

General remarks: Experts call the North Fork Class V run one of the most challenging river reaches in North America, if not the world, because of its continuous nature for over 15 miles. There's more than 20 named rapids or features on the North Fork, and dozens of others that aren't named. Anybody who's anybody as a

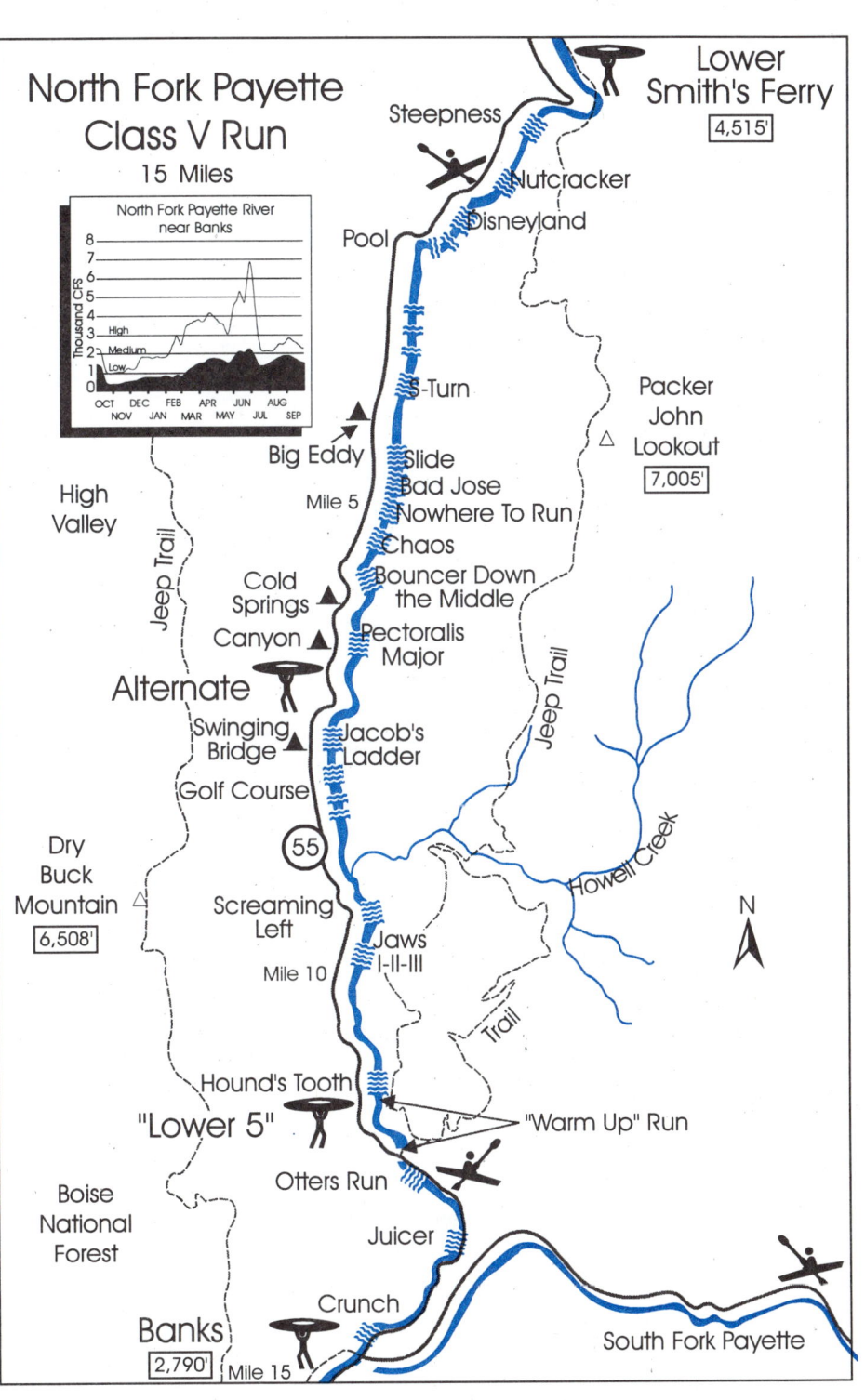

Class V kayaker has to test their skill on the North Fork. Wannabe world-class boaters haven't reached the stature of being truly "world-class" until they've successfully paddled the entire reach of the North Fork. "If you ain't been here, you're not there yet," says Rob Lesser, a Boise native who's been paddling the gnarly run for over 20 years. "The North Fork is a graduation river. You earn your diploma as a Class V paddler when you run it on your own ability." Bob McDougal, a well-known North Fork kayaker and world-class boater, compares the North Fork to "El Capitan" in rock-climbing circles.

Expert catarafters are attempting the North Fork in increasing numbers as well, and paddle rafters have run pieces of the top and bottom sections. Greg Stump and Alan Hamilton of Aire have run pieces of the North Fork in inflatable kayaks below 1,000 cfs. It's clear that as whitewater boaters increase their skill and equipment innovations make Class V rapids safer to run, the North Fork will become even more popular as time goes on. Please be prepared, however, for the single biggest downside of floating the North Fork: a potentially deadly Class V swim. Be prepared for self-rescue. When you attempt the omnipotent North Fork, experts say, "ultimately you are alone."

How do you know when your ready for the North Fork? This is a question that all experienced Payette River boaters have grappled with. Ultimately, of course, this is a personal call. For kayakers, experts recommend that you possess all of the abilities necessary to handle Class V water — a bomb-proof fast roll on both sides, a bomb-proof brace on both sides, the ability to catch tiny eddies, the ability to cope with getting stuck in holes, and excellent swimming ability. For catarafters, experts recommend that you have extensive rowing experience in Class IV-plus water, that you know how to punch holes, know how to hop to strategic locations on the boat or frame to prevent flips or flush out of holes, and that you know how to self-rescue in the event of flips and swims. Boise cat expert Brock Loveland believes catarafters should be able to respond to a flipped cat in the North Fork in 4-5 seconds. "Cats have opened this pandora's box," says Loveland, a river-rescue instructor. "The equipment has allowed new boaters to run Class IV water in a matter of hours, instead of years like it used to be. The equipment is so forgiving that it can deceive boaters into thinking they're ready for Class V water before they're a true Class V boater." In his opinion, catarafters must be prepared for self-rescue on the North Fork, or they're not ready to run it. "A boater is only as good as how they handle trouble — because on the North Fork, you are going to get in trouble," he says.

The Float: To begin, head out from the lower Smith's Ferry launch point and suck it up, for the rapids start to come at you right around the corner. After the North Fork takes a sharp right-hand bend, boaters will approach **Steepness**, the first Class V drop. This rapid was named by North Fork pioneer Mike Lyons due to the steep five-foot shelf the North Fork pours over at a narrow slot between the highway and a cliff wall. The river tends to push you to the right here, away from a nasty hole on the left. Rapids are continuous below here for a half-mile until a short pool leading up to **Nutcracker**, one of the toughest drops on the entire 15-mile run. The distinguishing feature in Nutcracker is a large rock or hole in the center of the narrow, powerful drop. John Wasson, who ran most of the North Fork with a group of five expert kayakers in 1979, says they named this drop as such because it is shaped like a nutcracker, with the hole or rock serving as the "nut," but the rapid has a nice double-meaning, too. If you fail to avoid the "nut" feature, you're likely to get squeezed as if you're between the clamps of a nutcracker. What a lovely thought. Experts advise a close study of this drop before running it. The river is chock full of holes and continuous drop for about a mile below Nutcracker until it flattens out for a second and forms a distinct horizon line above another steep drop called **Disneyland**. Wasson named this one after the ultimate E-ticket ride in

Rob Lesser

Don Banducci blasts through Nutcracker.

Disneyland, the best of the bunch. "Even though it looks bad, it usually just turns out to be a great ride," Wasson says. Below the rapids, the river pools up by the Big Eddy wayside stop and a nice beach.

The river begins to drop precipitously again below the pool and heads into several S-turn curves, thus the name **S-turn**. A cable foot-bridge spanning the river marks the beginning of **Slide,** a fairly steep drop with no distinguishing features. Lesser recalls naming that drop because it looks like and feels like a slide as you paddle through, but there's some bad stuff ahead.

Bad Jose is next, referring to some holes as the river bends left. Don Banducci, who was with Wasson and the gang in that first top-to-bottom run in '79, named that one. Immediately following Bad Jose is a wall of holes with no descernible route. Lesser named it **No Where to Run** originally "because you were going to get hammered wherever you went," he says. Later, a number of boaters looked at the drop in positive terms, Know Where to Run, a possible path through chaotic hydraulics. More holes and rocks present themselves below here in **Chaos**. The river bends slightly to the left for a wild ride through **Bouncer Down the Middle**, which has a number of nasty holes on the left and in the center. Lesser recalls naming this one as he paddled down the river with Wasson. They were cruising along through the Class V madness, and Wasson quickly looked over his shoulder to Rob and asked, "What's this one?" Lesser responded, "Oh, it's just a bouncer down the middle." And a hair-raising one at that. Overall, Lesser rates this as the third most challenging drop of the entire reach, comparable to No Where to Run and Jaws (below Screaming Left).

After Bouncer, there are no named drops for the mile until a series of rocks and holes present the rapid **Pectoralis Major,** a creative name bestowed upon this rapids by Lesser, Wasson, McDougall and other locals. This drop can be scouted directly across from Canyon Campground. From here, the river slackens

Brock Loveland high-sides in Jacob's Ladder.

a bit and bends right before the brink of **Jacob's Ladder,** the big kahuna on the North Fork.

Jacob's drops about 265 feet in less than a mile. Experienced North Fork boaters have a precise step-by-step progression they use to run this drop. Be sure to scout. No discernible "route" exists in Jacob's — just a ton of chop, holes and assorted rocks. "One of the most awesome sights is looking into the abyss as you come up on Jacob's," Lesser says. "All hell is breaking loose down there as far as you can see. But you have to put it out of your mind and concentrate on what's in front of you."

The idea in Jacob's is to get in a favorable position to plunge off the "rock drop" into a huge river-wide stopper hole without getting totally munched, because the next feature, a large whip-action hole on river right known as the "taffy puller" awaits below. "You don't want to get tipped over here because you'll definitely get slammed," Lesser says. The next feature is the "ocean wave," a huge yawner of a wave in left-center.

It's unclear to the Kentucky North Fork pioneers of '77 who named Jacob's Ladder, and Lesser thought the Kentucky boaters named it. So who knows? But it's such a got a great double-meaning, stemming from the Biblical reference to climbing the stairway to Heaven ... if you survive. If not, at least you'll ascend to paddling heaven on Jacob's Ladder.

Aire paddle rafters bust a hole in Golf Course. Mark Lisk

Below Jacob's, boaters will be presented with a seemingly endless series of holes and rocks called **Golf Course** for the next mile or so. The Kentucky boaters who ran the full reach of the North Fork for the first time in 1977 named Golf Course, but they referred to a section around Nutcracker. Since the '79 group named Nutcracker and it stuck, the cool name of Golf Course drifted downriver to its current location. Of course, there's more holes in this frothing morass than an 18-hole course, but the pin placements really keep boaters guessing. Below Golf Course is the Swinging Bridge take-out/put-in. The action begins below here with some Class III rapids that grow with intensity and steepness as boaters approach **Screaming Left Turn** or **Island** rapids.

This drop looks like one of the ugliest of the bunch as it's full of

Kayakers bounce through Screaming Left.

holes that may endo kayakers or cause catarafts to surf unintentionally. But most boaters cruise through it without much difficulty. It can be scouted easily from the highway. Screaming Left's name may be as apt as any on the North Fork, but it was apparently imported from the Susitna River. As boaters reach the bottom toe of the island, a series of nasty holes called **Jaws I, Jaws II** and **Jaws III** come up next. Lesser rates these series of holes as the fourth-hardest area of the North Fork.

Hound's Tooth is the next Class V drop below the Jaws series. It was named by Kentucky boater Bob Walker "after that big bicuspid" in the middle of the

Rob Lesser

Waves bury John Wasson in Hound's Tooth.

river, he says. There are actually two big teeth sticking up at the entrance of Hound's Tooth, and large holes behind them. The typical run is on the right side of the left tooth. Hound's Tooth marks the beginning of the Lower Five section of the North Fork, typically the section where first-time North Fork boaters test their ability. About 1.5 miles of "warm-up" Class III and Class IV features lie between the bottom of Hound's Tooth and the first Class V, **Otters Run**. Payette pioneer Mike Lyons named this one in 1975 after he saw three otters swim through the hole-ridden drop. "We watched them drop off some rocks into the rapid, and we thought they were going to get thrashed," Lyons says, "but they didn't. They dropped into these holes and they'd squirt out no problem. It looked like they were laughing and having a great time. They had a great run through there, so we named it Otters Run." A pull-out off of Idaho 55 by a railroad bridge provides an excellent scouting vantage point for Otters. Below here, boaters have about a mile of easier water until the next Class V drop, **Juicer**. Lyons named this one with fellow paddler Dick Getch. "We felt it was like an osterizer with all of those waves hitting you at once," Lyons says. Juicer has a long runout of rocks and holes, depending on the water level, and then the last big drop, **Crunch,** crowns off the North Fork Class V run. Lyons named this one after he totally crunched the bow of his Hollowform boat at about 1,200 cfs. The entrance to Crunch is best taken toward the right-center side, but Lyons got pushed left — as many do. "It was pretty vertical in there and I slammed

A paddle crew hits the blender in the top of Juicer.

a rock absolutely dead-on," Lyons recalls. "I thought maybe I had broken both of my feet. Then I looked down and I saw the nose of the boat was staring me in the face. It had curled 180 degrees and it was looking up at me." Below the steepest part of Crunch, a series of holes and rocks provide more dodging action for the next 100 yards. Then, the North Fork flattens out a bit as boaters make the final approach to Banks. Wa-hoo!

Catarafters swallow a face full of water in Crunch.

RIVER CONSERVATION

Today, Payette River boaters enjoy a recreation resource that's second to none.

It didn't happen by accident.

In the early days, Idaho pioneers toiled to cultivate the Lower Payette Valley. They established ranches, orchards and farms, all of which needed water. Every spring, the mighty Payette River supplied tons of water for raising crops, but much of it flew by during the spring melt before farmers needed it. They needed a way to harness the flow and put it to work all summer long.

In the 1920s, farmers built small dams at the outlets of Payette Lake, Upper Payette Lake, Little Payette Lake, Granite Lake and Box Lake to increase storage. High dams were installed on the Deadwood River in 1931, and on the North Fork at Cascade in 1948. All of those projects catch snowmelt, and then release flows as farmers and the Bureau of Reclamation call for it as the summer progresses.

Boaters benefit greatly from these releases. We enjoy season-long flows on the Payette's Main Fork, which conveys water to farms downstream. The South Fork provides high flows through the spring, and then Deadwood Reservoir provides additional flows in July and August. The North Fork typically flows high during snowmelt, and then it may be shut down to minimum flows in July — sometimes as low as 200 cfs — and then it picks up again in August and September, depending on snowpack and irrigation demand.

Thus, previous development has provided a nice multiple-use blend on the Payette River that works for farmers and boaters. Let's hope we can keep it that way.

Dams proposed for Big Falls, South Fork

In the late 1970s, and again in the late 1980s, high power dams and other hydroelectric schemes were proposed on the Payette's south and north forks. Recreational boaters played a significant role in defeating those projects, as did local residents who oppose converting the scenic river into a kilowatt factory.

Sensing a need for more electricity as southern Idaho grew rapidly in the late 1970s, Idaho Power Co. proposed an ambitious plan to build four high dams on the South Fork, between Pine Flats Campground and the site of the old Grimes Pass Dam. Specifically, the company proposed to build a 120-foot-high dam at Gateway Rapids, just downstream from Pine Flats hot springs, a 120-foot-high dam at Big Falls, an 85-foot-high dam at Black Bear Creek, just upstream of the Danskin ramp and rest area, and an 85-foot-high dam at Grimes Pass, the site of the "Ultimate Play Wave." In short, the projects would have destroyed the South Fork "canyon" stretch.

Idaho Power Co.

Idaho Power Co. envisioned damming Big Falls and three other South Fork sites in the '70s.

Combined, the projects had a maximum rated capacity of 85 megawatts. Construction costs would have run $73.2 million (1978 dollars). Based on average streamflow data, the projects would have run at a maximum of 50 percent of capacity, Idaho Power Co. said. In a company brochure, Idaho Power made the preposterous statement that its proposal consisted of "run of river dams" and the environmental impact would be "minimal."

"Creating the necessary head for generation, the four dams would back up water less than a total of 12 miles, leaving some 43 miles of free-flowing river untouched," the brochure said. "About two and one-quarter miles of free-flowing river would remain between the upper end of the Black Bear pond and Big Falls Dam.... At 100-135 feet high, the dams would be miniscule by comparison in the project area characterized by lofty mountains and towering trees...."

In 1978, whitewater boating was still in its infancy on the

Payette River. Very few rafts plied the South Fork Canyon, and kayakers were still few and far between.

Rob Lesser, a Payette kayaking pioneer, sensed the gravity of the situation and formed the Idaho Whitewater Association. A small group in McCall, called Friends of the River, also was formed to oppose the South Fork dams.

Public Utility commissioners Conley Ward, Ralph Wickberg and Perry Swisher, were savvy about the utility business and they had a strong environmental ethic. Ward points out that the PUC had denied Idaho Power's proposals to build a coal-fired plant in southern Idaho in 1978, with strong public support. Instead, the far-seeing commissioners pushed cogeneration and energy conservation at a time when most utilities wanted to build mega-plants.

"The conventional wisdom was that we were against the wall for energy supplies," Ward says. "Politically, at least by Republicans, the PUC was seen as an ostreperous blockade to progress and we were all going to freeze in the dark."

Lesser, fellow boater Roger Rosentreter and others defended the South Fork's natural values. Anglers testified in support of the native trout fishery. Recreationists "made a strong showing," Ward says. "There had to be someone to put the argument on the record, because by law, we had to make decisions on the record."

On July 21, 1980, the PUC stopped the South Fork proposals cold. In its decision-order, the PUC noted that Idaho Power could produce the same amount of energy as the dam projects with water-heater insulation, electrical outlet gaskets and shower-flow restrictors. The costs of those measures "are negligable compared to the South Fork project," commissioners said. "The South Fork's value in its existing state exceeds its limited energy production potentional.... It is therefore ordered that the application of Idaho Power Company to construct the South Fork hydroelectric project is hereby denied."

The PUC did, however, approve Idaho Power's hydroelectric proposal for the North Fork. It was a 258-megawatt proposal to divert most of the North Fork's flow below Smith's Ferry and run it through a 16-foot diameter underground tunnel some 16.5 miles to Banks. It was an attempt to harness energy from the North Fork's 1,700-foot vertical drop. Idaho Power eventually received a hydro license from the Federal Energy Regulatory Commission

(FERC) to build the project. But in 1986, it allowed the license to expire, concluding that the $218 million cost could not be justified in a time of energy surplus. It was a wise move because IPC still has an energy surplus that's projected to extend into 2015.

Environmentalists have a saying about dam proposals: As long as water runs downhill, and there isn't permanent protection for a river, dam projects never die. Dam-builders will keep coming back with a new scheme.

That's what has happened on the North Fork. Even though IPC relinquished its license, a small irrigation district from Homedale, Idaho, proposed the same hydro project in 1987. Gem Irrigation District saw dollar signs in the North Fork's steep rapids after it made a tidy sum from retrofitting Owyhee Dam with hydro turbines. IPC's surplus didn't matter. A federal law encouraged private parties to develop "renewable" energy projects, and required utilities to buy power from those projects at a premium rate. As long as hydro developers could ram through a project in the political arena, finding a purchaser was a lead-pipe cinch.

Idaho Power Co.

A hydro-engineer's dream, running the North Fork through the mountains in a tube to a hydro plant below.

Meanwhile, the Idaho Legislature passed a protected rivers bill in 1987 that called on Water Resources to study all of the river basins in the state — one by one — for possible development and/or protection. A major reason the protected rivers legislation cleared the Legislature is because state river plans were supposed to give Idaho primacy over water rights and water development, and keep the federal government from intruding on state's rights. In a state like Idaho, nothing is more important to farmers and legislators than state control over water.

The legislation called on the Idaho Water Resources Board to develop a comprehensive river plan for the Payette's north, south and main forks.

In addition to the North Fork project, another hydro scheme had been targeted for the South Fork at Oxbow Rapids. Then-Boise engineer Marc Auth, co-owner of Intermountain Power Corp., hatched a 3-megawatt hydro plan for the old Oxbow mining tunnel. His idea was to divert the river into the tunnel and spin a turbine at the tunnel's exit point. He also had guarantees that Idaho Power would have to buy the project's power, as long as he could win support in the political and regulatory arena. Thus, the proposed Payette River Plan took on immense importance to the hydro developers, river conservationists and Boise County residents.

"There ought to be a law against somebody just coming in and developing a public resource for private gain."

It became clear to river recreationists that they'd have to organize a campaign to fight the dam projects. In the fall of 1987, a new group was formed out of a casual conversation between Wendy Wilson, an environmentalist, kayaker and canoeist, and John Watts, a political organizer and kayaker. Wilson and Watts met in an eddy on the Cabarton reach of the North Fork. They were hanging out, waiting to surf "Cocaine," and they started to chat about Gem's hydro proposal. "There ought to be a law against somebody just coming in and developing a public resource for private gain," Wilson told Watts.

Watts encouraged Wilson to organize a campaign and recruit volunteers. She announced her plans at an Idaho Whitewater Association meeting, where Scott Montgomery, a Hewlett-Packard software engineer, kayaker and rafter, raised his hand. "We had

207

zero money, zero organization and zero facts," Montgomery said. "We flat had nothing, and I didn't even own a tie. I had never done anything like this before." Montgomery and Wilson emerged as co-directors of the new group Friends of the Payette. It was a four-year campaign that drew volunteers from every walk of life, and importantly, business own-

Dave Walsh

Above from left, Liz Paul, Marti Bridges, Wendy Wilson — key players in the Friends of the Payette campaign. Right: Scott Montgomery was campaign co-director.

Glenn Oakley

ers and landowners from Boise and Valley counties. Gem had changed its original project design to create a reservoir in High Valley, above Smith's Ferry, and drown private property. A number of High Valley landowners, including Susie Brown, didn't like that idea at all.

Even so, a number of Boise County residents supported the hydro projects because they disliked the influx of whitewater boaters invading their home turf and they wanted to increase the county's tax base. The Legislature was inclined to support development over protection of the environment, so Friends of the Payette would have to mount an all-encompassing campaign and make it politically impossible for a majority of lawmakers to vote against them. It was a daunting task.

Friends of Payette wages cutting-edge campaign

Early on, Friends members drafted a 10-page action plan for developing the political campaign. They raised start-up funds by selling donated golf shirts and T-shirts. One of the volunteers designed a professional logo for the group, using the scenic Rainbow Bridge as an anchor. They received donated computer equipment. They had kayaker volunteers who were H-P engineers tear apart Gem's hydro plan. They took Water Board members and legislators on special VIP float trips on the South Fork, Cabarton and Main Payette and let the river sell itself. They publicly supported legislative candidates, including Republicans, who were favorably inclined to protecting the river. Down the stretch, they hired Liz Paul to head up the organizational arm of the campaign. Paul, former executive director of the Snake River Alliance and a Class V kayaker, was a no-nonsense organizer who had snuffed the Special Isotope Separator plutonium project proposed for the Idaho National Engineering Laboratory in eastern Idaho.

As the 1991 legislative session drew near, the Water Resources Board was putting the final touches on a draft Payette River comprehensive plan. Friends volunteers were involved in every phase of the plan's development. The Water Board had set up an advisory committee for writing the draft, and people like Garden Valley expert kayaker and Hollywood movie consultant Jon Wasson played an active role. The board held numerous public hearings on the plan, which turned into emotional fiery debates between pro-dam people and pro-river people. By the time the Water Resources Board voted on the draft plan, board members knew that a majority of Idahoans wanted to keep the Payette River as it is, even if they weren't a boater and just liked to lie on the river bank and watch the clouds roll by.

The hydro developers went berserk.

So the board proposed banning hydro development on the North Fork, the South Fork and the Main Fork to Horseshoe Bend. It was a controversial decision. The hydro developers went berserk. "For every single purpose conceived by the Legislature in enacting the Protected Rivers Act, the draft plan is a total, unmitigated failure," said Roy Eiguren, an attorney representing Gem.

Then-Water Board member Gene Gray termed those statements "a love letter" compared to what hydro developers had said in other letters of protest.

Friends of the Payette had won round one. Now round two would be held in the Legislature. So they cranked up the campaign another notch. They recruited hundreds of volunteers to lobby legislators on the Payette plan. They put up yard signs; they made buttons; they formed a phone bank; they wrote letters to the newspaper; they produced TV ads; they gave talks to service clubs. And they contacted boaters who lived in other areas of Idaho, and urged them to contact their local legislators and tell them to support the Payette plan.

The bill started in the Senate, where it survived a narrow vote in the natural resources committee and then on the Senate floor. In the House, it was even tighter. The plan cleared the House Resources and Conservation Committee by one vote. The floor vote was nearly as close, but it passed.

> "What part of the word 'no' do they not understand?"

Friends of the Payette had scored the most stunning environmental victory in the history of the Idaho Legislature. The group had raised 10,000 members and $150,000. The Payette River would be protected from new hydro schemes for five years.

Everyone celebrated. "It turned out to be the pinnacle of my conservation career," Wilson says.

Come 1996, the Payette plan could be revisited, and guess what? A new scheme has been hatched for the North Fork. Gem Irrigation District has proposed to divert 100 cfs out of the North Fork, run the water down the railroad right of way in a tube, and then through a powerhouse in Banks. The Idaho Northern & Pacific Railroad is an active sponsor of the project, Gem officials say.

"It is important that the 1996 Legislature be fully informed of this revised and limited project ... (so) Gem Irrigation District can provide for the enrichment of our state," said Gem's manager, Clyde Hutton.

Wilson responds to the idea by saying, "What part of the word "no" do they not understand?"

Boaters would be well-advised to stay tuned in to this proposal. For more information, call Idaho Rivers United, 343-7381.

Mark Torf

Plastic explosive blows rock to smithereens in Blackadar Rapids on the South Fork. Friends of the Payette's activities included bird-dogging the Banks-to-Lowman highway project to ensure boulders weren't carelessly dropped into the river and to protect the river's natural course.

FLORA & FAUNA

The chance sighting of a red fox on the river bank, a black bear foraging for berries, a rattlesnake on a river scout or a moose chomping on aquatic plants in the river can add spice to your paddling trip. Following is a short list of the birds, mammals, reptiles, plants and trees that you could see while paddling the Payette or hiking nearby. Please consult with a detailed guide for purposes of identification:

■ **Large birds:** Bald eagle, golden eagle, osprey, red-tailed hawk, Cooper's hawk, white pelican, double-crested cormorant, osprey, great-blue heron, black-crowned night heron, sandhill crane, gull, forest grouse, ruffed grouse, ring-necked pheasant, black-billed magpie, belted kingfisher, American crow, turkey vulture, great-horned owl, western screech-owl.

■ **Waterfowl:** Mallard, Canada geese, common merganzer (the ones with the rust-colored heads and tufts), western grebes, gadwall, green-winged teal, redhead.

■ **Water/shore birds:** Kingfishers, water ouzels, American dippers, killdeer, American avocet, black-necked stilt, western sandpiper, long-billed dowitcher.

■ **Small birds:** Lewis woodpeckers, mountain bluebirds, robins, ruby-throated hummingbirds, western tanager, lazuli bunting, American pipit, cedar waxwing, tree swallow, many others depending on time of year.

■ **Mammals:** Moose, elk, deer, otters, mink, beaver, red fox, black bear, mountain lion, wolverine, fisher, flying squirrels.

■ **Amphibians and reptiles:** Long-toed salamander, Idaho giant salamander, western toad, spotted frog, western chorus frog, tailed frog, northern leopard frog, sagebrush lizard, side-blotched lizard, rubber boa, gopher snake, western garter snake, western rattlesnake.

■ **Trees:** Douglas fir, grand fir, ponderosa pine (the big tall ones with orange, vanilla-smelling bark), western larch (the ones whose needles turn golden in the fall and fall off), Engleman spruce, lodgepole pine, hackberry, willow, cottonwoods.

■ **Plants:** Poison ivy, syringa, bitterbrush, sagebrush, lemon grass, several species of native bunchgrass, crested wheatgrass, medusa head wild rye.

KEY CONTACTS

Outfitted river trips

Four outfitters offer day and multi-day trips on several different whitewater reaches of the Payette River. If you haven't tried whitewater rafting yet, it's safest to go with an outfitter first.

Outfitters provide experienced guides, solid equipment, elaborate lunches, Dutch-oven dinners on multi-day trips, and interpretive information on your river journey.

Please inquire for your specific dates and needs:
- Bear Valley River Co., 1-800-235-2327.
- Cascade Recreation, 1-800-292-RAFT.
- Headwaters River Co., 1-800-800-RAFT.
- Idaho Whitewater Unlimited, 888-3008 in Meridian or 208-793-2512 in Banks.

Rentals

Boaters can rent rafts, catarafts, canoes, kayaks, wet suits and other river equipment from a variety of sources.

- Bear Valley and Idaho River Sports will rent boating equipment in Banks in 1996, including life jackets, rafts, helmets, and kayaks. 1-800-235-2327 or 336-4844 in Boise.
- Boise Army-Navy rents rafts, life jackets, dry bags and other gear. 322-0660.
- Boise State University rents a full array of boating equipment at the Outdoor Rental Center in the Student Union Building. Renters must be BSU students or alumni. Call first, their hours are strange, 385-1946.
- Cascade Recreation rents kayaks, life jackets, helmets and other gear at its headquarters near Cooper's wood-carving shop, between Horseshoe Bend and Banks. 1-800-292-RAFT.
- Gravity Sports in McCall rents canoes, touring kayaks, whitewater kayaks, and wet suits. 634-8530.
- Idaho Outdoor Outlet in Cascade rents canoes, innertubes, and whitewater rafts. 382-4909.
- Idaho River Sports in Boise rents canoes, kayaks, rafts, life jackets and helmets.

■ Idaho Whitewater Unlimited rents rafting equipment, life jackets and other gear.. 888-3008 in Meridian or 793-2512 in Banks.
■ Medley Sports in McCall rents canoes, 634-2216.
■ Silver Pig Enterprises at North Beach on Payette lake rents canoes and touring kayaks at the launch point for the North Fork "Meanders." They also provide shuttles to Fisher Creek. 634-4562.

Lessons

■ Boise State University's Outdoor Adventure Program offers kayak lessons at the BSU pool, rafting lessons and river safety courses. Call 385-1374 for information.
■ The Cascade Kayak School offers kayaking lessons. 1-800-292-RAFT.
■ Cascade Recreation offers river safety courses. 1-800-292-RAFT.

River flow information

For current information about Payette River flows, call the Bureau of Reclamation (year-round) at 1-800-635-7820 or the Idaho Department of Water Resources (March-October) at 327-7865.

Boaters can obtain river flow information on the Internet. For information, call the Idaho Department of Water Resources at 327-7988.

Forest information

For primitive road conditions and camping information, call the U.S. Forest Service:
■ Cascade, 364-7400
■ Emmett, 364-7000
■ Lowman, 364-4250
■ McCall, 634-0400

QUALITY AIRETIME

For Your Free AIRE Catalog of
RAFTS, CATARAFTS, KAYAKS
and the dealer
nearest you contact:

*If it's inflatable,
AIRE is required.*

P. O. Box 3412, Dept. PRG • Boise, ID 83703 • 208/344-7506 • Fax 1-800-701-AIRE

WE'VE GOT YOUR GEAR

IDAHO RIVER SPORTS

1521 N. 13th. Street
Boise, Idaho 83702
208-336-4844
1-800-936-4844   FAX 336-5897

See The Experts For Complete Selection Of:
•Rafts   •Kayaks   •Canoes   •Inflatables
•Gear Bags   •River Wear
•Equipment Rentals

"SOMETHING FOR EVERYONE!"

Half-Day, Full-Day, Two-Day
Guided River Trips
River Equipment Rentals
River Equipment Sales

Call or Write for FREE Brochures

Idaho Whitewater Unlimited
1042 E. Ustick Rd.
Meridian, ID 83642
(208) 888-3008

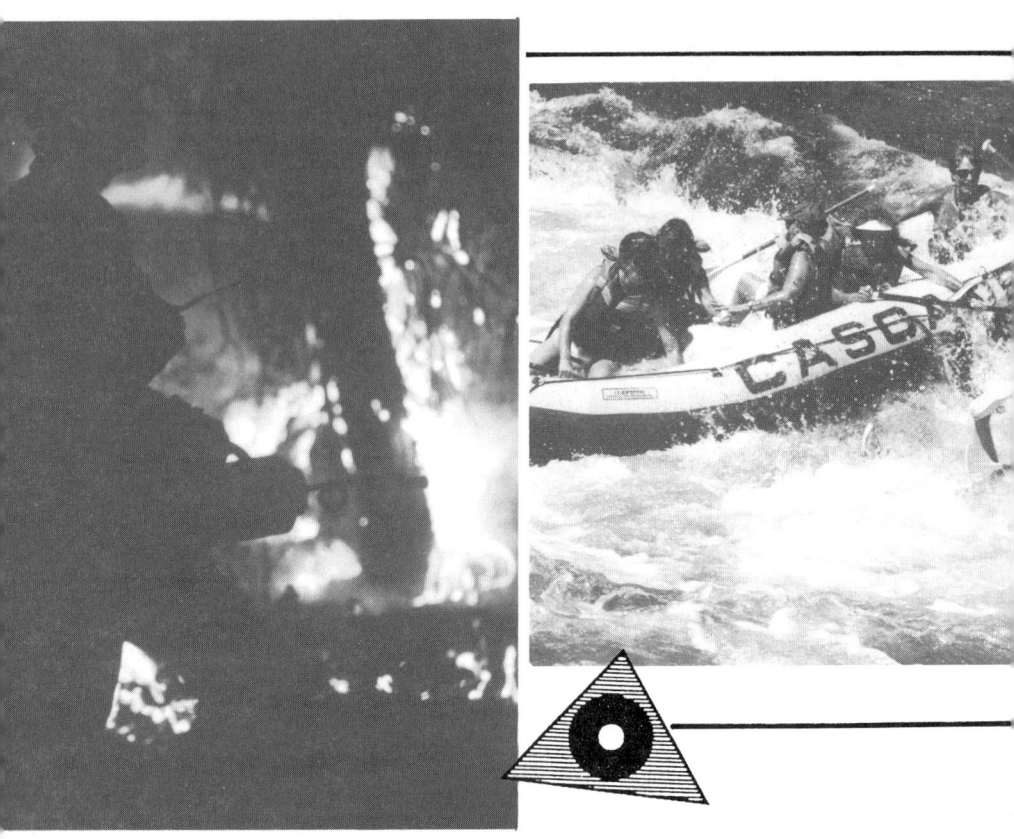

GET SHOT
. . . painlessly, professionally, peacefully . . . on any whitewater you choose . . . or in any action-packed (or quiet) activity

GET SHOTS
. . . local and global scenic, wildlife, wildfire, action adventure

PAYETTE VISIONS
assignment and stock photography almost anywhere . . . plus daily raft/kayak coverage on Idaho's Payette and Lochsa, working with top raft companies under Forest Service permit

call or write Karen Wattenmaker
HC 76 Box 2231, Garden Valley ID 83622
208-462-3524

HEADWATERS
RIVER COMPANY

1/2, 1, 2 & 3 DAY TRIPS ON THE
PAYETTE RIVERS
Professionally guided trips for all ages and levels of adventures. Centrally between Boise, McCall & Stanley

1-208-793-4325
RESERVATIONS
1-800-800-RAFT

SALES
SERVICE
RENTALS

Outdoor Specialists
Bicycling • Hiking • Climbing
Whitewater Boating • Canoeing
Skiing - Alpine & Cross Country

Open Daily 9am - 6pm
503 Pine Street
McCall, Idaho 83638
(208) 634-8530

Half, Full and Overnight Rafting Trips on the Payette River.

Office located in scenic Banks, only 34 miles from Boise.

CALL 1-800-235-BEAR (2327)

Cougar Mountain Lodge
9738 Hwy. 55
Smiths Ferry, Idaho 83611
208-382-4464

Hwy. 55 - 60 mi. north of Boise
on the
North Fork of the Payette River

Family Restaurant * Mini Mart * Souvineers

Breakfast * Lunch * Dinner
7 A.M. - 9 P.M. weekends
7 A.M. - 8 P.M. weekdays

Shuttle service available
with free parking
for rafting and kyaking

Close to camping, hiking and fishing

Cougar Mountain Nordic
provides cross country skiing on
30 kilometers of groomed trails
$4 half day
$6 full day

CANOE KAYAK RENTAL

- Float Idahos "Other" Water The Beautiful Upper North Fork of The Payette River
- Summer Months
- Shuttle Available
- West Side of North Beach

634-4562